ON THE QUEERNESS OF EARLY ENGLISH DRAMA

On the Queerness of Early English Drama

Sex in the Subjunctive

TISON PUGH

UNIVERSITY OF TORONTO PRESS

Toronto Buffalo London

NABUD
MAIN
PR
641
.P84
2021

© University of Toronto Press 2021
Toronto Buffalo London
utorontopress.com
Printed in the U.S.A.

ISBN 978-1-4875-0874-6 (cloth)
ISBN 978-1-4875-3887-3 (EPUB)
ISBN 978-1-4875-3886-6 (PDF)

Library and Archives Canada Cataloguing in Publication

Title: On the queerness of early English drama: Sex in the
subjunctive / Tison Pugh.
Names: Pugh, Tison, author.
Description: Includes bibliographical references and index.
Identifiers: Canadiana (print) 20200408305 | Canadiana (ebook)
2020041707X | ISBN 9781487508746 (hardcover) | ISBN 9781487538866
(PDF) | ISBN 9781487538873 (EPUB)
Subjects: LCSH: English drama – To 1500 – History and criticism. |
LCSH: Sexual minorities in literature. | LCSH: Gender identity
in literature. | LCSH: Sex in literature. | LCSH: Sexual orientation
in literature. | LCSH: Homosexuality in literature. |
LCSH: Desire in literature.
Classification: LCC PR641.P84 2021 | DDC 822/.10935266–dc23

University of Toronto Press acknowledges the financial assistance to its
publishing program of the Canada Council for the Arts and the Ontario Arts
Council, an agency of the Government of Ontario.

Canada Council   Conseil des Arts
for the Arts   du Canada

ONTARIO ARTS COUNCIL
CONSEIL DES ARTS DE L'ONTARIO
an Ontario government agency
un organisme du gouvernement de l'Ontario

Funded by the   Financé par le
Government   gouvernement
of Canada   du Canada

To Martha J. Bayless, Clare A. Lees, and F. Regina Psaki

For the greatest teachers, good is never good enough

Contents

Acknowledgments

Chapter 3, "Performative Typology, Jewish Genders, and Jesus's Queer Romance in the York Corpus Christi Plays," was originally published in *New Medieval Literatures* 20 (2020): 143–73. Chapter 4, "Excremental Desire, Queer Allegory, and the Disidentified Audience of *Mankind*," was originally published in the *Journal of English and Germanic Philology* 119, no. 4 (2020): 457–83. I appreciate the collegial support and exacting standards of the editors of these journals, particularly Kellie Robertson, Robert Meyer-Lee, and Matthew Giancarolo, as well as their permission to republish this material.

ON THE QUEERNESS OF EARLY ENGLISH DRAMA

Introduction

Quem quaeritis? Queerness in Early English Drama

The foundational scenes of early English drama, in the *Quem quaeritis* dialogues that are credited with softening the stance of Christian authorities against theatrical entertainments, established essential tropes for its subsequent queerness. As is well known, Western drama flourished during the first four centuries of the Common Era until the Christian Church, growing in prestige and influence, condemned theatrical productions and prohibited its faithful from attending them. During the ninth century the Second Council of Châlons and the Councils of Tours and Mainz forbad clergy from viewing the performances of mimes, and the Council at Aachen barred clergy from attending stage plays.[1] Drama mostly disappears from the historical record between the fifth and the mid-eighth century, returning in the early ninth century in the form of the *Quem quaeritis* dialogues, in which an angel queries the three Marys for whom they are seeking; the women answer, "Jesus," the angel announces that Jesus has risen from the dead, and the Marys rejoice and praise God.[2] As Timothy McGee summarizes, "Theater was officially frowned upon by the Church, and all performances took place in opposition to official Church policy. In contrast to secular theater, the *Quem quaeritis* dialogue was not only officially approved but liturgically promoted."[3] *Quem quaeritis* scripts appear in manuscripts throughout Western Europe,[4] and, as Anselme Davril notes, the introduction of the *Quem quaeritis* into local liturgical rites elicited further innovations of its form: "As long as it was alien, the ceremony could be rejected, but once accepted it became part of the local tradition." He further notes, "Whatever alterations to conform it to the accepted model were effected before the first performance of the chant in its new situation."[5] The *Quem quaeritis* was included in British liturgical rites as early as the tenth century, as documented in the *Regularis Concordia* of St. Ethelwold (965–75 CE), and thus it is with the *Quem quaeritis* that this study of queerness in early English drama begins.

It must first be acknowledged that tracing the roots of early English drama to the *Quem quaeritis* rites risks historical inaccuracy and confused categories of mimetic performance, for scholars disagree on the centrality of the *Quem quaeritis* to the resurgence of drama in the Middle Ages. For example, Michal Kobialka concludes, "The historical evidence indicates that ... the *Quem quaeritis* ceremony ... should be analyzed as a monastic practice and an inherent part of the tenth-century monastic document [i.e., the *Regularis Concordia*] rather than as a separate or unique description of a 'liturgical play.'"[6] It is beyond the scope of this monograph to include a history of early English theatre, a field that has mightily strived to overcome the long-standing evolutionary model of early drama, yet without reaching consensus on what precisely should replace it. Alexandra F. Johnston summarizes this predicament:

> The old theories argued an evolution along Darwinian lines from mimetic tropes associated with the Mass, to representational Latin plays on religious themes, to a vernacular religious drama performed by the laity that became increasingly secularized until it finally yielded to the polemic drama of the sixteenth century. Such theories will not stand in the face of our increasingly sophisticated understanding of western medieval culture and the cross currents of the politics and theology of the western Church. But there is yet to emerge a consensus that constitutes a "received wisdom" of the mimetic traditions of the millennium between the fall of the Roman Empire and the emergence of new vernacular dramatic forms.[7]

Within this ambiguous field, queerness circulates in surprising ways, and these queer currents of desire arising in early English drama serve as the focus of this study.

Many scholars view the *Quem quaeritis* ceremony as theologically conservative, yet the very act of its staging during the Easter service shifted the course of the Catholic liturgy and of Western theatre, and its inherent queerness could not be eluded. With four monks playing the roles of an angel and the three Marys, these pivotal productions, by necessity, incorporated cross-gender performance and costuming. The stage directions of the *Quem quaeritis* in the *Regularis Concordia* state, "quatuor fratres induant se" (let four brethren dress themselves) for their roles in the performance, and then establish the scene of their interactions: "Cum ergo ille residens tres velut erraneos, ac aliquid querentes, viderit sibi adproximare, incipiat mediocri voce dulcisone cantare" (When the seated angel sees the three women, approaching him wandering about as if looking for something, let him begin to sing in a pleasing voice of medium pitch).[8] In modulating his voice to a medium pitch, the monk who plays the role of the angel would need to consider the necessary modifications to his voice to better achieve the requirements of his performance. Furthermore, this production encourages tacit interaction between the performers and their audience, as the stage directions instruct, "deponant turribula, quae gestaverant in eodem Sepulchro, sumantque linteum et extendant contra clerum, ac veluti ostendentes, quod surrexerit Dominus et iam non sit illo involutus, hanc canant antiphonam" (let the women set down the thuribles they carried into the sepulcher, and let them pick up the cloth and spread it out before the clergy; and, as if making known that the Lord had risen and was not now wrapped in it, let them sing this antiphon). In enacting the liturgy for their fellow clergy, the actors of the *Quem quaeritis* envision the church qua theatre as a space of eternal truths espoused within the framework of performance, with cross-gendered casting and metatheatricality essential for the dissemination of Christian belief.

It is evident that the *Quem quaeritis* traditions influenced early English dramaturgy, as recorded in direct allusions such as those in *The Resurrection of Our Lord* and the Digby *Christ's Resurrection*. In the former the Second Angel asks, "Whom seeke you wemen, the lyvinge with the Deade / he ys not here, for he ys rysen in deede" (358–9), and in the latter Jesus asks Mary Magdalene, "*Mulier, ploras? Quem queris?* / Woman, why wepis thou? Whom sekes thou thus?" (602–3).[9] It is not, however, the intention of this study to trace a queer lineage from the *Quem quaeritis* plays throughout the English Middle Ages to the advent of the Renaissance, for such an argument would bolster the evolutionary and simplistic theory of dramatic history that the plays themselves do not support. Surveying the trajectory from church to theatre, Richard Axton avers, "The earliest plays and records cannot be said to support a notion of 'gradual secularization' of the Latin drama. Nor do they attest to much strength or variety of liturgical traditions in England."[10] For too long, assessments of early English drama assumed the aforementioned evolutionary model in which drama transitioned from the church to the city streets and private homes and finally to theatres; it also theorized that, as the Middle Ages ceded to the early modern era, the latter witnessed a magnificent flowering of talent. As an offshoot of this theory, it has been a long-standing truism of English literary history, though hotly contested in recent decades, of the inherent inferiority of medieval drama. An anonymous eighteenth-century critic, who penned the elaborately titled *A New Theatrical Dictionary, Containing an Account of All the Dramatic Pieces That Have Appeared from the Commencement of*

Theatrical Exhibitions to the Present Time, declares of the mystery and morality plays: "This period [of the mystery plays] one might call the dead sleep of the muses. And when this was over, they did not presently awake, but, in a kind of morning dream, produced the moralities that followed," although he concedes that "these jumbled ideas had some shadow of meaning."[11] John Addington Symonds, in his influential *Shakespere's Predecessors in the English Drama*, acknowledges the contributions of Shakespeare's forebears yet dismisses their achievements. "Without those predecessors, Shakespeare would certainly have not been what he is," he affirms; he then dismissively concludes, "But having him, we might well afford to lose them."[12] History, including theatrical history, is written by the winners or, in this instance, by the winners' sycophants.

Furthermore, in a curious correlation relevant to this study, much Renaissance drama is seen as outshining medieval drama not only in its literary quality but also in its performative queerness. Following the rise of queer theory in the 1980s and 1990s, scholars have investigated the ways in which plays written and performed throughout the Renaissance revel in queer tensions and torsions of identity, desire, and performance.[13] Indeed, the towering talent of the English early modern era, William Shakespeare, stands as his own subfield in this critical conversation, with his sonnets to a beautiful male beloved raising hints of queer desire in his personal life and with his plays teeming with gender reversals, cross-dressing, and homosocial desire verging on the homoerotic.[14] In contrast, early English drama, so often viewed through the lenses of its theological impulses, moral themes, and sociohistorical commentary, has largely resisted incursions of queer theory into its critical landscape.[15] Here again we see the standard, stereotypical divide thrust upon the artistic achievements of the Middle Ages. The early modern era breaks sharply with the past, ushering in a new era of art, narrative, and learning that rejects the models of the past. The Renaissance is a rebirth – or a "swerve," in Stephen Greenblatt's contested term – that veers Western civilization away from its forebears in the mistiness and mustiness of the Dark Ages.[16] Queerness, in subtle ways, plays a role in these discussions, in the persistent othering of the Middle Ages as the benighted past of sexual repression from which a fresh, vibrant, and energized Renaissance springs forth. The influence of medieval drama can be readily located throughout early modern theatre, in such examples as Christopher Marlowe's use of allegorical traditions and Shakespeare's reverence for Chaucer, and in a host of other such specimens that showcase continuity rather than an abrupt shift.[17] In light of these circumstances it is worth examining the ways in which the queerness of the Renaissance stage was inspired by the queerness of the medieval English stage, dating back to its earliest examples in the liturgical *Quem quaeritis* dialogues, while simultaneously rejecting an evolutionary model that presumes linear improvements from a foundational but debased past.

Given the insults, oversimplifications, yet intransigence of the evolutionary model, *On the Queerness of Early English Drama: Sex in the Subjunctive* explores the queerness that inevitably emerged in the penning and production of early English play-scripts, particularly in the ways in which conflicting meanings – including those that are subversive, coded, and perhaps even unintended – surface in the playful space of dramatic productions, if only temporarily. Notwithstanding the potential freedoms of this form, these dramatic subversions are simultaneously restrained by the ideological regimes governing both the culture and its modes of performance. As Clifford Davidson posits of medieval drama and its thematic treatment of evil, "If the theater at its most serious depends on evil against which its action may be positioned, drama also has a larger function in that it gives visible and audible shape to evil. As such the drama must be seen as embedding evil in symbolic form and hence providing a demonstration of it for the audience, which to be sure may not necessarily respond in conventional ways to the scenes that are presented."[18] Substituting *queer* for *evil* in Davidson's words reveals the ways in which a similar dynamic unfolds on the early English stage, as erotic actions and identities that cannot be endorsed within the prevailing ideological order find a space for expression. Moreover, interpretations and misinterpretations that unmoor a specific play from any morally sound foundations can be generated in this moment of expression.

Certainly, a good deal of dramatic criticism throughout the Middle Ages and into the early modern era condemned the theatre's treatments of sexual themes, if not the theatre's inherent licentiousness, as evils to be overcome, thereby illuminating the connections of sin, performance, and sexuality that create conditions for queerness to surface in various productions.[19] In his *Confessions* (397–400 CE), Augustine condemns the theatre for reinforcing his sinful inclinations: "Rapiebant me spectacula theatrica, plena imaginibus miseriarum mearum et fomitibus ignis mei. quid est quod ibi homo vult dolere cum spectat luctuosa et tragica, quae tamen pati ipse nollet?" (I was carried away by the stage shows, which were full of representations of my own unhappy experiences and added fuel to my flames. Why is it that in the theater people are willing to suffer distress when watching sad and tragic events that they nonetheless have no desire to endure themselves?)[20] For Augustine, the theatre threatens its viewers with moral dissolution, stoking their illicit passions. Roughly a thousand years later, the author of *A Tretise of Miraclis Pleyinge* (c. 1380–1425) similarly bemoaned the sins of the stage: "Myche more pleyinge of miraclis benemeth men ther bileve in Crist and is verre goinge bacward fro dedis of the spirit to onely signes don after lustis of the fleysh that ben agenus alle the deedis of Crist, and so miraclis pleyinge is verre apostasye fro Crist."[21] In his *Playes Confuted in Five Actions* (1582), Stephen Gosson execrates the stage, paying particular attention to its subversion of the male-female binary: "Whatsoeur he be that looketh narrowly into our Stage Playes, or considereth how, and which waye they are represented, shall finde more filthiness in them, then Players dreame off. The Law of God very straightly forbids men to put on womens garments, garments are set downe for signes distinctiue between sexe & sexe, to take vnto vs those garments that are manifest signes of another sexe, is to falsifie, forge, and adulterate, contrarie to the expresse rule of the worde of God."[22] For these critics of the early theatre, it stands as a dangerous medium owing to its dramatic and metadramatic staging of sin and sexuality, a seductive mode that threatens the actors and their audiences through their shared indulgence in proscribed pleasures.

Yet given the early English stage's evasive treatment of sexuality, the critiques of the author of *A Tretise of Miraclis Pleyinge* and Gosson are somewhat surprising. The salvation of a sinner's soul is a much more common storyline than one of heteroerotic romantic love, as Pamela Sheingorn wryly notes: "Young heterosexual couples who fall in love, marry, and produce children through sexual intercourse are virtually absent from a theatre that concerns itself with virginal saints, chaste marriage, immaculate conception, and, of course, virgin birth."[23] Proving Sheingorn's point through its counter-examples, only a very few early English plays focus on heteroerotic romance between human characters, including such comedies as *Fulgens and Lucrece, July and Julian*, and George Gascoigne's *Supposes*; the tragedies *Gismond of Salerne* and *Apius and Virginia*; and the romances *Common Conditions* and *Clyomon and Clamydes*. In line with Sheingorn's observation of the field's predominant interests in religious narratives and moral allegories, many erotic themes stress the miracle of divine intervention in human reproductive affairs instead of the couplings themselves. Rather remarkably, the N-Town Play includes stage directions for Jesus's conception: *"Here þe Holy Gost discendit with iij bemys to oure Lady, the Sone of þe Godhed nest with iij bemys to þe Holy Gost, the Fadyr godly with iij bemys to þe Sone. And so entre all thre to here bosom"* (following line 11.292).[24] This depiction of Jesus's conception, devoid of any hint of human eroticism, captures the tenor of many early English plays' evasive treatments of sexuality, in the focus on spirituality rather than carnality. In the Chester Mystery Cycle Adam approvingly alludes to intercourse – "Therfore man kyndely shall forsake / father and mother, and to wife take; / too in one fleshe, as thou can make, / eyther other for to glad" (2.157–60) – and the following stage directions instruct, "Then Adam and Eve shall stand naked and shall not bee ashamed."[25] Yet this scene is set before humanity's fall from grace, and so its apparent endorsement of sexuality is accompanied by the tacit caveat that prelapsarian pleasures have been lost in a post-lapsarian world.

Notwithstanding such rare dramatic moments that endorse sexuality in the mystery cycles, morality plays and interludes more often depict heterosexual affection as a sign of moral depravity, as evident in Wisdom's words in *Wisdom*: "The prerogatyff of my loue ys so grett / þat wo tastyt þereof þe lest droppe sure / All lustys and lykyngys worldly xall lett" (49–51).[26] The pleasures of this world, its lusts and likings of which surely eroticism is key, must be surpassed on the path to salvation. Many scenes that appear to endorse human sexuality prepare the audience instead to reject its pleasures. In *Jack Jugeler*, Dame Coye tells Boungrace, "Surelye I have of you a great treasure / For you do all thynges which may be to my pleasure" (929–30),[27] and Egistus similarly proclaims to Clytemnestra in *Horestes*, "So is my hart repleate with joye much more a thousand fould, / Oh lady deare, in that I do posses my hartes delyghte" (602–3), yet these relationships are revealed to be morally suspect as the play unfolds.[28] Similarly, Thomas Inglelend's *Disobedient Child* features the Wife's apparently sincere ode to marriage – "Yea, what can be more according to kind, / Than a man to a woman himself to bind?" – yet the play then dramatizes the horrors of marriage, with her husband suffering from her shrewish beatings.[29] As these brief examples demonstrate, early English drama rarely depicts human sexuality and eroticism approvingly, which thus hints at an even greater reticence about queer sexualities and identities.

Although queerness may not appear frequently on the early English stage, other taboo desires and practices, including bestiality, incest, abortion, and ménage à trois, are adumbrated in unexpected moments, thus hinting at the likelihood that queerness could not be fully erased from the dramatic record. In the Towneley Plays, Cain obliquely accuses Abel of bestiality: "Go grese thi shepe vnder the toute, / For that is the moste lefe" (2.66–7).[30] None of the mystery cycles depict such moments of biblical incest as Lot's daughters seducing their drunken father (Genesis 19:30–8), but Judas in the Towneley Plays confesses his patricide and his incestuous affair with his mother: "I slew my father and syn bylay / My moder der" (32.3–4). He also recounts his conception, with his father advocating abortion to his mother: "Lett hit neuer on erth go / Bot be fordon" (32.35–6). In Thomas Preston's *Cambises*, the eponymous anti-hero falls in love with his cousin, who attempts to reject his incestuous advances: "It is a thing that Natures course dooth utterly detest, / And high it would the gods displease of all that is the worst" (910–11).[31] Ill Report, the Vice character of Thomas Garter's *Virtuous and Godly Susanna*, accuses Susanna not merely of adultery but of simultaneous adultery: "Know you not Ioachims wyfe, / It is a peece with a mischeefe, / She must haue two at ones" (894–6).[32] In addition to condemning such sexual transgressions, early English dramas denounce erotic abuses particular to their social milieu, such as in *Hick Scorner* when Pity laments the forced marriages inflicted on widows by mercenary men seeking their wealth: "Widows doth curse lords and gentlemen, / For they constrain them to marry with their men, / Yea, whether they will or no" (109–11).[33] In plays that teach morality, sexuality cannot be altogether avoided, but its inclusion, even negatively expressed on a thematic level, introduces and performs through dialogue and gestures transgressive elements that should ostensibly be hidden from view.

But such is the crux of moral drama: in its blending of the sacred and the profane, early English drama in many instances seeks to entertain while enlightening, to portray sin while preaching virtue, deploying the pleasures available from both. Such disparate aims are broached in the words of the Poeta figure in *Candlemes Day and the Kyllyng of þe Children of Israelle*, as he calls to his audience in his opening prologue: "Besechying you to geve vs peseable audiens! / And ye menstrallis, doth youre diligens! / And ye virgynes, shewe summe sport and plesure, / These people to solas, and to do God reuerens!" (52–5).[34] To do reverence to God, Poeta hails an audience who will listen, minstrels who will play, and virgins who will offer solace – a verb that in many Chaucerian uses clearly indicates fornication – thus adumbrating the pleasures available on and around the early English stage.[35] Few lines summarize better the mixed intentions of much early English drama, and, as conceived by Poeta, heterosexual dalliances are welcomed into the theatrical arena. In another example of yesteryear's playwrights enacting their ability to stir erotic responses from their audiences, John Heywood's Vice figure, No Lover Nor Loved, in *A Play of Love* interrupts himself, when describing his beloved, to warn his audience – "To tell all to you: / I shall undo you" (437–48) – thus suggesting their own likely erotic fascination with her.[36] The early English stage's engagements with queer desires are similarly, if not more, elliptical and tentative in their references, yet as this brief survey of heteroerotic transgression indicates, they are surely as likely to register in numerous moments of suggestive phrasings, moral warnings, and comic energy.

Discussing the queerness of early English theatrical traditions presents challenging lexical issues, which this volume, and even its title – *On the Queerness of Early English Drama: Sex in the Subjunctive* – cannot escape and instead must embrace. The word *queerness* alludes to an ambiguous yet highly productive mode of critical inquiry, pertaining to disruptions of social, ideological, and sexual normativity that allow repressed, subversive, "sinful," or otherwise unexpected gendered and erotic identities to become visible. Within the realm of dramatic criticism, Nick Salvato employs queer theory "not to designate a static site of lesbian and gay identity but to gesture toward transgressive *movements* between and among different positions of sex, gender, and desire."[37] David Savran argues that queerness queries the provisional nature of every performance because it "is constituted in and through its practice. It is less a fixed attribute of a given text or performance than a transient disturbance produced between and among text, actor, director, and spectator."[38] Salvato and Savran speak of the queerness of modern American drama in their works, yet their critical approach, flexible but precise, applies equally to plays of other cultures in other historical moments, for it is attuned to the vagaries of desire and expression that so many dramas explore. Early English drama, more condemnatory than celebratory in its treatments of human sexuality, nonetheless allows the "transgressive *movements*" and "transient disturbance[s]" that Salvato and Savran identify, for erotic desire can never be fully circumscribed either on the page or in a production, with its conflicting surface and subtextual meanings continually in tension.

With regard to the term *early*, the plays examined in this study range chronologically from the 1300s to a *terminus ad quem* of the 1570s and are collectively demarcated as *early*, thereby to sidestep the categorical conundrum of whether particular specimens are better understood as medieval, Tudor, or (early) early modern. Histories of English literature typically date the end of the Middle Ages to 1485 with the accession of the Tudor dynasty, thus dubbing Sir Thomas Malory's and Robert Henryson's artistic sensibilities as medieval but assigning John Skelton, Sir Thomas More, and Sir Thomas Wyatt the Elder to the Renaissance. The Tudor era offers the advantage of clearly marked dates – 1485 to 1603 – yet it bridges the medieval and the early modern eras, and, as a result, scholars continually shuffle plays in and out of their respective purviews. John Coldewey's *Early English Drama: An Anthology* concludes with the Croxton *Play of the Sacrament*, dated to the second half of the fifteenth century, whereas the first volume of Glynne Wickham's magisterial four-volume study, *Early English Stages, 1300 to 1660*, ranges from 1300 to 1576. Several anthologies of medieval English drama impose an end-point of approximately the mid-sixteenth century: David Bevington's *Medieval Drama* concludes with John Redford's *Wit and Science* (c. 1530–48); Greg Walker's *Medieval Drama: An Anthology* concludes with the 1552–4 text of Sir David Lyndsay's *Ane Satyre of the Thrie Estaitis*; and Christina Fitzgerald and John Sebastian's *Broadview Anthology of Medieval Drama* concludes with Ulpian Fulwell's *Like Will to Like* (which was published in 1568, only a year before the last performance in the roughly two-hundred-year run of the York Corpus Christi Plays). In contrast, John Gassner's *Medieval and Tudor Drama* ends with Thomas Norton and Thomas Sackville's *Gorboduc* (1561), choosing an early ending date for a period that comfortably extends to Thomas Kyd, Christopher Marlowe, and William Shakespeare. Darryll Grantley, in his *English Dramatic Interludes, 1300–1580: A Reference Guide*, eschews any such adjective as *medieval, early modern*, or *Renaissance* in his title, instead employing 1580 as his "terminal date" because it is "around five or so years after the building of the first major permanent theatres in London, which signalled the emergence of a new commercial theatre."[39] In a striking example of how time periods are constructed differently for different fields and subdisciplines, and in deference to a range of scholarly opinions and classifications, the Middle Ages typically runs shorter for poetry and longer for drama, despite the paradoxical conundrum of why time might travel at different paces for the literary and the performative arts. Grantley's decision to separate the field before and after the rise of permanent theatres appears a judicious one, yet even it reinforces a division between the medieval and the early modern – as does this volume, too, in its necessary recognition of the simultaneously frustrating fatuity and organizational utility of chronological divisions that the use of *early* seeks to recognize but can never evade.

Regarding the use of the word *English*, the vast majority of the plays discussed in this volume are written in the English language by English authors and were performed in England, but in a chapter dedicated to Scotsman Sir David Lyndsay's *Ane Satyre of the Thrie Estaitis*, the meaning of *English* is called into question, for it raises the issue of whether Scots is a language in itself or, as it is often conceived and potentially disparaged, "English with a Scottish accent."[40] On a related note, should dramas written in Latin by English playwrights, such as John Foxe's *Titus et Gesippus* and *Christus Triumphans* and Thomas Watson's *Absalom*, be considered English plays? To describe all of the plays under consideration in this volume as *English* requires an admittedly expansive use of the adjective that risks subsuming them under a single banner, even as the ensuing analysis acknowledges the intersecting issues of language, culture, education, audience, and identity implicit in this designation. Throughout this volume the word *drama* applies in its broad sense to an entertainment designed for performance by actors assuming the roles of characters and enacting a storyline while reciting dialogue. In common parlance, *drama* is often used in contrast to *comedy* to suggest a work of deeper emotional resonance and subject matter, but many of these early English plays and interludes are nevertheless comic in tone. *Stage* or *theatre* might have been interchanged for *drama* in the title, yet these words are suspect as well because most of the plays were not performed on permanent stages or in theatres but outdoors in the city streets as part of civic cycles, or indoors at private homes, grammar schools, universities, the Inns of Court, and other such locations. The Croxton *Play of the Sacrament* refers to a stage in a stage direction – "*Her shall Ser Ysodyr þe prest spek ont[o] Ser Arystori, seyng on thys wyse to hym; and Jonatas goo don of his stage*"[41] – and Mr. S.'s *Gammer Gurton's Needle*, composed c. 1552–63 and printed in 1575, includes the specific notation that it was "played on stage."[42] The first purpose-built English theatre, the Red Lion, closed its doors quickly after opening in 1567, and more successful theatres opened later in the century (and thus were more safely tucked within the temporal borders of the Renaissance). The words *stage* and *theatre* are used throughout this volume, with the essential caveat that the terms refer to dramatic pastimes rather than to those specifically performed on a stage or in a theatre. Indeed, as Philip Butterworth details, a host of common words and phrases frequently used to describe early English drama – including *character*, *costume*, and *special effects* – are anachronistic and require proper contextualizing to understand this realm on its own terms.[43] Given these vexing taxonomical and philological quandaries, it is evident that the title *On the Queerness of Early English Drama* offers an intervention into a field that is itself hardly capable of definition. The amorphousness of this dramatic field matches the amorphousness of sexual queerness during the medieval and early modern eras, thus necessitating analysis calibrated for as much precision as possible while acknowledging – but not excusing – the inevitability of imprecision.

Following this introduction, the volume's first section, "Queer Theories and Themes of Early English Drama," ranges widely among the specimens of the field, in a survey of scripts that highlights their queer potential. This approach, in examining a variety of early dramatic genres that include mystery plays, morality plays, psychomachias, history plays, and interludes, is eclectic – and, for some critics, such an eclectic approach could be dismissed as merely scattershot. Whether it is termed eclectic or scattershot, however, this perspective is necessary for capturing the diffuse yet fleeting nature of queerness represented on the early English stage, which appears only very rarely on the surface level of a script but is more frequently contained in its subtexts and in the myriad possibilities of performance. Rainer Warning employs a similar approach in his *Ambivalences of Medieval Religious Drama*, arguing for the necessity of "a synoptic view of all the relevant plays" in order to have a better gauge of the inflections of meaning within particular works.[44] Such an approach has the additional advantage of further debunking the evolutionary theory of the transition from medieval to early modern drama. For any readers who might presume that the closer a play chronologically approaches the early modern period, the more likely it is to treat issues of sexuality openly, this supposition is debunked by such works as the notorious *Dux Moraud*, with its darkly incestuous storyline, which dates to the early- to mid-fifteenth century.

This section's first chapter, titled "A Subjunctive Theory of Dramatic Queerness," outlines four key perspectives for assessing the field's erotic subversions, in the possibility of queer scopophilia, queer dialogue, queer characters, and queer performances. Gazing at male actors can pique the audience's desires, with certain plays soliciting the audience's eroticized gaze towards male performers. In a similar vein, listening to suggestive dialogue that bears coded hints of homoerotic desire and transgressive identities, particularly through slang references, can build complementary levels of discourse in a single play, which necessitates that audiences attune themselves to a play's queer meanings – or simply overlook them. Early English playwrights envisioned in their casts a number of characters who transgressed rigid gender roles or otherwise eroded the binary between male and female, and various conditions solicited queer performances from the actors inhabiting these and other such roles. With cross-dressing expected for male actors playing female characters on the early English stage, queer energies could hardly be quelled in the transmission of a story from playwrights to actors to audiences.

Many early English plays, particularly those of and descending from the morality tradition, dramatize the benefits and dangers of men's homosocial friendships, with Vice figures leading protagonists astray, and Virtue figures leading them back to the path of redemption. While male friendships are venerated in many cultural contexts of the Middle Ages and the Renaissance, they also prompt anxieties concerning the possibility that asexual male friendships could evolve – or devolve – into sexual and sodomitical relationships. The following chapter, "Themes of Friendship and Sodomy," traces these tensions to demonstrate the ways in which male friendships both structure many dramatic narratives and subvert the framework of their moral lessons. As a grounding theme of much early English drama, homosociality bears within it the seeds of its own excess, which several playwrights exploit to present either the spiritual horror or the outrageous humour of sodomy. In light of the fluctuating values accorded to male homosociality, same-sex friendships could be staged for moral lessons of deep seriousness and for comic diversions of mirthful pleasure.

The volume's second section, "Queer Readings of Early English Drama," provides detailed interpretations of the subversive erotics depicted in pivotal plays and dramatic sequences of the period. The third chapter, "Performative Typology, Jewish Genders, and Jesus's Queer Romance in the York Corpus Christi Plays," explores the ways in which typology structures the meaning of these and other mystery cycles while undermining the teleology of Christian transcendence purportedly on display. Typology views the Jewish past as a precursor to eternal Christian truths, but within this play cycle it also entails the recoding of Jewish genders as predictors of Christian genders. Typology encourages certain interpretations over others, yet, particularly within the dramatic sphere, it cannot circumscribe the readings it unleashes. These issues are exacerbated in the encoding of the generic elements of romance in the later pageants of the York Corpus Christi Plays, thereby complicating the portrayal of a chaste and sexually temperate Christianity (represented by Jesus and Mary) against a Jewish population (portrayed as reproducing immoderately) – particularly given Jesus's and Mary's identity as Jewish characters. By ending with a queered image of Jesus chastely espoused to his mother, one that is derived from the secular tradition of chivalric romance, the York Corpus Christi Plays remind audiences of the torsions of gender ascribed to Jews, which then underscore the tenuousness of Christian genders, both earthly and heavenly.

In the chapter "Excremental Desire, Queer Allegory, and the Disidentified Audience of *Mankind*," the analysis turns to the queerness of allegory and performance in *Mankind*, one of the most energetic and frenetic of the morality plays. With its carnivalesque story of Mankind seduced into sin by a company of Vice figures, the play revels in scatological humour that cannot be divorced from the human body, as it concomitantly queries the metaphorical equivalence of the divine body as a model of humanity. Moreover, *Mankind* construes its protagonist's pathway to sin as inflected with homosocial desire to the extent that sodomy cannot be erased from its thematic message. With its allegory repeatedly subverting a coherent moral message, *Mankind* forces its audience to neither identify with nor reject its spiritual message but to disidentify with its themes by holding contradictory impulses together at the same moment, even if its redemptive theme must ultimately collapse. Too often viewers of morality plays are presumed to identify with a given play's protagonist and to learn alongside him a key spiritual lesson, but such a foundational assumption of the genre cannot withstand the queer currents of desire enacted on the early English stage and experienced by its audiences during the carnivalesque pleasures of performance.

In his allegorical interludes endorsing the Reformation, John Bale virulently attacks the Catholic Church as a sodomitical den of vice, and the following chapter, "Sodomy, Chastity, and Queer Historiography in John Bale's Interludes," analyses the fault-lines inherent in stagings of his theological critique. Bale aspired to depict regal authority in *King Johan*, hailed as the first English history play, as an exemplary virtue, thereby endorsing the Reformation and Henry VIII's role in it. Complementing this theme, Bale condemns sodomy vociferously, yet this key transgression figures so indeterminately in Reformation discourse and performance, including priestly chastity within its purview, that he cannot effectively distinguish between sodomitic and anti-sodomitic behaviours, particularly in their intersection with the presumed virtue of chastity. Bale includes Sodomismus as a character in his *Thre Lawes of Nature, Moses, and Christ*, but the deeper queer meaning of his interludes emerges in the challenge of staging such allegorical figures as England and such historical figures as King John being cleansed of sexual sin, and thus being ideal representations of a newly reformed England.

It is well known that the professional acting companies of early British drama featured male actors playing women's roles, and it is simply assumed in many interpretations of these plays that the actors sought to preserve the illusion of their cross-dressed performance. Such a baseline assumption no doubt captures the tenor of most such plays and performances, yet it cannot be extended to Sir David Lyndsay's *Ane Satyre of the Thrie Estaitis* without overlooking the farcical gender play that the dialogue demands. The concluding chapter of this section, "Camp and the Hermaphroditic Gaze in Sir David Lyndsay's *Ane Satyre of the Thrie Estaitis*," theorizes Lyndsay's farce as an early exemplar of camp, one that performatively undermines the pretence of gender in the theatrical realm. Furthermore, in its dissolution of the gender binary, *Ane Satyre of the Thrie Estaitis* reorients the audience's gaze to question gendered illusions and to perceive the hermaphroditic potential of all actors in all roles.[45] Seeing is not believing in this riotous romp, and Lyndsay exposes the campy façades of gender to depict dual levels of queer desire, both male and female, through his insistent direction that his actors accentuate their performative genders to the point of absurdity. The conclusion, "Theatrical Medievalisms, Terrence McNally's *Corpus Christi*, and the Queer Legacy of Early English Drama," briefly examines the persistence of early English settings and stories in contemporary drama, demonstrating the continued allure of medievalisms in the theatrical realm. Among the many post-medieval playwrights looking to the past for inspiration in the present, McNally stands out in his attempt to create a queer morality play, one directly inspired from medieval dramatic traditions, in his *Corpus Christi*. By reinventing Jesus as Joshua, a gay man from Corpus Christi, Texas, McNally rewrites the passion play from a queer perspective, yet the play was spurned by many critics, particularly with the dismissive assessment levelled at much queer theatre: that it sought to "preach to the converted." Such criticisms echo those earlier directed towards medieval drama, in that its attention to Christian tenets and morality led to plays that were simplistic rather than complex. The volume thus concludes by linking McNally's *Corpus Christi* and its critical vicissitudes to those of early English drama as a whole and suggests instead the necessity of evaluating drama that "preaches to the converted" on its own dramatic and thematic impulses.

As a whole, early English drama sought to uphold central tenets of Christianity while entertaining audiences with storylines that admitted the possibility of sin. Sin and other such transgressions spark the necessary conflicts for a plot and its resolution, with queerness serving as such a necessary transgression and frequently appearing furtively in the sideways interactions of the performers and their audiences, in actors encoding subversive elements in their roles, and in audiences viewing according to their personal sense of pleasure. Although early English drama, as a whole, eschewed direct treatments of sexuality, whether normative or queer, *On the Queerness of Early English Drama* examines noteworthy encounters that highlight early drama's indirect engagement with homoerotic desire and its representations. The theatrical realm, as Augustine, the author of *A Tretise of Miraclis Pleyinge*, and Gosson remind their readers, solicits no end of transgressive, salacious, and simply unexpected pleasures, and the queerness of early English drama, both in its blatant and latent enactments, stands as one of its chief, if often overlooked, delights.

PART ONE

Queer Theories and Themes of Early English Drama

A Subjunctive Theory of Dramatic Queerness

"In sensuall causys delyght is chefe maistres, /
Specyally recountying lovys bysynes."
Celestina, in Calisto and Mélebea (lines 566–7)

"Sometimes the place presumes a wanton mynde."
Bailo, in Jocasta (vol. 1, act 1, scene 1, p. 258)

As Celestina, in *Calisto and Mélebea*, informs her interlocutors and her audience, people enjoying talking about "lovys bysynes" – wooing, courtship, sex, and related shenanigans. Within the dramatic sphere it is likewise fun to imagine, act out, and view "lovys bysynes" for all those who partake of the theatrical realm, including playwrights, directors, actors, audiences, costumers, and set designers. Enacting such storylines nevertheless requires a host of independent and interlocking decisions about how to stage erotic desire, considering in particular the sociocultural mores of the early English stage. Moreover, as Bailo states in George Gascoigne and Francis Kinwelmershe's *Jocasta*, certain locations spark immoderate thoughts, with the theatre standing as an inviting site for imaginations ranging from the chaste to the lurid. In assessing the queerness of early English drama, we are confronted with the challenge of contemplating how transgressive desires were envisioned by contemporary playwrights, portrayed by contemporary actors, and interpreted by contemporary audiences.

To consider such issues solely in relation to the past, however, would freeze these plays in the historical moment of their creation and production and thus would deny the possibility that their ambiguities could be exploited when the plays are staged anew in the present and into the future. A script is relatively static, but a performance is always dynamic. Of course, many scripts resist scholarly attempts to determine their definitive editions, particularly owing to conflicting versions of manuscripts and early printed volumes. Describing a dramatic script as "relatively static" oversimplifies its creation, history, and editorial reconstruction, while recognizing its fundamental contrast with the ephemerality of its many performances. In a telling example of the challenges of textual fidelity and the early theatre's engagement with sexuality, John Daye, the printer of the 1570 edition of Thomas Sackville and Thomas Norton's *Gorboduc*, compares its previous publisher, William Griffith, to a rapist for his misdeeds against the play's meaning: "even as if by means of a broker for hire, he should have enticed into his house a fair maid and done her villainy, and after all to-bescratched her face, torn her apparel, berayed and disfigured her, and then thrust her out of doors dishonested."[1] In the complex and never finalized interplay between page and stage, and, as Tiffany Stern argues, between stage and page as well, springs forth an artistic space of endless interpretive possibilities.[2]

Grammatically, the subjunctive mood indicates not the actual but the anticipated, not the determined but the desired. It is "the mood of a verb that shows hopes, doubts, or wishes," Keith Folse explains,[3] and thus it captures the whirlwind of possibilities always swirling in the dramatic sphere, particularly in light of the conditional, potential, and aspirational quality of all playscripts. No script, even with multitudinous stage directions, can ensure that a given performance will align with the playwright's vision; no number of rehearsals, even with countless cajoleries, blandishments, or threats, can ensure that a given performance will align with the director's ambition. Recognizing these conditions, several dramatic theorists have characterized the subjunctive nature of performance. Victor Turner proposes that drama and other cultural performances reveal a society's "subjunctive mood," allowing a space where "taboos are lifted, fantasies are enacted," yet one where "ritual forms still constrain the order and often the style of ritual events."[4] Richard Schechner, outlining how cultural performances create conditions for the "restoration of behavior," discerns the inherent conditionality of drama: "Understanding what happens during training, rehearsals, and workshops – investigating the subjunctive mood that is the medium of these operations – is the surest way to link aesthetic and ritual performance."[5] Joseph Roach muses in a similar vein that "no action or sequence of actions may be performed exactly the same way twice; they must be reinvented or recreated at each appearance," a phenomenon he refers to as "repetition with a difference."[6] Within these parameters all actors must confront the range of potential meanings in a script and determine the *could*, the *would*, and the *should* necessary in interpreting words on a page and performing them on a stage. The eternal challenge of textual interpretation, along with the concomitant ambiguity of the multiple and conflicting readings that a given script might generate, establishes the great unpredictability of the dramatic experience for its creators, its casts, and its audiences.

The subjunctive qualities of the theatrical experience are particularly relevant to considering the queerness of early English drama, for, as discussed in the introduction, this is not a theatrical tradition deeply invested in detailing the passions of sexual desire, whether heteroerotic or homoerotic in its orientation. Mystery plays depict biblical narratives culminating in Jesus's passion and its aftermath, morality plays inevitably conclude with their protagonists redeemed (though after first falling to sinful temptations), and most interludes similarly stage Virtue figures allegorically triumphing over their Vice counterparts. Although sexuality is rarely foregrounded in these plot lines, it is too central an aspect of the human condition to be ignored, and so it enters into texts through their margins and their subtexts and then onto the stage through the decisions of the cast and crew – sometimes collectively, sometimes individually – to stress a particular aspect of the script. Recognizing these conditions, this chapter examines and theorizes four clusters of potential queerness in early English drama, including queer scopophilia, queer dialogue, queer characters, and queer performance. These clusters, it should be noted, cannot be cleanly divided from one another: audiences simultaneously look at actors acting while hearing the words they speak, and actors must perform the actions of the characters that they adopt. It should further be noted that the examples of these queer theatrical modes range widely among the specimens of early English drama; this ecumenical approach allows for an expansive view of the field's potential queerness but one that admittedly collapses disparate dramatic traditions under a unifying critical perspective, despite their variations in theme and tone. Fintan Walsh observes, in considering the queerness of the theatre, "From a certain perspective all live performance might be aligned with [queerness], as so often the contingency of the event, not to mention the indeterminacy of desire and identification among those present, speaks to the slipperiness of all identity."[7] Walsh's words apply well to the dramatic events portrayed on the early English stage, where various gendered and erotic identities, from the surreptitious to the brazen, were enacted, with queer possibilities surfacing not always for direct viewing but more for sideways glances, in the moment of wondering if what one just saw was really as queer as one might think.

Queer Scopophilia

"It does me good to feed mine eyes on him" (scene 8, line 21), declares Damon of his friend Pythias in Richard Edwards's *Damon and Pythias*, in a statement acknowledging the pleasure of gazing on the male figure.[8] Paul Woodruff describes the dramatic experience as an "art of watching and being watched,"[9] and the theatre as a visual medium offers a range of scopophilic pleasures. George Rodosthenous posits, "Theatre is a voyeuristic exchange between the performer and the audience, where the performer (the object of the audience's gaze) and the audience (the voyeur of this exchange) are placed in a legalized and safe environment for that interaction." He further theorizes that scopophilic voyeurism occurs not only when actors depict amorous or provocative encounters but also "when the audience has an excessive interest watching the performers in everyday (non-sexual) scenes."[10] It is evident that early English playwrights considered the audience's gaze as a constitutive factor of the theatrical experience, such as when Idleness of Francis Merbury's *Marriage between Wit and Wisdom* selects a particular man in the audience to taunt simply because he is watching the play that has been staged for his pleasure: "What, I ween all this company are come to see a play! / What lookest thee, good fellow? didst see ne'er a man before? / Here is a gazing! I am the best man in the company, when there is no more!" (88–90).[11] In this moment of metadramatic discourse, Idleness mocks this audience member for participating in the theatrical experience through his gaze, while simultaneously foregrounding himself as the object of the man's attention.

As evident from this example, all theatrical events must be corporealized by the actors upon whom the audience focuses its attention, and, to enhance this narrative and performative bond, playwrights clearly envision certain roles for good-looking performers. These foundational precepts, within the homosocial world of early English drama, necessitate that handsome men frequently stand as the focalized object of other men's gazes.[12] Good-looking characters should be played by good-looking actors, and even when a character's physical allure is not essential to a role, and excepting circumstances when perfect beauty is represented by a mask, attractive actors often receive prominent parts. Given these casting conditions, the early English stage solicits queer currents between its male viewers and the males they view. Along these lines, several characters of dubious morality pride themselves on their physical allure, with the playwrights encouraging their audiences to indulge in the pleasures of the gaze. In Thomas Watson's *Absalom*, the eponymous anti-hero, rebelling against King David's authority, approvingly admires himself: "Hos forma contemptus recusat, et decor / vultu refulgens" (1.1.108–9; My fine physique and the comeliness glowing in my face protest against these scorns);[13] this figure, as Gila Aloni and Shirley Sharon-Zisser confirm, long stood as an "object of androgynous beauty and polymorphic desire, including the desire of his father, who is described as having 'long[ed] for him' (Samuel II 14:1)."[14] *Thersites* features another eponymous anti-hero who solicits the audience's gaze: "When I consider my shoulders that so brode be, / When the other partes of my bodye I do beholde" (120–1), he begins and soon adds, "Beholde you my handes, my legges, and my feete! / Every parte is stronge, proportionable, and mete" (147–8).[15] In a further example it would certainly be a stunning case of miscasting for a man even of average looks to be cast as Youth, the protagonist of *The Interlude of Youth*. In his opening lines this young man celebrates his beautiful body:

My hair is royal, and bushed thick,
My body pliant as a hazel stick;
My arms be both fair and strong,
My fingers be both fair and long,
My chest big as a tun,
My legs be full light for to run. (47–52)[16]

Such a self-blazon is indicative of the sin of pride, and in this tale of moral redemption Charity chastises Youth for his egotism: "You had need to ask God mercy. / Why did you so praise your body?" (64–5). Charity's words, which discern the body as the suspect source of human frailty, carnality, and sin, align with the play's redemptive theme that Youth must concentrate on his spiritual future rather than on his hedonistic present. Notwithstanding Charity's prudent advice, some audience members, whether male or female, would likely recognize in Lady Lechery's words their own desires for the actor playing Youth: "And when it please you on me to call, / My heart is yours, body and all" (460–1). Handsome actors playing antagonists, anti-heros, and unredeemed sinners do not dampen their physical appeal, and in these instances the audiences are interpellated into the play's moral themes if they accede to the pleasureful eroticism of gazing at good-looking men.

Whereas the previous scenes staging Absalom, Thersites, and Youth as objects of desire do not explicitly underscore their homoerotic appeal, John Skelton's *Magnyfycence* features Lyberte – a male character addressed as "syr" by Felycyte (26) – who presents himself as the object of illicit desire, both heteroerotic and homoerotic:

I am so lusty to loke on, so freshe, and so fre,
That nonnes wyll leue theyr holynes and ryn after me;

Freers, with Foly I make them so fayne
They cast vp theyr obedyence to cache me agayne,
At Lyberte to wander and walke ouer all,
That lustely they lepe somtyme theyr cloyster wall. (2145–50)

With these lines satirizing the sexual appetites of nuns and friars, Liberty's attractiveness must be apparent to all audience members, and, as with Lady Lechery's lascivious assessment of Youth, certain audience members would likely agree with these nuns and friars about Liberty's desirability. Through the theatrical construction of queer scopophilia, audiences are drawn into the transitory earthly pleasures that *Absalom, Thersites, The Interlude of Youth,* and *Magnyfycence* thematically condemn.

The queer potential of handsome actors is complicated, but not necessarily lessened, when they play holy figures. In the Towneley Plays, John the Baptist calls Jesus "the semelyst that ever was seyn" (15.266),[17] and Secundus Angelus of the Chester Mystery Cycle likewise praises his attractiveness: "Comely hee ys in his clothinge, / and with full power goinge" (20.109–10).[18] Earlier, this cycle depicts Jesus naked, with Cayphas stating exasperatedly, "Men, for cockes face, / howe longe shall pewee-ars / stand naked in that place? / Goe nayle him on the tree!" (16A.149–52).[19] Surely the audience did not see a naked Jesus on the stage, but they must have seen Jesus in some state of undress or in costuming such as a leather smock to indicate undress, and if the actor playing Jesus is "comely" subsequently, he must be "comely" in this scene, too. The mystery cycles encourage their audiences to contemplate the divine magnanimity of Jesus's crucifixion, but in this instance certain audience members would quite possibly desire the scourged and stripped actor playing this role. With spiritual desire surging for Jesus in his sacrifice and sexual desire surging for the actor playing him, the mystery plays inspire intersecting levels of spirituality and eroticism from their scopophilic delights.

Several morality plays feature naked protagonists, with the muddying factor that they are imagined as characters of indeterminate age who are recently born yet capable of speech. Susannah Crowder affirms that "nakedness was seen in this period as a way of revealing the true self" and documents the prevalence of leather garments for depicting nudity.[20] In *The Castle of Perseverance*, Human Genus recounts his birth: "I was born þis nyth in blody ble / And nakyd I am, as ȝe may se" (284–5).[21] In *Mundus et Infans*, Infans describes himself as a newborn, mentioning the "forty weeks I was freely fed / Within my mother's possession" (40–1) and lamenting, "Now into the World she hath me sent, / Poor and naked – as ye may se" (44–5).[22] Both plays stress the visuality of the moment with an identical rhetorical flourish – "as ʒe may se" – demanding that the audience gaze upon and contemplate the actor's naked body. *The Castle of Perseverance* and *Mundus et Infans* do not address the question of whether their protagonists are first played by child actors – a possibility that, in light of their treatment of temporal themes, seems less likely for *The Castle of Perseverance* but more likely for *Mundus et Infans*, and almost certainly true for *Gismond of Salerne*, in which Cupid introduces himself as "a naked boy, not clothed but with wing" (1.1.2).[23] A later morality play, T. Lupton's *All for Money*, comments ironically on such birth scenes in its dramatization of Sin's birth – or more accurately, his birth from his father's vomit – with the character then explaining his adult size: "And although I be young, yet am I well grown" (244).[24] In Henry Medwall's *Nature*, the Worlde proclaims his desire for Man, the naked protagonist: "Ye are the parsone, wythout faynyng, / That I have evermore desyred to se. / Come let me kys you! O benedycyte, / Ye be all naked!" (430–3).[25] The Worlde represents sin and Man's downfall in this interlude, and his desire for a kiss would be more thematically consistent with his character if it were staged as lasciviously as possible, with Man's nudity enhancing the scene's voyeuristic appeal. Envy undresses Prosperity in *Impatient Poverty* – "Off with this lewd array. / It becometh you nought, by this day!" (681–2) – with his words suggesting that Prosperity would become more attractive with either different or no clothing.[26] Of course, these actors did not appear in the nude; William Tydeman documents that early English productions relied on "the medieval equivalent of the modern body-stocking or leotard and tights," which are referred to as *lybkleider* (body clothing) in several accounts.[27] The illusion of undress nonetheless creates provocative effects, and an actor's call for audiences to gaze upon him heightens the oscillating experience of seeing a man in dramatic costuming that simultaneously encourages them to visualize him naked.

In a manner similar to nudity, costuming can powerfully pique the audience's desire, for, as Stephen Orgel pithily summarizes, "clothes make the woman, clothes make the man: the costume is of the essence."[28] In "Woman Taken in Adultery," the N-Town Plays stage an illicit liaison as recorded in John 8:1–11, with the audience seeing not an erotic encounter but its aftermath: *"Hic juuenis quidam extra currit in deploydo, calligis non ligatis et braccas in manu tenens"* (following 24.124; Here a certain young man runs outside in his underwear, with his boots untied and holding his pants in his hand).[29] In this surprisingly frank depiction of adultery, the character's costuming imbues this encounter, likely staged comically, with a soupçon of scopophilic pleasure. Whereas the visuality of this scene depends on an actor in a state of sinful undress, a complementary theme of early English drama condemns excessive fashions, either execrating men who bedeck themselves in sumptuous finery or exposing the ploys of Vice characters who advocate the latest couture, such as Tutivillus in the Towneley Plays (27.339–51), Galavnt in the Digby *Mary Magdalen* (491–506),[30] and Nichol Newfangle in Ulpian Fulwell's *Like Will to Like* (58–68).[31] In John Foxe's *Christus Triumphans*, Satan acts as a costumer, dressing himself as the Angel of Light and his minions in deceptive finery (5.1.13–28),[32] and the stage directions of *All for Money* stress the importance of his shocking costume: "*Here cometh in SATAN the great devil, as deformedly dressed as may be*" (following 347). As discussed in chapter 4, the Vice characters of *Mankind* take a noted interest in the eponymous protagonist's dress and literally fashion him according to their desires. On the early English stage, such clothing would have marked the sinfulness of male characters bedecked in vestments of similar excess, with queer potential evident in the heady intersection of homosociality, fashion, and desire.

While many actors, whether costumed in alluring finery or standing in a state of undress, become objects of desire when the eyes of their audience members are locked on them, it is not always clear whether viewers should believe characters who proclaim their handsomeness, such as when Torturer 1 of the Towneley Plays affirms, "For I am right semely and fare in the face" (21.192), and when Herod in the York Corpus Christi Plays similarly declares, "Lordis and ladis, loo, luffely me lithes, / For I am fairer of face and fressher on folde" (16.16–17).[33] Antagonists and Vice characters frequently deceive protagonists, audiences, and themselves, and so this character might be played by an unattractive man for the comic disjunction between his self-perception and the audience's assessment of him. Despite this necessary caveat, and as the previous examples illustrate, many early English playwrights sought to amplify the appeal of their productions through the allure of their characters and of the actors playing them, with the visuality of their costuming similarly enhancing their stage presence – even when these attractions are construed as sinful. The desires unleashed through these and other such visual pleasures could hardly be quarantined from queerness.

Lastly on this point, and while pederasty should not be conflated with homosexuality, it would be remiss not to mention that the adolescent actors of early English drama could spark a wide range of erotic attractions, not only those of homoerotically inclined adult men. The Prologue character of *Tom Tyler and His Wife* divulges first his intention for his audience – "To make you joy and laugh at merrie toyes" – and then the means for accomplishing this goal – "I mean a play set out by prettie boyes" (6–7).[34] Several early English plays foreground the theme of adolescent males led astray by corrupt advisers, such as when Gorboduc's secretary Eubulus warns him, "Traitorous corrupters of their pliant youth / Shall have unspied a much more free access" (1.2.386–7). In *Damon and Pythias*, Grim the collier states of his antagonists Will and Jack, "Who invented these monsters first, did it to a ghostly end / To have a male ready to put in other folks' stuff" (scene 13, lines 93–4). Grim's words are a bit obscure, but as Ros King explains of the multiple levels of punning on *male* as a travelling bag, as a hole qua anus, and as the Latin *male*, or evil, these lines "comment ironically on the anti-theatrical attacks frequently made by Protestant divines on boy actors as objects of homosexual desire," which construes them as the "sink and repository of other people's filthy thoughts."[35] Alan Bray documents that Nicholas Udall, author of *Royster Doyster* and headmaster of Eton, "was involved in a scandal because of the homosexual relationship he had had with one of his former pupils. The events are somewhat mysterious, but the affair seems to have come to light during an investigation by the Privy Council into the theft of some school plate in which the boy had been involved."[36] While one cannot construe much from these misty events, it seems apparent that, during his dramatic pastimes, Udall looked at the actors on the stage and liked what he saw. Surely he was not alone in divining the queerly scopophilic pleasures available on the early English stage for all to gaze upon.

Queer Dialogue

Many scenes in early English drama assume queer (or queerer) intonations if readers view those most venerable of linguistic research tools, the *Oxford English Dictionary* (*OED*) and the *Middle English Dictionary* (*MED*), with a healthy dash of scepticism in their assessments of the slang meanings of medieval words in literary contexts. More so than with their denotations, the colloquial connotations of words inhabit a linguistic underworld long before they can be codified semantically. In several intriguing passages in early English drama, words whose sexual meanings are confirmed in William Shakespeare's usage remain undefined – or, perhaps more accurately, predefined – for the Middle Ages. Again, such circumstances require a subjunctive analysis, for to argue that the *OED* and the *MED* should not in all instances be viewed as appropriately impartial and respected arbiters of a word's meanings is itself a controversial claim. As the following discussion of snippets of dialogue from early English plays indicates, the contextual usages of many words strongly argue that the *OED* and the *MED* should recognize that the denotations of various words include queer connotations and that many early modern slang words trace their roots to the Middle Ages.

To begin with a fairly obvious example, *capon* – that is, a castrated chicken – conveys slang denotations of emasculated and thus potentially queer men, although the *OED* and *MED* do not register these usages. In Nicholas Udall's *Royster Doyster* the masculinity of Rafe Royster Doyster sparks much humour, with Mathew Merygreeke referring to him as "Malkyn" (1.2.114) – that is, according to the *OED*, either a "sluttish woman" or an "impotent or effeminate man."[37] Dobinet Doughtie says, "Oft is hee a wower, but never doth he speede" (1.4.10), and Merygreeke likens him to a capon (1.2.29). The *OED* and *MED* hit close to the mark by including *eunuch* in their definitions of *capon*, but this appears too restrictive a definition.[38] The audience, unless a group of committed literalists, has no reason to suspect that Royster Doyster is indeed castrated, whereas *capon*'s figurative meaning as an emasculated or queered man more accurately captures the play's gendered humour. In this instance, both the *OED* and the *MED* do not register this obvious metaphorical usage, which, it should be noted, need not even be the grounds of a criticism: to define a word in its entirety could not possibly entail including all of its potential metaphorical applications, although it raises the issue of the point at which a prevalent metaphorical usage becomes another subsidiary definition.

To push this example further, *capon* appears to serve as a double entendre for a male prostitute in *Four Elements*. Humanyte, falling to the depravities of life with his new friend Sensuall Appetyte, is hungry and wishes he "had a good stewyd capon" (576).[39] Sensuall Appetyte replies that "all capons be gone" and offers instead, "Yet I can get you a stewed hen / That is redy dyght" (580–2). *Stewed* puns on the *stewes*, or brothels, as evident in Sensuall Appetyte's following line that this chicken qua prostitute "lay at the stewes all nyght" (586). Also, whereas *dighten* typically means "to prepare, get ready for use," the *MED* confirms its slang meaning "to have sexual intercourse with (a woman)."[40] Within this interlude's comic vulgarity, the double entendre conflating hens, sexual intercourse, and prostitutes is unquestioned and virtually unquestionable, and so Humanyte's wish for a "good stewyd capon" – even if we imagine that the character does not realize himself to be punning on a male prostitute in a brothel – imbues the scene with a deeper comedy, particularly with Sensuall Appetyte's satiric assessment that the capons have all been taken by the king (577–9). Based on the congruence between a stewed hen and a stewed capon within roughly twelve lines of dialogue, the queer connotations of the latter should be allowed as a likely, albeit coded, meaning, precisely because queerness so often must be occluded owing to the socio-cultural conditions of the era and even more so when one is satirizing the sexual appetites of the royalty.

In a particularly thorny passage of Middle English slang in John Skelton's *Magnyfycence*, Magnyfycence, Fansy, and Felycyte exchange pointed barbs expressing queer antagonism. Responding to Felycyte's words, Fansy declares, "In fayth, I set not by the worlde two Dauncaster cuttys," to which Magnyfycence replies, "Ye wante but a wylde fly-eng bolte to shote at the buttes" (293–4). Paula Neuss glosses *Doncaster cuts* as "daggers," noting that "Doncaster daggers were proverbial,"[41] whereas Greg Walker explains that Doncaster cuts were "horses with cropped tails."[42] Neuss translates *buttes* as "marks," "buttocks," and "casks of ale"; Walker translates it, perhaps more likely, as "targets," with the combined possibilities of meaning facilitating a double entendre. Magnyfycence then says, "For whiche ende goth forwarde ye take lytell charge" (296) – a line that, following the suggestion of a wildly flying bolt, elliptically admits the possibility of anal penetration – and then adds, "Wel, wyse men may ete the fysshe, when ye shal draw the pole" (300). First, it is unclear whether Middle English *pole*, modernized as *pool* in Neuss's edition, refers to Modern English *pool* or *pole*. Neuss asserts that the passage refers to the proverb "Fools lade the water and wise men catch the fish." Indeed, this is the likelier meaning of the phrase, but the possibility of a double entendre should not be overlooked, particularly owing to the phonic similarity of *pool* and *pole* in late Middle English. Like Freud's cigar, which is sometimes just a cigar, a fish and a fishing pole may simply represent themselves, yet *fish* has long been employed as a vulgar euphemism for women and female genitalia. This usage is evident in Shakespeare's *Henry IV, Part 1*, when Falstaff insults the Hostess: "Why? she's neither fish nor flesh, a man knows not where to have her" (3.3.128).[43] Skelton was likely aiming for a similarly crude joke with his *fish*. The *OED* confirms *pole*'s usage as *penis* to the early 1600s, but this signification likely pre-dates its earliest documented meaning.[44] The *OED* and *MED* are silent about the slang meanings of *fish*, although Eric Partridge confirms its meaning as "a girl or woman, viewed sexually, especially a prostitute," in his *Shakespeare's Bawdy*.[45] One need not read Skelton's passage as laden with queer allusions to anal penetration and hand jobs, yet the comedy of the scene – and it is most certainly a comic scene – is heightened if these double entendre are allowed as likely, but occluded, interpretations that some in the audience would catch but others would miss. Medieval authors frequently relied on plausible deniability to excuse their bawdy fictions, as in Chaucer's retraction to his *Canterbury Tales* and in the plea of the author of *Four Elements* "to regarde his only intent and good wyll" (14). In a similar manner, Skelton could deny any queer significations to these passages at the same moment that they were startlingly present.

In an intriguing passage of *Lusty Juventus*, Hypocrisy encourages Juventus to indulge in sinful pastimes, exhorting him: "We shall have merry company, / And I warrant thee if we have not a pie, / We shall have a pudding" (706–8).[46] Pies have long been connected to female genitalia, and puddings, in their British culinary association with sausages, have been correspondingly connected to male genitalia. The *OED* records the meaning of *pudding* as "penis" to 1693, as registered in Thomas Urquhart and Peter Anthony Motteux's translation of *The Third Book of the Works of Mr. Francis Rabelais*.[47] Rabelais died in 1553, and so the word's meaning as "penis" in French pre-dates Urquhart and Motteux's translation by roughly 140 years, but this connotation likely carried over into English slang much earlier: as Garrett P.J. Epp notes, "puddings – bags or entrails stuffed with something else … are referred to with … sexual innuendo" in the works of John Bale.[48] In *King Darius*, the Vice figure Iniquity insults his counterpart Equity – "And here, John Puddingmaker, / Here is for thee a taper / With a pair of beads" – with the phallic imagery of a candle and two beads making explicit the symbolism of the insulting epithet.[49] A pudding is used as a phallic stage prop in George Whetstone's *Promos and Cassandra* when Dalia flirts with Grimball: the stage direction states, "*She takes out a white pudding*" (part 1, following 4.7.8), with flirtatious banter following. Grimball complains, "You powte me, if that you got, my Pudding awaye"; she rebuts, "Nay good sweete, honny *Grimball*, this Pudding giue mee" (4.7.9–10).[50] Similarly, in *July and Julian*, the servant Fenell says to Nan, "Put a podinge in ye pott, y^t I may haue somewhat," to which she replies, "For all thi mocke, I will not sticke wth the for that" (244–5).[51] The play ends with July and Julian engaged, and the servant Wilkin commenting approvingly of their match: "here ys as mett a grement as a podinge for a friers mouth" (1292) – an apparent allusion to fellatio that correlates with the many sodomitical insults levied against fraternal orders.[52] As these examples illustrate, the phallic connotations of puddings frequently elicit queer interpretations that align with a play's satiric and humorous themes.

With these examples and others, readers must consider the circumstances of the scene and the likelihood of a given word denoting vulgarly, and in many instances it is exceedingly difficult to determine whether an erotic subtext should be recognized. In *Lusty Juventus*, Juventus, jealous of "some whoreson villain" (804) who has fornicated with Abominable Living, threatens this unidentified figure: "Tell me,

I pray you, who it was, / And I will trim the knave, by the blessed mass!" (807–8). The *OED* misses the mark widely on the slang meaning of *trim*, dating its meaning to 1955 as "sexual intercourse with a woman" and ascribing its usage to the United States.[53] Yet this meaning is readily apparent in Shakespeare's *Titus Andronicus*, in Aaron's cruelly punning account of Lavinia's rape: "Why, she was wash'd, and cut, and trimm'd, and 'twas / Trim sport for them which had the doing of it" (5.1.95–6).[54] Willful Wanton in *The Tide Tarrieth No Man* desires a husband who "would trimly bebrave" her (809),[55] and Sin in *All for Money* says of Mother Croote, who desires a young husband, "Oh, she will be a trim bride, that day she is wed!" (1301). Some would surely argue that it stretches the bounds of credible interpretations to envision Juventus as threatening to avenge himself sexually on this "whoreson villain," but it is equally worth considering that we may be bowdlerizing our interpretations by not leaning in to the full range of the word's meanings and its homoerotic threat. More so, even if the *Lusty Juventus* playwright did not intend such a meaning, his intentions would not preclude an audience member from hearing an unintended allusion to a sodomitical revenge, for from contemporary usage it is abundantly clear that *trim* frequently carries a connotation, and at times a denotation, of sexual intercourse.

As this brief overview indicates, the history of queer slang in medieval England remains to be written, and the field would benefit greatly from its own Eric Partridge to document the full range of obscenity, vulgarity, and sexuality likely intended by early English authors.[56] Scholars of Shakespearian bawdy language tend to date the connotations of vulgar words to the Renaissance era, thus further accentuating a perceived sharp divide between the medieval and early modern eras rather than their many continuities. Numerous Renaissance slang words evince hints of their prehistory that can be fruitfully explored in their appearance in early English drama, as they were likely enhanced by comic gestures and performances on the stage. In the following pages of this chapter and book, the authority of the *OED* and the *MED* is repeatedly challenged to document that early English playwrights were often as obscenely and vulgarly humorous as their early modern counterparts.

Queer Characters

Several characters of early English drama blur the rigid borders between male and female that were common to the Middle Ages and the Renaissance, and the actors embodying these roles were called to subvert preconceived notions of gender distinctions between the sexes. Musing over cultural constructions of gender, Derek Neal postulates that "every society presents its members with a set of meanings imputed to biological sex,"[57] and Caroline Walker Bynum delineates the predominant binaries of medieval gender paradigms: "*Male* and *female* were contrasted and asymmetrically valued as intellect/body, active/passive, rational/irrational, reason/emotion, self-control/lust, judgment/mercy, and order/disorder."[58] Characters who challenged the male-female binary, particularly emasculated men and masculine women, appeared frequently in early English drama, and the unremarkable nature of many of their depictions indicates that, despite the rigidity of medieval gender roles, their ultimate porosity was acknowledged as well. The following pages discuss a wide range of such characters who upset the male-female binary, including cross-dressers, hermaphrodites, eunuchs, and characters alternately perceived as male and female within a given play.

Recognizing the gendered imbalance between actors and their roles, playwrights could enhance the humour of their plots through the lability of the border between male and female, and in several instances male characters are ridiculed for their effete masculinity, thus disproving any biological ontology to gender. Christina Fitzgerald observes that early English plays revel in the contradictions of masculinity, and she details the ways in which these works, while "attempt[ing] to discipline masculine bodies and shape individual and corporate identity," simultaneously "reveal masculinity as something performed or played, as a show or a game, and therefore unessential, unstable, and not in earnest: something easily appropriated, usurped, or lost."[59] During the Middle Ages effeminate men were viewed as inferior to their more masculine counterparts, although, as Elspeth Whitney explains, effeminacy registered differently than it does today, such as in the fact that "hypersexuality or an *excess* of attraction to women … was identified as effeminate because femininity was aligned with lack of restraint and masculinity with self-control."[60] Characters of early English drama frequently evaluate one another according to their performance of gender, such as in Esau's barbed assessment of his mollycoddled sibling in *The History of Iacob and Esau*: "Nay, he must tarrie and sucke mothers dugge at home" (118).[61] Little indicates that Iacob's subsequent performance should be inflected with his brother's dismissive assessment of his masculinity, but when such slights and insults accumulate, and when they can be parlayed into a more detailed profile of a character, a queer personality may begin to emerge.

Further along these lines, in playing effeminate or otherwise emasculated men, actors could emphasize this aspect of their characters to heighten the comic effect of their performances. For instance, in the Digby *Candlemes Day and the Kyllyng of þe Children of Israelle*, Watkyn beseeches Herod to let him join the other soldiers in the slaughter. "For oon thyng I promyse you: I wille manly fight, / ... / Though I sey it myself, I am a man of myght" (137–9), he says with words that protest too much, and Herod dubiously replies, "Be thi trouthe, Watkyn, wold-est thu be made a knyght? / ... / But thu were neuer provid in bataile nor in fight" (145–7).[62] Another man of dubious masculinity, Gib in *The Shepherds (2)* of the Towneley Plays presents himself as overmatched by his wife: "She is as greatt as a whall; / She has a galon of gall. / By hym that dyed for us all / I wald I had ryn to I had lost hir" (9.153–6). The more the actor playing Gib accentuates the character's fear of his wife, the greater the humour. Furthermore, Gib shares the stage with his fellow shepherds Coll and Daw, and so any corollary decisions related to his gestures, mannerisms, and costuming would better individual-ize this character. A more emasculated Gib becomes a more individu-ated Gib, who thus becomes a more memorable character: following the logic of this dramatic syllogism, a queerer Gib becomes a better role for the actor to play. This principle would apply to a range of pitiful, unsuc-cessful, or cuckolded lovers in early English drama, including the title characters of *Tom Tyler and His Wife* and John Heywood's *Johan Johan*. In *The Tide Tarrieth No Man*, Courage's soliloquy envisions "the goodwife [who] giveth her husband a blow / And he for reward doth give her a kiss" (646–7), and in the fragment *The Prodigal Son* the Pater's wife taunts him:

An housbande I haue
And he is but a knaue
And I am a wyly pye
I set him on the score
And tell hym before
That a cokold he shall dye. (15–20)[63]

Men married to overbearing wives serve as a standard humorous trope of much medieval and early modern drama and literature, and emphasiz-ing this humour through its exaggeration within the theatrical sphere could well result in characters that exceed the boundaries of "normative effeminacy" – a construct itself bordering on the oxymoronic. As effemi-nacy was often allied with excessive heterosexual desire in the late medieval and early modern eras, conclusions about the queerness of a par-ticular scene must be treated with great caution, and as in so many instan-ces, the variability of performance gives rise to contrasting possibilities.

These henpecked and cuckolded characters of early English theatre raise the corresponding issue of whether their effeminacy could pique questions regarding their sexuality. In *Occupation and Idleness*, Ydelnes presents himself in feminine and coquettish terms: "And if ye wyl ataste me, / Ye shul fynde me queynte. / Queyntly go Y, lo, / As pretty as a py, lo" (81–4).[64] It is well established that *queynte* denotes both *craftiness* and *vagina*, as evident in Chaucer's famed account in *The Miller's Tale* of Nicholas's vulgar "seduction" of Alison: "As clerkes ben ful subtile and ful queynte; / And prively he caughte hire by the queynte" (lines 3275–6).[65] With the word repeated in its adjectival and adverbial forms in *Occupation and Idleness*, surely the actor should stress them. Upon espying Occupacioun, Ydelnes determines to "begile" (line 115) him, and the play proceeds with Ydelnes disguising himself as Besynes and proceeding with his plans. The age difference between the characters is established as well, with Ydelnes referring to Occupacioun as "good man" (line 100), the latter referring to the former as "yonge man" (line 101), and Doctrine calling him a "boy" (line 452). Occupacioun later warns Doctrine, "Sir, this boy wyl you begyle" (line 496), suggestive of Ydelnes's homoerotic and pederastic appeal. Similarly, the eponymous Vice figure of *Common Conditions* declares of himself, "I am somewhat feminative" (p. 190), yet little in the play expands on this point. Another character, Nomides, rebuffs his female suitor, declaring of himself, "I am none such that lives by love, I serve not Venus' train" (p. 216).[66] He later falls in love with the beautiful Clarisia and resorts to cross-dressing to pursue his affections, requesting the assistance of her handmaid and fool: "How sayest thou, my lady Lomia, wilt thou change coats with me?" (p. 243). The object of Nomides's desire is female, yet his seductive practices require his feminization. In these various examples the characters openly proclaim their effeminacy, and the actors therefore face the challenge of the degree to which their performances should stress this key aspect of their roles. At the very least, it is difficult to envision an actor reciting the words, "Queyntly go Y, lo, / As pretty as a py, lo," without accentuating their effeminizing valence.

Another quandary arising from the subjunctive nature of the theatre is that in several instances it is unclear whether a character should be played more masculinely or more effeminately, in a manner similar to the question of whether characters proclaiming themselves to be attractive should be cast as such. In *Damon and Pythias*, Grim the collier aligns himself with an adult and puissant masculinity through his self-description: "Go to then lustily, I will sing in my man's voice, / I've a troubling base buss" (13.265–6). If Grim's voice registers as a bass, it would in this instance be redundant for the actor to state as a fact that which the audience would simply hear, which calls into question the accuracy of his self-assessment. Jack repeatedly satirizes Grim's masculinity, threatening his genitalia – "And though we are cockerels now, we shall have spurs one day / And shall be able perhaps to make you a capon" (13.76–7). Jack also taunts, "Yet your wife told me you were an ox" (13.274), with *ox* connoting a castrated bull or a cuckold. Surveying the shades of masculinity from exaggerated to normative to effeminate, actors would opt for the valence they perceived to be the most appropriate for their characters. By stressing a character's effeminacy, they could enhance a play's humour and individuate their characters, often with scene-stealing performances. Furthermore, a given actor's choices could never define these roles in perpetuity, whether the actor stressed or overlooked any queerness in them.

Similar to the dramatic effects of effeminate men, masculine women would contrapuntally highlight the flimsiness of gender as a social construction. The strong wives who dominate their husbands in *Tom Tyler and His Wife*, *Johan Johan*, *The Prodigal Son*, and *The Tide Tarrieth No Man*, along with similar characters in other such plays, challenge their performers to determine the appropriate pitch of shrewishness, strength, rage, overweening erotic desire, or of any other such trait that the narrative action requires for the effective impersonation of these women. For example, in *Johan Johan*, Tyb must be portrayed as sufficiently strong to cower her husband, as indicated by the play's final stage direction: "*Here they fyght by the erys a whyle and than the preest and the wife go out of the place*" (following line 664).[67]

Several plays depict women not only outwitting or cuckolding men but physically emasculating them. Whereas few scenes from biblical drama should be as harrowing as the Slaughter of the Innocents, its grim terror in the Towneley Plays is leavened when Woman 3 attacks one of the soldiers: "Take thee ther a foyn. / Out on thee, I cry! / Have at thi groyn / Anothere!" (12.552–5). Following this debilitating attack on his genitals, Soldier 3 begs her, "Peasse now, no more!" (12.557), but then presents himself to Herod as a model of martial masculinity: "Had ye sene how I fard / When I cam emang them!" (12.612–13). In Thomas Preston's *Cambises*, one of the three ruffian characters, appropriately named Ruf, threatens Meretrix, "By Gogs hart, my dagger into her I wil thrust" (line 258).[68] As the stage directions explain, she defeats him in the ensuing scuffle: "*He falleth down, she falleth upon him and beats him and taketh away his weapon*" (following line 272). The comedy of a woman fighting a man – and winning – is soon repeated in the encounter between Marian May-Be-Good and Ambidexter, with the Vice character conceding the woman's victory – "Even now I yeeld and give you the maistery" (line 838) – and then fleeing. In R.B.'s *Apius and Virginia*, the supporting characters Mansipulus and Mansipula spar sharply, with the latter threatening her husband, "Have with ye, have at ye, your manhode to try!" (line 224), thereby counterbalancing the play's tragic themes with the low humour of their insults and scuffles.[69] The Towneley Plays share little in common with *Cambises* and *Apius and Virginia* thematically, yet in their depiction of women physically dominating men, they build their humour not merely through the conflict itself but through the symbolic emasculation of the men: the debilitating kick to Soldier 3's groin, Ruf's loss of his phallic dagger, and the challenge to Mansipulus's "manhode." In these instances a more emasculated Soldier 3, Ruf, Ambidexter, and Mansipulus set the conditions for a queerer performance. By leaning into the emasculating potential of their performances, the actors can heighten the humorous effect of these scenes, likely making themselves comic scene-stealers in otherwise dramatic plays.

In a unique instance of women challenging stereotypical expectations for sexed bodies, Celestina in *Calisto and Mélebea* resists the male-female binary in her descriptions as a "berdyd hore" (395) and a "berdyd dame" (784), thus positioning her on the border between male and female. As A.R. Braunmuller notes, "However common an aging woman's beard-like hair might have been or be, however commonly perceived and recorded by medical practitioners ancient and modern, a bearded woman violated some ingrained cultural assumptions and distinctions."[70] To fully gauge Celestina's queer effect, it is necessary to consider her casting and costuming. Although many female roles were played by adolescents, a man with a full beard playing Celestina would enhance the play's farcical humour, and so once again we see that a character's queerness enhances the actor's ability to create a memorable performance.

The various emasculated men and masculine women of early English drama display the tenuousness of gender as a social construction, and various other queer figures, including cross-dressers, hermaphrodites, and eunuchs, further fracture the gender binary. The apocryphal Pope Joan, whose disguise failed when she gave birth, is cited in *Damon and Pythias* (13.181), and Ill Report dresses as a woman in Thomas Garter's *Virtuous and Godly Susanna*: "In womens geare I am alone, it is my whole delight" (516).[71] In part 1 of George Whetstone's *Promos and Cassandra*, Cassandra must dress as a page for her assignation with Promos (act 3, scene 7, in which the stage direction states that she enters *"apparelled like a Page"*), who threatens her brother with execution if she refuses his advances, thus creating the queer metadramatics of a male actor dressing as a female character who then dresses as a man for the express purpose of having sex with another man.

Hermaphroditism further blurs the categories of male and female in early English drama. Trappola in *The Bugbears* includes hermaphrodites among a litany of monsters and spirits, which indicates that he construes them among the supernatural and unearthly (3.3.71).[72] Apius, contemplating his unrestrained passion for Virginia in *Apius and Virginia*, wishes to relive the Ovidian tale of hermaphroditic etiology: "Oh that Virginia were in case as somtime Salmasis, / And in Hermafroditus steede my selfe might seeke my blisse" (361–2).[73] In John Bale's *Thre Lawes of Nature, Moses, and Christ*, Idololatria appears as a female character in the narrative present, but as Infidelity remarks, "sumtyme thu wert an he!" (425), in an intriguing indication of the character's transgender experience that is left unexplored in the remainder of the interlude.[74]

In alluding to biblical accounts of eunuchs, early English plays further query the varieties of embodied masculinity. George Gascoigne's *Glasse of Governement* mentions the episode recounted in Acts of the Apostles in which "by harkning unto *Phyllip* the Apostle, the *Eunuch* was converted,"[75] and *The Enterlude of Godly Queene Hester* includes in its cast of characters the eunuch Arbona.[76] It seems doubtful that the staging of the play would remind audiences of Arbona's status as a eunuch in King Assuerus's court, although costuming could distinguish him from the other figures, including the three advisers and a herald.[77] Modelling his Pardoner in *The Pardoner and the Frere* on Chaucer's Pardoner in the *Canterbury Tales*, Heywood was inspired by his forebear's character of ambiguous gender, who has been variously identified as a eunuch, a hermaphrodite, and a homosexual.[78] In the antagonistic exchange between Heywood's Pardoner and Frere, the latter accuses the former of fighting like a woman – "Ye, horeson, wylt thou scrat and byte?" – to which the Pardoner replies, "Ye, mary wyll I, as longe as thou doste smyte!" (543–4).[79] With Chaucer's Pardoner as his model, Heywood envisioned a character of similarly indeterminate gender whose antagonistic behaviour towards the Frere could easily be elevated for comic effect.

In other such instances, queer characters transform from one sex to another as part of their performances, thus again confronting audiences with the arbitrariness of the human body as a theatrical signifier. In "Adam" of the Chester Mystery Cycle the Demon assumes the shape of a serpent with a woman's face – "A maner of an edder is in this place / that wynges like a bryde shee hase – / feete as an edder, a maydens face – / hir kynde I will take" (2.193–6). With this costuming, Eva's temptation is imagined as a lesbian seduction, although she later refers to the Serpens as "lord" (2.241) and then as a "shee" (2.294). Avarice in *Somebody and Others, or The Spoiling of Lady Verity* identifies herself as female – "For I am she that moost often dooth rule / Ouer the people my name is Auaryce" (16–17) – but Mynster refers to her as "Good syr Auaryce" (48).[80] Henry Medwall's *Nature* presents Innocencye with similarly conflicting gendered terms. The Worlde adjures her, "Be pece, fayre woman!" (442), and later demands, "Leve yt woman, leve yt, for yt ys nought" (511), but then advises Man of Innocencye, "To put thys man from your company" (631). Sensualyte dismisses Innocencye as "but a boy" (657). Alan Nelson argues that "this inconsistency would hardly have been noticed if Innocency was played by a boy,"[81] and although one may concede this point for the audience viewing the play if the character were costumed androgynously, it does not explain why Medwall would characterize Innocency in conflicting terms.

As this brief survey indicates, gender transgressive characters appear or are alluded to with relative frequency in early English drama, allowing audiences to witness the demolition of the gendered binary. Furthermore, as evident in the portrayal of Anima in *Wisdom*, gender-switching characters can structure the thematic development of a play. The Latin etymology of Anima's name indicates her femininity, and the stage directions identify her as female: "Here entrethe ANIMA as a mayde, in a wyght clothe of golde gysely purfyled wyth menyver" (following 16).[82] Anima's costuming is somewhat androgynous, as it includes "a cheueler [wig] lyke to WYSDOM," with this headpiece linking her to the play's similarly coifed male protagonist. Moreover, she declares herself to be a masculine, or at least an androgynous, figure: "I þat represent here þe sowll of man" (101). Notwithstanding Anima's name and her designation as a "mayde," Wisdom perceives her as a male character and advises her by quoting Proverbs 23:25 – "Fili, prebe michi cor tuum" (79; My son, give me thy heart) – and then describes her resemblance to God: "Yt ys þe ymage of Gode þat all began; / And not only ymage, but hys lyknes ȝe are" (103–4). While audiences should consider sceptically the words of Lucifer, he too affirms the relationship between humanity's external appearance and the divine model: "Of Gode man ys þe fygure, / Hys symylytude, hys pyctowre" (349–50). *Wisdom*'s interest in cross-gendered characters deepens when Wyll introduces a "sprynge of Lechery" (747), for which the stage directions outline a doubled gendered transformation: "Here entreth six women in sut, thre dysgysyde as galontys and thre as matrones, wyth wondyrfull vysurs congruent" (following line 752). It is possible, as David Klausner suggests, that female actors played these parts: "There seems to be no ambiguity about Will/

Lechery's dancers: they are six women, three of them cross-dressed as gallants." Klausner cites the essayists of Pamela Allen Brown and Peter Parolin's *Women Players in England, 1500–1600: Beyond the All-Male Stage* to discount the oversimplification of an all-male stage prior to the Reformation.[83] Yet whether the scene requires six men to play three "galontys" and three "matrons," or whether it requires six women for these roles, half of the actors must play the opposite gender, testifying to the play's insistent thematizing of cross-gender casting, despite the fact that the play's moral themes condemn such gender play. Wyll, who represents wilfulness, celebrates this ambiguously gendered dance as indicative of humanity's fallen nature: "Thys dance of þis damesellys ys thorow þis regyn" (760).

Building on the indeterminacy of Anima's gender, the *Wisdom* playwright later depicts the character as a monster – "Here ANIMA apperythe in þe most horrybull wyse, fowlere þan a fende" (following line 902) – with this entrance thus linking her indeterminate gender, potentially registered as hermaphroditism, to monstrosity. Wysdom's amorous words to Anima – "Ye haue wondyde my hert, syster, spowse dere, / In þe tweyn syghtys of yowr ey" (1085–6) – apparently solidify her gender as female, yet the previous oscillations of her identity cannot be undone. Whether Anima is played by a female or a male actor, this vision of a courtly romance between Wysdom and Anima fails to quell the perverse energies previously staged. Lucifer hopes to seduce humanity into sin, denigrating "þe flesche of man þat ys so changeable" (360) and detailing his ambitions to "tempte" (361) and "perwert" (362) the "Soule" (363). Anima's narrative journey through genders and monstrosity builds the play's valedictory speech, in which she prays to Jesus, "Nowe ye mut euery soule renewe / In grace, and vycys to eschew, / Ande so to ende wyth perfeccyon" (1159–61). To end with the "perfection" of the world's gendered order restored, Anima travels through a queerly sinful path, one that undermines any certainties an audience might previously have held about the immutability of gender.

Given the tradition of male actors playing female roles, in many instances an audience might not be able to discern the gender either of an actor or of his character, or even of both, and thus experience a destabilizing moment in their expectations for the ensuing performance. In an intriguing moment in Nicholas Udall's *Royster Doyster*, Dobinet Doughtie espies Tom Truepenie approaching and cannot distinguish his sex: "But yonder commeth forth a wenche or a ladde" (2.2.21). Wherever *Royster Doyster* might have been staged, surely the actors playing Dobinet Doughtie and Tom Truepenie were not standing terribly far away from each other, and so Dobinet Doughtie's words highlight the difficulty of determining not only whether a male actor is playing a female role but whether he is playing a male role, too. Soon after, Christian Custance upbraids Tibet Talk-Apace, "Is all your delite and joy / In whiskyng and ramping abroade like a Tom boy" (2.4.5), which casts this character as gender transgressive. In light of the gender play evident throughout much early English theatre, an audience would be challenged to confront the protean possibilities that occurred when the actors assumed their assigned characters, disguising the reality of their biological bodies with the costumes and prosthetics of the stage so that viewers were often unsure of what was hidden underneath.

Queer Performance

Theorizing the queerness of performance in the Middle Ages and the Renaissance requires an oscillating perspective between past and present, between how various identities were staged in early English drama and how modern theorizations of gender and erotic identity can help us to understand their conflicting valences better. Several scholars have considered the performativity of queerness and the queerness of performativity in intersecting theories of ideology, subjectivity, and theatre. Judith Butler, contemplating the creation of gender and identity both within and against ideology, argues that "performativity ... is to be read not as self-expression or self-presentation, but as the unanticipated resignifiability of highly invested terms."[84] For Eve Kosofsky Sedgwick, queer performativity is inherently related to the marginalized status of LGBTQ+ people, proposing that it is "the name of a strategy for the production of meaning and being, in relation to the ... fact of stigma."[85] Desire constitutes the self in many theories of performativity, and Sue-Ellen Case argues of the theatrical practices behind this process that "gestural systems are devised to reveal ... desire as perceived through the body"; she envisions such performances as integral to understanding the actor's construction of desire within and beyond the theatrical event.[86] These theories, while admittedly anachronistic to early English drama (as are virtually all literary and performative theories), showcase the deep connections between acting and the individual, with the theatrical metaphor of performativity connecting self to society. The quest for examples of queer performances on the early English stage, then, requires considering the ways in which actors might participate in creating a system of gestures and identities through which queer identities could be perceived and queer audiences could see themselves, if only through the refractions of a funhouse mirror. As Jody Enders argues, "a theatrical gesture was in and of itself a speech act,"[87] and Garrett P.J.

Epp provocatively posits that all acting evokes queerness: "The actor, simply by acting, sodomises social and textual authority."[88] In this light, the early English stage serves as a fertile site for considering the production of cultural codes that resonate to this very day.

With male actors called to perform female roles and to dress themselves in women's clothing, early English drama elicits queer performances, yet, at the same time, this queer tension in most instances is implicitly quelled.[89] The script of *Robin Hood and the Friar* introduces Maid Marian with the following stage direction: "*The man playing the Marian presents himself.*" Then, the Friar ravenously speaks of his lust for her: "Here is an huckle duckle an inch aboue the buckle / she is a trul of trust, to serue a friar at his lust."[90] A man playing a woman who then piques a male character's desire: a key aspect of the queerness of early English drama arises in the frequent impossibility of a so-called straight performance, for even the most committed of these performances cannot help but expose the seams of the dramatic construction. All early English plays with female roles bear the potential for queer interpretations that explore the tensions arising from the actors' artistic decisions in embodying these characters and then interacting with others. Certainly, the necessity of males playing female roles troubled early drama critics such as Stephen Gosson, who condemned the gender-switching central to so many plays and interludes: "If [a play] shoulde bee Plaied, one must learne to trippe it like a Lady in the finest fashion … Therefore whatsoeuer such Playes as conteine good matter, are set out in print, may be read with profite, but cannot be playd, without a manifest breach of Gods commaundement."[91] The possibility of men "tripping it like ladies" caused great concern for Gosson and others of his ilk, for they believed sinfulness to be inextricable from transvestite performances. Notable, too, is that Gosson sees profit in reading plays but not in performing them, suggesting that even an unimpeachable moral message would be undermined by a performance that could not help but assume queer connotations. Every performance by a man in a woman's role is imbued with queer potential, and, as discussed in chapter 6, a proto-camp sensibility may even be discerned in some of these performances, such as when the maid Willful Wanton in *The Tide Tarrieth No Man* bewails her virginity: "I am as able as they with a man to lie" (774). A "straight" performance of this line is funny, but a queer performance could easily be funnier, with the actor emphasizing the distinction between his male body and his female role.

The subjunctive conundrums surrounding medieval and early modern depictions of homosexuality are apparent in the fact that it can be hazily discerned in suggestive and elliptical language that can be made explicit through performance, with scenes from John Skelton's *Magny-fycence* illustrating this point. Liberty declares to Magnyfycence, "I am presydent of prynces; I prycke them with Pryde" (2082). According to the *OED* and the *MED*, it is unlikely that Skelton is punning on *prick* as a slang term for penis in this line; the play dates to approximately 1515–23, but the *OED* dates the usage of *prick* as "penis" to 1555 in the tract *A Manifest Detection of the Moste Vyle and Detastable Vse of Diceplay*.[92] Yet it is readily apparent that *prick* denotes "penis" in earlier plays. In John Heywood's *Foure PP*, Potycary puns on women's fashions by employing *prycke* as a double entendre: "But prycke them and pynne them as myche as ye wyll, / And yet wyll they loke for pynnynge styll" (275–6).[93] In *Thersites*, Mater worries that her malevolent son will murder her, crying, "He wyll pricke me! / He wyll stycke me" (626–7). *Pricke* and *stycke* are obvious synonyms of *stab*, with the former word capturing Mater's fear of her son's incestuous and rapacious desire. Thus, if one concedes the likely possibility that Skelton uses *prick* similarly, this pun could be made apparent by the actor placing his arms akimbo and thrusting out his crotch. Whereas this scene was probably not staged for its mostly negligible queerness, Skelton's satiric treatment of sinful religious figures more openly allows for queer stagings. Counterfeit Countenance, speaking of the duplicities he has learned from the religious orders, states, "To counterfet this, freers haue lerned me; / This nonnes nowe and then, and it myght be, / Wolde take, in the way of counterfet Charity" (487–9). Greg Walker proposes, "If 'This' is accompanied by an obscene gesture, the stanza becomes a satirical mockery of the sexual misdemeanours of nuns and friars."[94] This stanza concludes with the intriguing line "Monkys may not for drede that men sholde them se" (493), but again, owing to the elliptical phrasing, one cannot be sure that Skelton alludes to homoerotic transgressions. We will never know when men jutted out their crotches on the early English stage, but as Walker proposes, it is likely that they would do so at comically appropriate moments, and so we must ponder when such moments could have been exploited by the actors.

The viability of a queer performance is particularly evident in a common plot point: when male actors kiss their fellow actors who are playing female characters. In such moments, actors must confront and deploy tropes of masculinity and theatrical narrative that concomitantly allow spaces of queer visibility. Kisses are mentioned infrequently in stage directions in early English drama, yet when they do appear, the actors face the challenge of how amorously to embrace. In many instances, kisses would require no frisson of desire and would be such as those between family members. In the Towneley Plays the stage directions instruct Abraham to kiss Isaac – "*Et osculatur eum*" (following line 4.278; And he kisses him) – and Isaac requests a kiss from Esau, "Com nere, son, and kys me" (5A.1; cf. 5A.66), although Jacob duplicitously fulfils this request. Kisses involving Jesus rarely entail erotic undertones, such as when Maria Magdalena kisses his feet in the Chester Mystery Cycle (14.105–8; cf. Towneley Plays 23.610) or when Judas traitorously kisses him (15.309; cf. Towneley Plays 17.685). When Primus Pastor in the Chester Cycle encourages his fellows, "Therfore lend me your mouth, / and frendly let us kysse" (7.683–4), the dramatization need require little more than a peck on the cheek, as would likely be the case in *Impatient Poverty* when the Vice character Envy pretends to mourn Conscience's departure, requests a kiss ("Yet kiss me or ye go," 506), and then laughs riotously behind his back. When employed as a gesture of familial affection, respect, or simple friendship, a kiss, as the classic song intones, is just a kiss.

Scenes from other plays indicate that playwrights assessed the dramatic effects of kissing and sought to magnify or diminish its erotic timbres. John Redford's *Wit and Science*, a secular re-imagination of the psychomachia in which Tediousness seduces Wit from his female beloved, Lady Science, features some attempted but failed kisses played for humour. Wit requests, "Let me have a kis at this our meeting" (727)."[95] Rebuffed, he would apparently try again when stating, "Cum now, a bas, my nowne proper sparling!" (741). Comedy frequently flows from the travails of courtship, and the humour of this scene would be enhanced through its exaggeration, with Wit hungrily approaching Science as she then forcefully reprimands him. Despite Wit's failed attempts to kiss Science, the play concludes with their marriage, which would appear an appropriate narrative moment for an embrace, yet Lady Science instead declares: "Well than, for the end of all dowtes past / And to that end whiche ye spake of last, / Among our wedding matters heere rend'ring, / Th'end of our lives wold be in rememb'ring" (1086–9). The play ends without a kiss, at least according to the script, thus indicating that Wit and Lady Science can flirt with, but not consummate, any physical display of affection. Kisses, however, are not the only means of displaying intimacy, and, in an outward expression of his earlier debauchery, Wit positions himself in Idellnes's lap ("*And when the galiard is doone, Wit saith as folowith, and so fal[l]ith downe in Idellnes' lap*"; following line 330). Resting one's head in another's lap could be seen as even more intimate than a kiss, yet *Wit and Science* allows such intimacies during Wit's seduction into sin rather than allowing a kiss for the united virtues.[96]

In other instances, it would be difficult for actors to quell the erotic energy of a kiss without subverting the obvious arc of the storyline, such as in *Royster Doyster* when the eponymous protagonist seeks to embrace several characters. He kisses Mage Mumble-Crust (1.3.99) and Dame Christian Custance's other servants, declaring, "I will kisse you too mayden, for the good will I beare you" (1.3.101), with this scene played for humour, as Tibet Talk-Apace derides his osculatory skills: "Yea sir? I pray you when dyd ye last kisse your cowe?" (1.3.110). If Royster Doyster had merely pecked the servants on their cheeks, Tibet Talk-Apace's response would not make logical sense, and so it is apparent that he must kiss them on the lips and do so over-enthusiastically. In a contrapuntal scene intended to dramatize proper courtship, Gawyn Goodlucke declares his intention to kiss his fiancée, Christian Custance: "Howe much I joy in your constant fidelitie, / Come nowe kisse me the pearle of perfect honestie" (5.4.11–12). We have only Gawyn's words to gauge the passion of this kiss, but surely "Howe much I joy" should be spoken joyfully, and thus a passionate embrace would appear more congruent with his desires than a mere peck.

When Vice characters kissed on the early English stage, their sinfulness would have been appropriately enacted through languid, lascivious embraces – even if they were never portrayed in such a manner. In *The Contention between Liberalitie and Prodigalitie*, Tenacitie, a miser, proclaims his passion for Money – "Oh, my sweeting, my darling, my chewel, my joy, / My pleasure, my treasure, mine owne prettie boy" (835–6) – and then requests a kiss: "Oh, forbid me not to kisse my sweete Money" (838).[97] The Vice character Wantonness kisses Wit in *The Marriage between Wit and Wisdom* (following line 180), and the stage directions also note that she has "*sung him asleep upon her lap*" (following line 201). Without accompanying stage directions, we can only surmise the nature of the kiss, or even if it was staged at all. Several plays feature female sex workers, who are called upon to kiss male Vices. In *Nice Wanton*, Iniquity kisses Dalila, who has fallen into prostitution. "God a mercy, Dalila, good luck, I warrant thee!," with the stage direction noting, "*He kisseth her*" (191); he soon compliments her as the "best whore in England" (208).[98] In *Misogonus*, Misogonus desires to kiss another character of the meretrix tradition, Melissa: "Ah, mine own henburd, I must needs lay thee o' th' lips" (2.2.284).[99] A similar situation occurs in *Cambises* when Ambidexter, the Vice character, propositions Meretrix, a prostitute: "Mistres Meretrix, I thought not to see you heer now. / There is no remedy, at meeting I must have a kisse" (234–5). The stage directions indicate the fruition of Ambidexter's desire: "*Kisse*" (following 236). Meretrix demands more affection from Ambidexter: "Nay, soft! I swere, and if ye were my brother, / Before I let go I wil have another," with the stage directions indicating "*Kisse, kisse, kisse*" (240). With Meretrix avowing her willingness to indulge in an incestuous kiss with her brother rather than to forgo the delights of Ambidexter's lips, these kisses should proceed beyond pecks to more amorous osculation.

The kisses of *Lusty Juventus* are similarly emphasized. Of Juventus's approaching rendezvous with Abominable Living, Hypocrisy advises, "You must her embrace / Somewhat handsomely" (779–80), and Juventus envisions her in a state of dishabille: "I could find in my heart to kiss you in your smock" (800). Juventus's first kiss may appear somewhat perfunctory – "To kiss her since she came I had clean forgot" (817), he says – but his second attempt is expressed enthusiastically: "Full greatly I do delight to kiss your pleasant mouth" (844). The stage direction confirms, "*He kisseth.*" Juventus then urges her to join him for greater intimacies in a more private setting: "I long to talk with you secretly, therefore let us go hence" (846). The audience is left with the image of Juventus paired with Abominable Living and expressing his longing for time away from the prying eyes of others, which emphasizes the sinful nature of their passion and the queer undertones of the actors' embraces. In John Foxe's *Christus Triumphans*, Pseudamnus, who represents the Antichrist and the Pope, kisses Pornapolis, who represents the Whore of Babylon: "Vah, ut dulci te osculo capio, / Mea lux" (4.8.30–1; O, with what a sweet kiss I hold you, my light). A more sinful embrace than that between the Antichrist and the Whore of Babylon could hardly be envisioned within a medieval and early modern Christian worldview, and thus the moral turpitude of the kiss would be heightened by its amorousness.

With these scenes and others of their ilk, acting troupes faced a vexing performative conundrum: to stage the kiss in congruence with its narrative tenor and thus to heighten the play's metadramatic homoeroticism, or to stage the kiss as passionlessly as possible and thus to undermine the play's heteroerotic surface. In a sharp irony, queer performances enhance many of these plays' narrative interest in heterosexuality while calling into question the very possibility of portraying heteroerotic attraction in an all-male venue. Furthermore, between these two performative poles stands no median mode of enacting the scenes so that they would be devoid of queer meanings, and so the queerness of performances, in these instances, stands not as an exception but as a grounding condition of early English drama.

In various ways theatrical experiences are predicated upon multiple and overlapping forms of desire. Foremost, the theatre relies on the audience's desire for entertainment, in the persistent human enjoyment of a story enacted in an engaging manner, and yet one can never circumscribe the range of desires enacted and experienced within the theatrical realm. As the preceding discussion of queer scopophilia, queer dialogue, queer characters, and queer performance divulges, erotic energies cannot be stripped even from productions – including biblical plays, psychomachias, and interludes inspired from allegorical traditions of sin and redemption – that are designed to inculcate their audiences into the mysteries of the Christian faith. Early English playwrights, guilds, and theatrical companies created a space for queer characters and plots to become visible, if only momentarily and often unintentionally, but nonetheless with lasting repercussions to drama.

Chapter Two

Themes of Friendship and Sodomy

Two related yet contrasting themes percolate throughout much early English drama: the moral benefits of male homosocial friendship and the immoral perils of sodomy. As numerous studies have demonstrated, homosocial friendships were valorized throughout the Middle Ages and the Renaissance as the epitome of masculine honour and fidelity;[1] this fraternal tradition can be traced back to the classical era, as evident in Cicero's homage to friendship in *De amicitia*.[2] For a brief example from the field of early English drama, *Everyman*, long viewed as the paradigmatic morality play, takes as one of its primary themes the protagonist's realization, "In prosperyte men frendes may fynde, / Whiche in aduersytye be full vnkynde" (309–10).[3] Everyman's many friends, including Fellowship, Kindred, Cousin, Goods, Dyscressyon, Strength, Fyve Wyttes, and Beautye, forsake him, with only Good Deeds remaining faithful at the moment of death: "Thou shalt fynde me a good frende at nede" (854). Expanding on such fraternal dynamics, several early English dramas celebrate the depths of male friendship and privilege homosocial bonds over heteroerotic marriage, with these conditions at times confusing any presumed boundary between asexual friendship and homoerotic affection. Other plays consider the possibility of male sodomy, either to condemn it as a moral affront or to wield its humorous and satirical edge. In both such instances, and in a range of other dramatic circumstances, male homosociality and homosexuality offer a means to query the ways that illicit desires can be simultaneously repressed and expressed in the dramatic realm.

Homosocial Friendships in Early English Culture and Drama

Accounts of male friendship, including those with erotic undertones, appear throughout the literary record of the Middle Ages and the Renaissance, including the poetry of Paulinus of Nola (353–431),

Hrabanus Maurus (776–856), Walafrid Strabo (809–849), Marbod of Rennes (1035–1123), and Hilary (c. 1225).[4] In addition, literary accounts position Jove's cupbearer Ganymede as an emblem of same-sex desire, with accompanying paeans to the pleasures of homoerotic affection.[5] Stories of male homosocial friendship appear in much medieval literature, including the romances *Amis and Amiloun*, *Eger and Grime*, Chaucer's *Knight's Tale*, and the Balin and Balan stories of the Arthurian legend. During the Tudor era, Thomas Eliot, in *The Bankette of Sapience* (1534), cites a variety of classical authorities on the value of friendship (Amitie), including Augustine ("I suppose this to be the very true law of amitie, a man to loue his frende no lesse nor no more than he loueth hym selfe"), Solomon ("A faithefull frende is a sure protection, he that findeth such one, findeth a treasure"), and Isidorus ("That is trewe frendeshyppe, that looketh for nothynge of his frende, but onely his fauoure, as who saythe, without mede loueth his louer").[6]

Medieval and early modern friendships included within their purview the concept of sworn brotherhood, in which two men pledged an oath of support for each other in a recognized ceremony. As Robert Stretter observes, "The practice of sworn brotherhood, which ritually transformed men, usually of aristocratic station, into 'wed brothers' with an array of legal, social, and moral obligations, appears frequently in medieval romance from the eleventh to the fifteenth centuries."[7] In the 1450s, Richard Strangways documented the heraldry of such brothers in arms and the great affection between them: "There were ii knights ... and there fell so great love betwixt them that they were sworn brothers, and that one of them bore his arms with a bend; and for the great love that his sworn brother had to him he forsook his own arms and said he would bear his brother's arms and took the same arms, saying that he laid the bend up on the left side: and heralds considered the great love betwixt them and granted thereto."[8] Although the historical record contains several such accounts of sworn brotherhood, the study of these friendships and their potential intimacies generates debate, amply evident in the sharp criticisms of John Boswell's controversial *Same-Sex Unions in Premodern Europe*.[9] It is beyond the scope of this chapter to definitively assess the queerness evident in the full spectrum of male friendship that the historical record contains, but James A. Schultz identifies a much-needed middle ground on this issue, arguing for an analytical perspective "that does not assimilate male couples of the Middle Ages to modern homosexuality but that also does not refuse them the possibility of erotic involvement."[10] This chapter adheres to Schultz's model of homosociality, one that does not simply assume homosocial friendships align with queerness but that concurrently acknowledges this possibility.

In travelling the path from sin to redemption that is dramatized in so many early English morality plays and interludes, male protagonists benefit spiritually from their homosocial friendships with the Virtue figures who catalyse their salvation – in contrast to the manifold hetero-erotic transgressions that characterize their descents into sin with the male Vice characters who lead them morally astray. From this perspective, male homosociality serves as a grounding condition of the genre, in its attention to both vice and virtue. As discussed in greater detail in chapter 4, *Mankind*, with no female characters in its cast, exemplifies this paradigm of homosocial friendship leading to sin and salvation: Mankind, after terminating the dissolute shenanigans sparked by Mischief, New Gyse, Nowadays, Nought, and Titivillus, is redeemed through his friendship with Mercy. Even most exceptions to this overarching pattern conclude with proper masculinity restored, such as in Richard Wever's *Lusty Juventus*. This play features the title character seduced into sin by male and female characters (respectively, Hypocrisy and Abominable Living), with the theme of friendship emerging when Hypocrisy disguises himself as Friendship to lure Juventus into sin (527). Juventus learns not to trust false friends, according to the advice of Good Counsel: "Let not flattering Friendship, nor yet wicked company, / Persuade you in no wise God's word to abuse" (1131–2).[11] By the play's conclusion, his homosocial bond with Good Counsel leads him to redemption, demonstrating the necessity of carefully choosing one's homosocial relationships. As is well established, the roles of women, compared to their percentage of the population, are lopsidedly under-represented in early English drama, with many dramatis personae failing to list a single female character. Plays such as *Nice Wanton* (with three female characters, Dalila, Eulalia, and Xantippe) and *The Bugbears* (with four female characters, Tomasine, Iphigenia, Catella, and Phillida) are rare; *The Castle of Perseverance*, with its multiple female characters, is exceptional. With women absent or under-represented in early English drama, the relationships of men with one another take centre stage – both literally and figuratively.

As evident from *Everyman, Mankind,* and *Lusty Juventus,* many morality plays and interludes employ a lexicon of brotherhood and friendship to dramatize the morally beneficent nature of such close relationships. In *Wealth and Health*, Wealth proclaims, "O, brother Health! thou art, indeed, / More preciouser than gold,"[12] and the fragment *Love Feigned and Unfeigned* begins with Familiarity pledging his devotion to Unfeigned Love: "Oh wellcome sure vnfayned love right welcome loving brother / whome I (as nature doth me bynd) I love above all other" (9–10).[13] The lead characters of *The Four Cardinal*

Virtues – Temperance, Prudence, Justice, and Fortitude – are depicted as brothers, as evident when Justice welcomes Fortitude: "And as our brother be thou shall" (175).[14] *Hick Scorner* presents a doubled story-line of male friendship and its spiritual benefits, dramatizing Pity and Contemplation's efforts to redeem Free Will and Imagination from their sinful ways. At the play's beginning, Contemplation affirms his strong alliance with Perseverance: "But Perseverance oft with me doth meet / When I think on thoughts that is full heavenly; / Thus he and I together full sweetly doth sleep" (68–70).[15] Nothing in these lines sug-gests that their spiritual intimacy leads to – or is corrupted by – sexual intimacy, and even the image of the two men sleeping together should not be taken to construe their homoerotic passion, as bed-sharing was a common feature of medieval and early modern life.[16] Yet the play's focus on homosocial friendship is stressed such that belonging to a male couple provides an invaluable path to salvation. *Hick Scorner* concludes with Free Will and Imagination reformed, as the erstwhile sinners pair off with their moral mentors Perseverance and Contem-plation, with Free Will telling Imagination: "Sir, wait thou now on Perseverance, / For thy name shall be called Good Remembrance. / And I will dwell with Contemplation, / And follow him wherever he be come" (1006–9). Imagination, the former warden of brothels, is redeemed through his relationship with another man, as he casts aside the lustful heteroerotic temptations of his former life.

In several interludes a homosocial friendship between men estab-lishes a narrative foundation for an erotic triangle, against which the feminine is perceived by one of the men as a threat. Eve Kosofsky Sedg-wick, in her groundbreaking analysis of erotic triangles, limns its homo-social underbelly, pointing to the ways in which male relationships are established through and against a female beloved.[17] Such a tension is apparent in *The Marriage of Wit and Science*, in which Wit proclaims his friendship for Will – "As dere to me as myne owne dere brother / Who-soever be one, thou shalt be an other" – with Will glumly responding, "Yea, but your wyfe wyl play the shrew; perdy, it is she that I feare" (2.1.327–9).[18] The play ends with Wit joyously married to Science, as the title implies, but Will's actions throughout much of the play – allegori-cally and thematically wilful – evince his propensity for male friendship to the extent of undercutting his friend's marital hopes, such that queer-ness can seep into the performance and the character's motivations. One of the great mysteries of Shakespearian drama is Iago's motiva-tion for sabotaging Othello's marriage to Desdemona, with queerness potentially answering a virtually unanswerable question; in *The Mar-riage of Wit and Science*, the audience knows Will's motivation – again, wilfulness – yet his excessive attention to his friendship with Wit casts him outside the range of normative homosociality and inside the range of potential queerness.

Two comic plays, Nicholas Udall's *Royster Doyster* and Ulpian Ful-well's *Like Will to Like*, take advantage of the humorous potential of male friendships as funhouse reflections of marriages. *Royster Doyster* interrogates the meaning of masculinity in many scenes, such as when Mathew Merygreeke dubiously assesses Rafe's masculinity and exhorts him, "Too hir then like a man, and be bolde forth to starte" (1.2.171).[19] Although Merygreeke's comic role in the play obscures his motivation, he declares his regret that he cannot be Royster Doyster's wife:

> That I am not a woman myselfe for your sake,
> I would have you my selfe, and a strawe for yond Gill,
> And mocke [make] much of you though it were against my will.
> I would not I warrant you, fall in such a rage,
> As so to refuse suche a goodly personage. (3.4.104–8)

They continue discussing Merygreeke's potential engagement to Roys-ter Doyster, repeatedly phrasing the possibility of such a relationship in the subjunctive. "And I were a woman" (3.4.109), Merygreeke states, as well as, "And I were the fairest lady in the shiere" (3.4.117). Similar themes are addressed in *Like Will to Like*, in which Nichol Newfangle promises to introduce Tom Tospot to Rafe Roister and aligns them with other couples: "Yonder cometh Rafe Roister, an old friend of mine. / By the mass, for thee he is so fit a mate / As Tom and Tib for Kit and Kate" (274–6).[20] Within such humorous plays, male friendships are likened to heteroerotic marriages for the inherent comedy of the juxtaposition, with the tone barely registering as satiric. Indeed, even if one were to claim these lines as satiric, their tone is assuredly more Horatian than Juvenalian.

Whereas many early English plays treat homosocial friendship as a prominent theme, in a few plays it is the pre-eminent one. John Foxe's *Titus et Gesippus* illustrates the view of homosocial friendships as the epitome of human relationships, surpassing the bonds between hus-band and wife, for even when they are suffering from heteroerotic lovesickness, the friendship of the title characters exceeds their love for women. Foxe's play of the Titus and Gesippus legend descends from a long line of such brotherhood stories, most notably Boccaccio's eighth tale of the tenth day of his *Decameron*.[21] As Titus tells Phormio, when discussing Gesippus's approaching nuptials, "Deinde Gesippum illum vnice animo meo / Semper charissimum, huic qui datur in coniugem?"

(1.1.40–1; Then you know that Gesippus, who's marrying her, has always been singularly dear to my heart).[22] In a later scene Gesippus discusses his love for Semprona in tepid terms, while celebrating his friendship with Titus:

> Quamquam neque negare possum eam me
> Amare quoque, sed non adeo ut non amico meo facile
> Postputarim omnia etiam si vita haec effundenda sit, quae mihi
> Charior est, ut ne tanti putes esse mihi iacturam foeminae. (1.9.37–40).

(Though I certainly can't deny that I love her too, I don't love her so much that I would not readily put my friend ahead of everything, even if it meant losing my life, which is dearer to me than she is. So don't think the loss of a girl is of such importance to me.)

Not long after these words, Titus reiterates the depth of his friendship with Gesippus in amorous terms: "Sed vbi / Gesippus nunc est, quem nimis his vlnis amplecti / Atque osculari gestio, ac vbi requiram cogito" (2.2.18–20; But now where's Gesippus? I long to hold him in my arms and kiss him. I wonder where to look for him). Their mutual devotion does not escape the notice of others, and Martius comments approvingly, "Neque enim quid sit satis commentari queo / Nisi ex amore factum sit iuuenes quia / Conflagrant mutuo" (5.3.4–6; I can't conceive of what this means unless it's done out of love – unless these young men burn with mutual love). Titus and Gesippus's mutual devotion guides the plot, and the women they ostensibly love serve as exchangeable goods to prove the depth of their friendship, not their heteroerotic passion. Considering the staging of this play and its subjunctive queerness, Garrett P.J. Epp observes that "Foxe downplays the physicality of all the play's central relationships alike, yet he does not entirely avoid thereby all implication of effeminacy and sodomy. Theater is physical; some of the physicality here is sexualized, and all of it involves male bodies."[23]

Richard Edwards's *Damon and Pythias* similarly exalts male friendships over heteroerotic unions. Witnessing these men's abiding affection, the executioner Groano compares his marriage unfavourably to their friendship: "I have a wife, whom I love well, / And if I would die for her – would I were in hell! / Wilt thou do more for a man, than I would for a woman?" (10.319–21).[24] Aristippus describes the perfect union realized in Damon and Pythias's friendship: "for in two bodies they have but one heart" (14.44). Yet as discussed in the previous chapter regarding queer performance, the script leaves unanswered the question of how to stage the men's homoerotic intimacy. Damon calls for Pythias immediately prior to his own execution, "Let me kiss thee ere I die" (15.195). Witnessing the extent of their affection, Dionysius miraculously transforms from the scourge of the men to their admirer, leading him to declare, "Eubulus, my spirits are suddenly appalled, my limbs wax weak, / This strange friendship amazes me so, that I can scarce speak" (15.199–200). Damon and Pythias's "strange friendship" mesmerizes Dionysius, but what is striking about their kiss is that it must register both as normative – surely the audience is not intended to perceive their friendship as sodomitical – but at the same time it is exceptional to the very point of queerness in that it registers so beyond the norms of typical male friendships. Edward's recurring interest in stories of homosocial friendship is further evident in his lost play *Palamon and Arcite*, an adaptation of Chaucer's *Knight's Tale*.[25] The popularity of this story of homosocial brotherhood is further evident in its incarnation as a song, documented in the theatrical world by a stage direction in John Philip's *Pacient and Meeke Grissell*: "*Here Grissell Singith a songe, to the tune of Damon & Pithias*" (following line 485).[26]

The title characters of *Clyomon and Clamydes* begin as adversaries but end in friendship, as evident in their paired dialogue. Clamydes commences, "Well then my *Clyomon*, to take our leave to court let us repare," to which Clyomon genially responds, "As your friend and companyon *Clamydes* every where" (1868–9).[27] Unlike in *Titus et Gesippus* and *Damon and Pythias*, Clyomon and Clamydes's friendship does not overwrite the play's heteroerotic themes, as it concludes with the respective pairings of the protagonists with their heteroerotic love interests, Juliana and Neronis. *Clyomon and Clamydes* introduces a final queer twist, similar to that employed by William Shakespeare in *As You Like It* and in *Twelfth Night*, when a female character, Neronis, who has previously disguised herself as a shepherd's boy, reveals her true identity to her beloved Clamydes. The play thus reinstates heteroerotic affection while simultaneously tracing its roots to a homosocial friendship – at least from the perspective of the biologically male character. Male friendships take some surprisingly queer turns: in this instance, in the possibility that a male beloved might actually be female and so that the friendship can be sexually and legally consummated.

Yet as much as male friendships guide protagonists from sin to redemption in morality plays, and as much as they may represent the highest devotion possible between humans in other dramas, the flip side of this coin is, as mentioned previously, the frequent depiction of protagonists led into sin through their male friendships. Homosocial friendship itself need not be morally salutary or morally opprobrious, a theme evident in George Gascoigne's *Glasse of Governement*, which features four pairs of friends: the fathers Phylopæs and Philocalus, their elder sons Phylautus and Phylosarchus, their younger sons Phylomusus and Phylotimus, and the Vice figures Eccho (the Parasyte) and Dick Drumme (the Royster). Phylocalus avows to Phylopæs, "It were not reason *Phylopæs* that having so many yeares contineued so neare neighboures ... we should now in the ende of our time become any lesse then entiere frendes, and as it is the nature and propertie of frendshippe to seeke alwaies for perpetuity, so let us seeke to bring up our Children in such mutuall societie in their youth."[28] While these men benefit from their strong ties, as do their younger sons, their elder sons support each other in their debauchery, and the Vice figures view friendship as more transactional than affective in nature, with Dick Drumme admitting of his friendship with Eccho that "in deed we were sworne brethren," but then abandoning any emotional connection: "but what for that?"[29] The men's debasement of sworn brotherhood bespeaks their sinful ways, which the elder sons replicate and the younger sons reject.

As the example of Dick Drumme and Eccho implies, early English drama relies heavily on the theme of men exploiting friendship for base purposes. Vice characters engage in morally dubious relationships with other men, often while applying a lexicon of friendship, devotion, and sworn brotherhood but perverting such relationships of their salutary effect. In the fragment *Albion Knight* the eponymous hero mistakenly pledges an oath with Iniury – "Then by your othe I am content / To haue your frendshyp with good assent" (57–8) – although Iniury's true companion is his "olde mate called Dyuycion" (153).[30] *Four Elements* features Humanyte seduced into sin by Sensuall Appetyte, who employs the language of sworn brotherhood when he promises that he will "do you good and trew servyce, / And therto I plyght my trouthe" (530–1).[31] This interlude's conclusion has been lost, but it seems safe to assume that, in the end, Humanyte returns to Studyous Desire: "For yf you forsake my company so / Lorde Nature wyll not be contente" (482–3). Given the long-standing vision of Nature as a female allegorical figure, this regendering of Nature as a Lord is surprising.

Along with these storylines of misdirected male friendships and sworn brotherhoods, traces of homoeroticism can frequently be found. When Belyal laments Saul's conversion in *The Conversion of St. Paul*, his words hint at their queer affection: "Ho! Ow3t, ow3t! What, haue we loste / Our darlyng most dere, whom we lovyd moste?" (466–7).[32] In *The Conflict of Conscience*, male Vice characters are effeminized as Circes, which suggests their attempts to seduce other men into sin; Conscience asks, "What Circes hath bewitched thee thy worldly wealth to love / More than the blessed state of soul?" (1504–5).[33] In W. Wager's *Enough*

Is as Good as a Feast, the Vice character Covetous pledges his fraternal devotion to Inconsideration and Temerity. "Fare ye well both, give me your hands one after another. / I love ye as dearly as the children of my mother" (597–8), he requests of them, and later he similarly appeals to Precipitation, "I love you as well as mine own born brother" (736).[34] The play expands its consideration of true and false friendships when Precipitation declares, "A true friend more than kinsfolk is to be esteemed" (798), with Enough replying, "No more are all friends that friendship pretend, / As is approved with many in the end" (801–2). The play concludes with Satan promising his affection – "And doubt you not but with you I will play the loving lad" (1463) – accompanied by the image of Satan bearing Covetous on his back: "*Bear him out upon his back*" (following line 1471), in an image potentially carrying sodomitic undertones.

As these examples illustrate, men's friendships can be salvific or damning, yet in either case they bear queer potential in the tension between normative and non-normative relationships, in the possibility that some men might like other men just a little too much. Furthermore, the question of staging remains intriguing yet ultimately unanswerable. To enhance the homosocial storyline of a given play, actors could have captured the deep emotional connection of a beneficial friendship with affectionate gazes and close physicality, or they could have portrayed the dangers of a morally bankrupt friendship with lascivious stares and inappropriate gestures. As stage directions are so infrequently included in early English plays, we can only surmise how actors would have employed gestures to capture the complexities of characters engaged in friendships and sworn brotherhood, yet surely the better performances captured the ways in which homosocial surfaces could only imperfectly camouflage homoerotic depths.

Sodomy in Early English Culture and Drama

Given the common themes of homosocial friendship and the moral trajectory from sinful seduction to homosocial salvation staged in much early English drama, accompanying treatments of sodomy illuminate the conflicting responses to male homoeroticism in the corpus. Although many Western literary and cultural traditions venerated male friendships, others viewed them as potentially leading to homoerotic sin, as evident in the writings of Aelred of Rievaulx and Guibert of Nogent. After discussing the benefits of spiritual friendship, Aelred condemns other alliances, particularly in his reference to carnal friendship: "Verum amicitiae carnalis exordium ab affectione procedit, quae instar meretricis diuaricat pedes suos omni transeunti, sequens aures et oculos suos per uaria fornicantes" (The real beginning of carnal friendship proceeds from an affection which like a harlot directs its step after every passer-by, following its own lustful ears and eyes in every direction).[35] He further fears that such friendships will fall to greater evils, those that remain unnamed but are nonetheless suggestive of sexual intimacy: "Est et amicitia quam pessimorum similitudo morum conciliat; de qua dicere supersedeo, cum nec amicitiae nomine digna, ut superius diximus, habeatur" (Then there is the friendship which is based on a likeness in evil. Of this type I refrain from speaking, since, as we have said before, it is not to be considered even worthy of the name of friendship).[36] As C. Stephen Jaeger summarizes of Aelred's opinions of friendship, "Spiritual friendship matures out of a boyish affection which is 'always mixed with impure loves,' and which 'obscures and corrupts the true character of friendship' by drawing it to the desires of the flesh ... 'Wanton' affection (*affectionis lascivia*) must be governed by the 'foresight of reason.'"[37] Barbara Newman states that Guibert of Nogent was "deeply troubled by the threat of erotic friendships between monks" because they might lead to "harmful intimacies" and "fatal love"; Guibert advocates such friends be separated in a manner that is "so harsh and abrupt that no hope of repairing the love again may remain."[38] Aelred and Guibert fear that sodomy will outweigh the moral benefits of homosocial friendship, and recognize that the line between the two can be difficult to discern.

Sodomy is a vexed term in the Middle Ages and the Renaissance, denoting a range of transgressions ranging from the spiritual to the sexual. As Glenn Olsen documents, "In the early Middle Ages, the 'sodomite sin' could refer either to something very specific, anal intercourse; to a 'short list' typically including masturbation, intercrural ... or femoral intercourse, and anal intercourse; or to a variety of usually unspecified 'sins against nature.'"[39] These meanings persisted in the Tudor era, with the word developing additional nuances, including idolatry, impiety, and even clerical celibacy, amidst the rhetorical wars of the Reformation. Building on the work of Alan Bray, Jonathan Goldberg explains, "Sodomy is not ... so much a set of forbidden acts as the performance of those undefined acts – or the accusation of their performance – by those who threatened social stability – heretics, spies, traitors, Catholics."[40] And so even when John Bale includes Sodomismus in his cast of characters for *Thre Lawes of Nature, Moses, and Christ*, the audience does not necessarily envision and certainly does not see before them an enactment of anal sex, yet at the same time the connections between sodomy and homosexuality could never be fully severed.

Along with the theatre critics cited in the introduction who railed against the sexual mores of the stage (Augustine, the author of *A Tretise of Miraclis Pleyinge*, and Stephen Gosson), several moralists denounced the perversions of dramatic pastimes for their connections to sodomy. John Northbrooke's *A Treatise against Dicing, Dancing, Plays, and Interludes, with Other Idle Pastimes* (1577), an allegorical discussion between Age and Youth, denounces the stage in harsh and eroticized terms, damning it as modern Sodom: "Loke backe no more to filthy Sodom, least it happen to you as did to Lot's wife; neither turne to your vomet like a dogge, neyther get to your filthy puddle and myre, like a swyne, for, if you do, your portion wil be with those that shal be shut out of God's kingdome."[41] Castigating theatrical pastimes in similar terms, Philip Stubbes, in *The Anatomie of Abuses* (1583), condemns not merely their subject matter and performance tactics but also their sinful effects on audiences: "Then these goodly Pageants being ended, euery mate sortes to his mate, euery one brings another homeward of their way very friendly, and in their secret conclaues (couertly) they play the Sodomits, or worse."[42] Margaret Janke Kidnie, while recognizing the wide range of *sodomy*'s significations in Tudor England, notes, "The likelihood is that sexual attraction between men was a feature of the public theaters, and it seems unnecessary to rule out entirely the possibility that Stubbes at least nods towards same-sex relations in his use of the term 'Sodomits.'"[43] As a site both for learning the moral benefits of homosocial friendship and for falling to the manifold sins coming under the rubric of sodomy, the early English stage was variously construed as salvific and damning, with the confused cultural values of male homosociality creating a vexed atmosphere.

Although more often in the margins of texts and virtually (although not universally) unperformable on the stage, sodomy becomes visible at key moments in early English drama, including allusions to the Sodom narrative of Genesis, sharp insults from one character to another, and the transgressive humour of parodically enacting this denigrated expression of sexual desire. The biblical narrative of Sodom is cited in several plays of the era, including Thomas Watson's *Absalom* (1.3.137), *King Darius* (p. 74), *Occupation and Idleness* (386–7), and *Pacient and Meeke Grissell* (379–80).[44] In W. Wager's *The Longer Thou Livest*, Exercitation declares, "Idleness taught the Sodomites impiety" (1902), and in Wager's *Enough Is as Good as a Feast*, Satan derides Wordly Man as "a filthy sodomite" and "a very dunghill and sink of sin" (1441 and 1443). *Misogonus*'s Eupelas lambastes Sir John as "thou abominable sodomite! Thou execrable sot!" (2.2.330).[45] John Bale's interludes, as discussed in chapter 5, abound with references to Sodom and sodomites.

Sodomy, owing to the multiplicity of the term's signification, often remains a spectral presence even when it is allegorically embodied by an actor in performance, but numerous plays openly engage in the humour of anality and anal insults through references to analingus and the *osculare fundamentum*. In *Like Will to Like*, Nichol Newfangle complains to Lucifer of his anal abuses: "Thou carest not whom thou killest in thy raging mind. / Dost thou not remember since thou didst bruise me behind? / This hole in thy fury didst thou disclose, / That now may a tent be put in so big as thy nose" (85–8). J.A.B. Somerset explains of Newfangles words: "Nichol suggests that the Devil's nose be used as a tent – a surgical appliance to distend and cleanse a wound (here, Nichol's fundament)."[46] In *The Bugbears*, Trappola insults Biondello: "Stoop down alow / And kiss my round rivet while I claw thine elbow" (1.2.13–14).[47] Dulypo in George Gascoigne's *Supposes* purposefully mistakes the name of Erostrato, his alter ego, as "arsekisse," and Lytio insults Cleander, wishing that "your nose were in … an hole in another place."[48] Several of John Heywood's characters refer to analingus, including Potycary in *The Foure PP*, who insults Pardoner and his relics:

> Thys kysse shall brynge us muche promocyon –
> Fogh! By Saynt Savyour, I never kyst a wars!
> Ye were as good kysse All Hallows ars,
> For by All Halows, me thynketh
> That All Halows breth stynketh. (499–503)[49]

In Heywood's *Play of the Wether*, Mery Report taunts Gentylman, "As lefe ye kyste myne ars as blow my my hole soo" (255, cf. 1064), with Launder providing a rare instance of a female character offering such an insult: "Byr lady, I wolde ye had kyst myne ars to" (871).[50] *Tom Tyler and His Wife* features the eponymous wife, appropriately named Strife, similarly directing her nemesis, Tom Tayler, to kiss her anus; Patience invites a reconciliation between the two – "Tom Tayler also, shall you kiss ere you go, / And see you be friends" – to which Strife replies, "I would he had kist both the endes" (828–30).[51] With so many references to anality, early English plays employ the carnivalesque humour of analingus – an inversion of normative sexuality – to remind their audiences of sexual possibilities that were unlikely to be staged but could nonetheless be adumbrated for their comic potential.

Reaching beyond such insulting references to analingus, several plays refer more directly to anal penetration and sexual sodomy. In *The Enterlude of Godly Queene Hester*, Hardydardy recounts the story of Perillus, who built a torture device in the shape of a bull for King Phalaris but was then himself executed in it, with Hardydardy concluding to King Assuerus, "I wene, by God, he made a rodde / For his own arse!" (1028–9).[52] *Lusty Juventus* adumbrates sodomitic themes when Juventus promises Knowledge that he will maintain their homosocial friendship: "And I will never forsake your company / While I live in this world" (322–3). Juventus fails to maintain this beneficial homosocial friendship and falls to the heteroerotic allure of Abominable Living, with Hypocrisy outlining his sodomitical plans to trap humanity: "I set up great idolatry / With all kind of filth[y sodomitry], / To give [mankind a fall]" (402–4). In sum, *Lusty Juventus* envisions proper male friendship as an antidote both to sinful heteroerotic pursuits and to Hypocrisy's sodomitic plans for humanity's downfall. Returning to George Gascoigne's *Supposes*, this play pursues its interest in sodomitical insults when Dulypo, attempting to convince Cleander that Pasyphilo has betrayed him in his courtship of Polynesta, declares that Pasyphilo is defaming him as a sodomite: "And he saith, that you desire this yong gentlewoman, as much for other mens pleasure as for your owne." Cleander asks for clarification, and Dulypo continues, "Peradventure that by hir beautie, you woulde entice many yong men to your house." Cleander cannot decode the queer insinuation – "Yong men? to what purpose?" – with Dulypo's response silently emphasizing the sodomitical allegations: "Nay, gesse you that" (p. 209). Dulypo's queer insult exemplifies the cagey ways in which early English plays alluded to homosexuality and sodomy while not explicitly naming them, leaving the audience to interpret the obvious insinuation of his words, and couching them in sufficient silence so that the unmentionable vice remains unmentioned.

The familial relationships among Vice figures often take on queer and sodomitical connotations, particularly in discussions of parentage. In W. Wager's *The Longer Thou Livest*, Idleness declares himself to be Incontinence's father: "Then thy parent I must needs be. / Thou art a vice by all men's consent; / Therefore, it is like that I begat thee" (611–13). With no mention of Incontinence's mother, the relationship assumes a queer coding, in which male Vice figures sire male offspring without the necessity of heterosexual intercourse. Thomas Lupton's *All for Money* traces sodomy to Satan through the undeclared parentage of monstrous progeny. Three of the play's primary Vice characters – Money, Pleasure, and Sin – appear as grotesquely maternal figures, with their hermaphroditic corporeality contributing to the play's concluding message concerning immoderate, and thus potentially queer, homosociality. Following the prologue and an introductory conversation among Theology, Science, and Art, the play's dramatic action begins with three scenes of vomitous parturition: Money gives birth to Pleasure, Pleasure gives birth to Sin, and Sin gives birth to Damnation. Throughout these parodic scenes Money, Pleasure, Sin, and Damnation discuss their gestations and births, thus creating a vision of the outwardly male body as inwardly female. Sin complains of the cramped quarters of his gestation in Pleasure, "I could not once turn me, in my father's belly" (237), and he subsequently worries of a breached birth of Damnation: "The whoreson's head is so great and he so ill-favored made / That I must needs be ripped, I am greatly afraid!" (280–1).[53] Upon Damnation's delivery, he sighs in relief, "It is the heaviest lubber that ever man did bear! / ... / How say you, masters, is not this a well-favored baby / That I, Sin, have brought forth so painfully?" (291–4). Damnation thanks his father for the "pains and labor" required "in bringing forth of me" (307).

All for Money does not directly address whether the births of Pleasure, Sin, and Damnation should be construed as resulting from asexual or sexual reproduction, but Satan soon appears in the play, delighted in these newborn offspring and humorously quarrelling with Sin, whom he repeatedly refers to as "my friend Sin" (374, 386, 415). With this affirmation of their friendship stressed three times, the audience is cued to look for signs that this homosocial relationship veers into the homoerotic, with evidence forthcoming when Sin requests of Satan "a piece of thy tail" (462). Satan refuses and queries the necessity of this request, to which Sin replies:

> Then your nose I would have, to stop my tail behind,
> For I am cumbered with colic, and letting out of wind,
> And if it be too little to make thereof a case,
> Then I would be bold to borrow your face. (467–70)

With this image of Satan's nose buried in Sin's buttocks, Lupton compels his audience to conceive of their relationship as an inversion of heterosexual intercourse. Building on the play's homosocial themes of sin and damnation, Sin warns the audience not to marry his son:

> Therefore, if any chance to marry my son hereafter,
> Let them not blame me, for I have told his behavior.
> Before you proceed therefore in this marriage,
> Weigh well with yourself the danger and charge. (1325–8)

Sin does not limit his advice to the women of the audience, and so these words admit the possibility of men marrying Damnation, as he himself has committed himself to Satan. To posit that Satan begets Pleasure,

Sin, and Damnation requires one to conjecture about their moment of conception, and it must be admitted that the play does not depict or otherwise confirm their joint parentage. Satan, however, stands as the only reasonable candidate for their paternity. With Satan's delight in their births, his fraternal relationships with the acknowledged fathers who grotesquely birthed them, and Sin's admonitions about marrying Damnation, sodomitical procreation, as paradoxical as such a vision must be, stands as the explanation that the play cannot portray on its surface but can only broach through its suggestively queer themes.

Despite the overarching silence enveloping sodomy in early English drama, in some rare instances it became visible on the stage, even if not directly named as such. In Henry Medwall's *Fulgens and Lucres*, the erotic competition between A and B escalates from homosocial competition to sodomitical farce. With words and gestures focusing the audience's attention on male genitalia, B comments on men's shifting fashions: "A codpece before allmost thus large, / And therin restith the gretist charge!" (1.734–5).[54] B's words *thus large* indicate that the actor would likely use his hands to approximate, and likely exaggerate, the size of the penis under his codpiece, with his double entendre on *greatest charge* suggesting its mighty puissance; as Greg Walker comments, "the line was no doubt accompanied by a suitably impressive gesture."[55] By focusing on his character's penis, Medwall establishes the homosocial competition between A and B in anatomical terms, with the conflict escalating. The two characters soon skirmish over their respective desire for Ancilla, Joan, with the play depicting B's successful efforts to kiss her. The stage directions first indicate, "*Et conabitur eam osculari*" (following line 1.994; And he will try to kiss her), and then state, "*Et osculabitur. Intrat A*" (following line 1.1004; And he will kiss her. A enters). Upon witnessing this kiss, A reacts waspishly: "Now a felychip, I the beseche / Set even suche a patche one my breche!" (1.1005–6). *Set a patch on my breech* roughly translates as "kiss my ass,"[56] with these words inverting the play's erotic themes: a man kisses a woman on the mouth, and then another man demands – threateningly to his amatory adversary, humorously for the audience – that similar attention be directed to his anus.

A and B's erotic competition escalates through singing – "*Et tunc cantabunt*" (following line 1.1125; And then they will sing]) – and wrestling – "*Et deinde luctabuntur*" (following line 1.1146; And then they will wrestle) – until B proposes, "Let us just at farte prycke in cule" (1.1169). As Christina Fitzgerald and John Sebastian explain of "farte prycke in cule," "From the text, it becomes clear that A and B will each be somehow tied bent-over double, holding wooden sticks or staffs with which they will attempt to poke the other in the anus."[57] Men poking sticks at each other's buttocks parodies sodomy, but this scene provides more than merely vulgar humour; it is, on the contrary, germane to the play's amorous themes. In many ways this scene of *Fulgens and Lucres* dramatizes the similar queer tension between Chaucer's *Knight's Tale* and *Miller's Tale*, which depends on the latter's humour of parodic sodomy to elevate, if also to question, the former's veneration of courtly love. The romance of the *Knight's Tale* concludes with Palamon and Emily pledged in marriage, but, as much as the majority of the Canterbury pilgrims appreciate this tale, the Miller famously threatens, "By armes, and by blood and bones, / I kan a noble tale for the nones, / With which I wol now quite the Knyghtes tale" (3125–7).[58] *The Miller's Tale* features a battle between two men – Nicholas and Absolon – over their shared beloved, Alison, and their erotic contest ends with Nicholas's parodic penetration: "And he was redy with his iren hoot, / And Nicholas amydde the ers he smoot" (3809–10). The *Knight's Tale* ends with the genteel promise of marriage, yet prior to any possibility that Palamon and Emily could consummate their affections, whereas *The Miller's Tale* satirizes the courtly promises of romance through the bawdy humour of adulterous intercourse and parodic sodomy. In this light the farcical scenes of attempted anal penetration in *Fulgens and Lucres* imbue a deeper meaning to its primary plot line of heteroerotic romance, pointing through humorous contrast to the necessity for a woman to make her own decisions in love, particularly when her suitors are more concerned with demonstrating their prosthetically phallic superiority over each other than their admiration for her.

Anal shenanigans similar to those in *Fulgens and Lucres* infuse the uproarious humour of Mr. S.'s *Gammer Gurton's Needle*, in which a frantic search for Gammer Gurton's lost needle is resolved when it pierces her servant Hodge's backside, for this needle, in a strikingly unsubtle metaphor, represents a penis. The *OED* documents the use of *needle* as a slang term for "penis" to the late sixteenth century, citing John Lyly's *Gallathea* (1592) as its first usage, with Cupid promising: "I say I will pricke as well with my needle, as euer I did with mine arrowes."[59] Although *Gammer Gurton's Needle* pre-dates this usage by roughly forty years, it appears evident that the needle of this play functions similarly as in Lyly's lines for Cupid, as Lindsay McFadyen convincingly argues in his essay "What Was Really Lost in *Gammer Gurton's Needle?*"[60] McFadyen points out that the "descriptions of the needle … are consistently phallic," noting Gammer Gurton's description of it as "my joy, / My fair, long, straight nee'le that was mine only treasure. / The first day of my sorrow is, and last end of my pleasure" (1.4.4–6).[61] Hodge similarly employs phallic imagery in describing it: "A little thing with an hole in the end, as bright as any silver, / Small, long, sharp at the point, and straight as any pillar" (2.1.43–4).

Of course, an anus is required for anal penetration, and Hodge fulfils this requirement. The prologue announces:

As Gammer Gurton, with many a wide stitch
Sat piecing and patching of Hodge her man's breech,
By chance or misfortune as she her gear tossed,
In Hodge's leather breeches her needle she lost. (prologue, 1–4)

As the *OED* documents, the primary denotation of *breech* is a "garment covering the loins and thigh," which evolved to indicate trousers. In an example of metonymic semantic expansion, *breech* also refers to "the part of the body covered by this garment; the buttocks, posteriors, rump, seat," with the *OED* dating this usage to the late sixteenth century in Robert Greene's *Comicall Historie of Alphonsus, King of Aragon*.[62] The prologue further suggests anal penetration when the audience is apprised, "Suddenly the nee'le Hodge found by the pricking / And drew it out of his buttock where he felt it sticking" (prologue, 17–18). As established in the previous chapter, *prick* often denotes the penis, and so the play opens with the image of Hodge anally penetrated by his mistress's phallic needle. Of course, within the performance itself, Gammer Gurton is played by a male actor, and so this performative phallus, whether accorded to the female character or to the male actor, or even to both simultaneously, establishes Hodge as the passive partner in an anal encounter, with its eroticism sublimated to the play's farcical humour.

Along with the missing needle qua penis of its title, *Gammer Gurton's Needle* revels in vulgar humour, and, given these conditions, it is difficult not to see sexual puns in its unfolding action, even in Tib's apparently innocuous line concerning her mistress: "If she hear not of some comfort, she is, faith, but dead; / Shall never come within her lips one inch of meat ne bread" (1.3.17–18). The *OED* documents that the usage of *meat* as "penis" is roughly contemporaneous with *Gammer Gurton's Needle*.[63] Gammer Gurton's boy is named Cock, and her roosters (that is, her cocks) also play a part in the story, with the bedlam figure Diccon reporting to Dame Chat, "Here is Gammer Gurton your neighbour, a sad and heavy wight: / Her goodly fair red cock at home was stole this last night" (2.2.37–8), as he orchestrates the women's impending battle over their lost goods. Accentuating the play's sodomitical themes, Diccon reports of this cock: "And Doll, your maid, the legs she hid a foot deep in the dung" (2.2.66). A cock – or more specifically, a cock's legs – in dung conjures images of anal penetration that the play returns to in its conclusion. Diccon urges Hodge, "But Hodge, take good heed now thou do not beshite me!" (5.2.290), with the accompanying stage direction indicating "*And gave him a good blow on the buttock.*" The lost needle is found as Hodge cries, "He thrust me into the buttock with a bodkin or a pin!" (5.2.293), and soon adds, "Chwas almost undone, 'twas so far in my buttock!" (5.2.307). As William Toole assesses, "the coordination of scatological imagery and action ... gives the play a kind of comic inevitability," and its interest in anal penetration makes explicit the erotic undertones of its humour.[64] In sum, *Gammer Gurton's Needle* barely camouflages the sodomy that is central to its thematic and comic significations, but, in camouflaging that which should be apparent, it testifies to the fact that the queerness of the early English stage virtually always appeared shrouded in latency, even when the humour demanded blatancy.

Finally, although this chapter has addressed the homosocial and homoerotic potential of various male relationships in early English drama, it would be remiss not to address the play with the greatest potential for a lesbian reading: the Digby *Mary Magdalen*. Scholarship on female friendships in the medieval and early modern era has explored the ways in which women's friendships both found inspiration in and diverged from male models of friendship such as those espoused by Cicero in *De amicitia*.[65] Robert Mills details in his *Seeing Sodomy in the Middle Ages* that women's friendships could pose similar anxieties to men's friendships, in the possibility that a spiritually beneficial relationship would degrade into a carnal affair.[66] And as much as many discourses of sodomy in the Middle Ages simply overlook the potential for women to engage in homoerotic encounters, Chaucer's Parson provides a key example of the elasticity of this sin (which could ensnare women as well as men), when discussing lechery: "The fifthe spece is thilke abhomynable synne, of which that no man unnethe oghte speke ne write; nathelees it is openly reherced in holy writ. / This cursednesse doon men and wommen in diverse entente and in diverse manere" (10.909–10). As Karma Lochrie observes in her reading of this passage, "Medieval writers on Sodomy who write primarily about male-male sexual activity often represent it as being derived from a wanton, libidinous, essentially *feminine* (because unchecked by masculine reason) desire," demonstrating the ways in which femininity is used as a social construct to shape masculinity.[67] Francesca Canadé Sautman and Pamela Sheingorn discuss the implications of sodomitical discourses for women: "Thus, if the invention of sodomy held grave consequences for the ways male sexuality was to be regulated and circumscribed, it held as many for the construction of sexuality as a network of ideologies, practices, and discourses. And it held momentous consequence for the construction of women's sexuality, regardless of the object choices in their lives, for it strengthened women's role in the maintenance of the heteronorm and rendered their search for alternative positions and modes of pleasure more obscure, hidden, forbidden, and hence dangerous."[68] Within the field of early English drama, with women marginalized from plot lines and performances, male homoeroticism stands as an ever-present possibility, which should not then obscure the ways in which women's desire is staged.

Queerness potentially emerges when male actors playing female roles embrace each other, as evident in the Digby *Mary Magdalen*. This play integrates biblical and apocryphal narratives with the typical allegorical features of the psychomachia, while also framing the seduction into sin as a lesbian encounter. The playwright stresses that Lechery is a female character, with Flesch referring to her as "Lady Lechery" and praising her as the "flowyr fayrest of femynyte!" (422–3).[69] The scene adopts the rarefied language of courtly romance, with Lechery awed by Mary Magdalen's stunning beauty – "Bryter þan þe bornyd is your bemys of bewte, / Most debonarius wyth your aungelly delycyte!" (443–4) – and asserting her desire, "Your servant to be, I wold comprehende!" (446). In seeking to serve her female beloved, Lechery is a female character inhabiting a male social role, and Mary Magdalen finds herself rapturously enthralled by her suitor's becoming words and demeanour: "Your debonarius obedyauns ravyssyt me to trankquelyte!" (447). She soon elaborates, "Forsothe, ye be welcum to myn hawdyens! / Ye be my hartys leche! (460–1). Should the audience envision these two women as consummating their lesbian flirtation? Good Angyll admonishes her, "Fleschly lust is to þe full delectabyll" (593), hinting at the sensual delights that she has enjoyed. Lechery also acts as a bawd, encouraging Mary to pursue an illicit encounter with Gallant – "Lady, þis man is for ʒow, as I se can, / To sett yow i[n] sportys and talkyng þis tyde!" (507–8) – which testifies to the shifting nature of illicit desire throughout the play.

Certainly, the lesbian nature of Mary Magdalen's seduction builds the play's spiritual themes as she shifts from a corporally erotic relationship with a woman to a spiritually eroticized relationship in which she is chastely married to Jesus. In a scene reminiscent of the *Quem quaeritis* dialogues, her costuming signifies her reclaimed chastity: "*Here xall entyr þe thre Mariis arayyd as chast women, wyth sygnis of þe passyon pryntyd ypon þer brest*" (following line 992). Newly chaste, Mary sees herself as Christ's lover. Not yet recognizing him, she proclaims, "For I have porposyd in eche degree / To have hym wyth me, werely, / The wyche my specyall Lord hath be, / And I hys lovyr and cavse wyll phy" (1065–8). Although Mary Magdalen now renounces sexuality in favor of a relationship with her saviour, she miraculously aids barren women, and the play ends with sexless procreation during her travels in Marseille. Mary Magdalen tells Rex, "Thy wyffe, she is grett wyth chyld! / Lyke as þou desyerst, þou hast þi bone!" (1666–7). Regina confirms her pregnancy – "A, ʒe! I fel ytt ster in my wombe vp and down! / I am glad I have þe in presens!" (1668–9) – and realizes that only Mary Magdalen can provide the succour she craves: "A, þe chyld þat betwyx my sydys lay, / Þe wyche was conseyvyd on me be ryth – / Alas, þat wommannys help is away!" (1757–9). From her lusty encounter with Lady Lechery to her re-embodiment as a chaste bride of Jesus to her miraculous midwifery of a child conceived without conception, the play concludes with abstinence, and Mary Magdalen proclaims, "In charyte my werkys I woll grave, / And in abstynens, all dayys of my lyfe" (1993–4). As Theresa Coletti observes, "it is not just Mary Magdalene's renounced sexuality that exemplifies the potential benefit of a much-desired discipline but a more broadly based, equal opportunity sublimation of earthly eros that the play seems to admonish, and over which the saint's acquired virginal purity presides."[70] The play's thematic development depends on Mary Magdalen's initial seduction into lesbianism, which would (subjunctively) argue for the actors to accentuate the eroticism of these earlier encounters in order to portray more fully her progression into chastity.

Within the primarily male world of early English drama, homosocial relationships guide the unfolding of many plots, whether to salvation or to damnation, or for another thematic goal altogether. At its core, friendship serves as a foundational premise for these plays, and audiences are called to assess gradations among morally beneficent and spiritually dubious alliances, with homoeroticism potentially adumbrated in the thin line between the two. Given these conditions, it would be surprising if queerness did not seep into the storylines, asking audiences to question the moral valence of a given relationship for the protagonists, particularly those of morality plays and moral interludes. From the spiritual turpitude of homosocial relationships in *All for Money* to the humour of anal jousting in *Fulgens and Lucrece*, from the mock references to male marriage in *Royster Doyster* to Mary Magdalen's lesbian seduction, early English drama employed homosocial friendships for a variety of dramatic purposes, with a variety of queering consequences to their depiction and reception, from which sodomy could never be fully vanquished.

PART TWO

Queer Readings of Early English Drama

Chapter Three

Performative Typology, Jewish Genders, and Jesus's Queer Romance in the York Corpus Christi Plays

The York Corpus Christi Plays, in depicting a panoramic account of Christian experience from creation to doomsday, must by necessity depict Jewish experience as well. Within the Christian typological imaginary, events and figures from the Hebrew Bible, redubbed and reconfigured as the Old Testament, are conceived as prophetic predictors of Jesus's fulfilment of eternal truths. In positing a radical rupture between the Jewish past of the Old Testament and the Christian present and future of the New Testament, typology insists upon the linearity of time leading inexorably to Christian transcendence, yet Christianity can never supersede its roots in Jewish traditions. Judaism and Christianity stand side by side in the pages of the Christian Bible, yet they simultaneously stand at odds, with Jewish texts conscripted to serve as the foundation of a faith that is separate from its own traditions, and with the New Testament using these texts to fortify its pronouncement of new eternal truths. In staging biblical scenes for the edification and entertainment of their audiences, the York Corpus Christi Plays thematize Christianity's supersession of Judaism yet concomitantly depict the impossibility of typology, owing to the disruptive queerness inherent in portraying biblical genders, sexualities, and erotic ideologies. Speaking to a distinct yet related topic in medieval drama, Miriamne Ara Krummel affirms the utility of queer theory for understanding the performance of Jewish identity in the York Corpus Christi Plays, stating that the "porousness of the division between Christian and Jew, given the importance of Jesus and the Jewish Patriarchs to the Christian faith, requires a careful (re)construction of what/who is and is not Jewish"; she then posits that "a closeted Jewish identity is one that the text conceals; an outed Jewish identity is one that the text denotes."[1] These gendered and erotic tensions percolate throughout the cycle and cluster around the intersecting issues of typology and Jewish and Christian identities. In his classic study *The Play Called Corpus Christi*, V.A. Kolve describes this cycle as a playful but serious artistic enterprise, one that was conceived as "a lie designed to tell the truth about reality," the aim of which "was to celebrate and elucidate, not even temporarily, to deceive."[2] Playful dramas, however, rarely unfold as straightforwardly as their playwrights might intend.

As is well known, the York Corpus Christi Plays date to the late fourteenth century, and their early foundations and development remain the subject of much scholarly debate.[3] Their fundamental structure and content were registered in the "Ordo paginarum ludi Corporis Christi," a 1415 document detailing the pageants, their characters, and the trade guilds that produced them.[4] Following the Reformation, the celebration of Corpus Christi was abolished in 1548, and the plays were last performed in 1569 on "Tewisday in witsone weeke."[5] A variety of authors penned the cycle's constituent pageants, and the so-called York Realist in particular was celebrated for his artistic accomplishments.[6] Several of the pageants appear as well in the Towneley Plays (noticeably altered), suggesting a vibrant cross-pollination among the playwrights and performers of the various cycles. The unruly hermeneutic conditions surrounding the York Corpus Christi Cycle – in the multiplicity of authorship across its constituent pageants, in the influence of other cycle pageants on it and its influence on these other cycles, and in the variability of performance across a span of two centuries, with hundreds of actors, costumers, pageant designers, and other such artists contributing to their staging – undermine attempts to offer definitive interpretations of their meaning, performance, and reception. Moreover, various guilds oversaw the staging of the individual pageants, which further contributes to the diversity of "authorship" in these productions.

Despite these historically contingent circumstances, it is widely agreed that typology structures the theological message of the York Corpus Christi Plays and other such pageants, thus providing interpretive ballast to this dramatic cycle that was penned by different authors yet unified by a shared theme.[7] At its core, typology posits that the actors and actions depicted in the Old Testament prefigure the actors and actions of the New Testament, thereby reformulating Jewish textual traditions for emerging Christian ones. As Walter Meyers explains, "Typology begins as a system of Scriptural exegesis that maintains that God intended certain biblical persons, objects, or events to prefigure later persons, objects or events ... Most frequently, the type is an Old Testament person or event prefiguring someone or something in the New."[8] Typology establishes interpretive horizons for audiences of the York Corpus Christi Plays, and in her noteworthy reading of the cycle Sarah Beckwith eloquently remarks that the plays "remember and argue over memory, in the most tangible of ways, as they embody and transform the very shape of Corpus Christi in the plastic medium of the city of York." She further demonstrates the ways in which the plays grapple with the meaning of Christian truth within the realities of their contemporary location.[9] Typology, like memory, attempts to structure the audience's interpretation of these plays within the urban and dramatic confines of York.

Yet as typology encourages viewers to look for connections between the Old and New Testaments, it underscores the inherent ambiguity of the break between past and present and the confused relationship between Jews and Christians. In a real sense, typology and typological interpretations attempt to contain and constrain the interpretation of medieval drama, positing an inherently conservative reading of a performative genre inherently open to carnivalesque play. Anthony Gash rightly notes that "the relationship between written text and performance is a fluid one" in light of "the dynamics of live performance," concluding that "what is diabolic 'perversion' from one point of view ... is festive reversal from another."[10] Robert Sturges proposes that typology attempts to guide the staging and reception of medieval drama, but he advocates "resisting this harmonizing Christian reading" and exploring instead the dissonant possibilities that these dramas enact.[11] Consider, for instance, Claire Sponsler's reading of the staging of Christ's body in the Corpus Christi Plays, in which a "central irony" emerges from their "representations of violence against the bodies of Christ, women, and children," which ultimately "question[s] the ideology of social wholeness and its cultural work."[12] Between ideology and representation, as well as between typology and performance, arise countless possibilities for the plays' religious message to take on unruly and unexpectedly queer significations.

In multiple scenes the York Corpus Christi Plays query the meaning of Jewish and Christian genders and sexualities and thus destabilize the interpretive certainty promised by its typological foundations. Kathleen Biddick argues that typology – a "fantasy of supersession" – "may be regarded as constitutive of the Christian unconscious," which must constantly struggle "to ward off the shattering threat of typological reversibility."[13] In transforming typology from a hortatory into a performative mode – that is to say, from the themes of sermons into the themes of dramas – the York Corpus Christi Plays create theatrical differences between Jews and Christians that simultaneously unleash the queer potential of a theological production. Such transpositions of gender culminate in the plays' depiction of a Jesus who, through typological logic, must cleanse the story of his life from any sense of erotic transgression, while representing so many Jewish forebears, regardless of their own erotic histories and gendered identities. Within the typological imagination the plasticity of Jewish genders allows the reconstitution of Christian identity as liberated from prior traditions; yet it also suggests a similar plasticity for Christian genders, particularly given Jesus's Jewish identity. In the play's generic interest in the romance tradition, the clash between typology and gender is further intensified, as Jesus's new role as a knightly protagonist cannot fully withstand the typological pressures unleased throughout the preceding pageants. As Theresa Tinkle rightly cautions, "All things considered, we would not necessarily expect a coherent Jesus to emerge from the playwrights' episodic treatment of his body, costumes, theatrical properties, and voice."[14] Moreover, the performances of the York Corpus Christi Plays, unlike the reconstituted scripts, were unlikely to uphold a strictly linear plot line, with audience members potentially seeing plays from transtemporal moments of biblical history, and the role of Jesus would be played by several different actors. Jesus's gender, built on the inherently unstable foundations of typology, calls into question the supersessionist logic of typology generally; it does so through the queer effects of literary genders produced by the York drama's representation of his religiously and ethnically marked gender.

Performative Typology, Gender and Sexuality, and the Hermeneutic Jew

Throughout medieval England, members of the religious orders preached sermons based on typological interpretations of scripture, and therefore the general populace would recognize the centrality of typology to their understanding of their faith and its relationship to Judaism, even if they remained unversed in its exegetical underpinnings. Typology served as a common theme of medieval sermons, as evident in John Mirk's *Festial*, which was widely distributed among English parish priests, to the extent that Susan Powell concludes, "Not only was the *Festial* the most widely read English sermon cycle in the fifteenth century, it would also appear to have been the most frequently printed English text before the Reformation."[15] In the prologue to his *Festial*, Mirk addresses his readership of fellow priests and offers his sermon collection as a handbook for moral instruction – "therein he schal fynde redy of alle the principale festis of the ȝere a schort sermon nedful for hym to techy[n] and othur for to lerne"[16] – and he repeatedly stresses typological interpretations of the Old Testament. In one such example he posits Moses as a figure of Jesus: "þus was Moyses a fugur and a tokyn of Criste. For Moyses com before and ȝaf þe lawe, and Criste com aftur and ȝaf grace and mercy and trewthe. For ryght as Moyses fatte þe pepul oute of Egypte þorogh þe see to þe hul of Synay, rygh so Cryste, whan he com, be hys preching and miracles doing, fatte þe pepul oute of darkenesse of synne and of ele lyving þorogh þe watur of folowyng to þe hul of uertues."[17] In another such reading, Mirk identifies Abraham and Isaac, in the patriarch's willingness to sacrifice his son, as typological figures of God the Father and Jesus: "þan [by] Habraham ȝe schul vndurstande þe Fadur of heuen, and be Ysaac, hys Sone Ihesu Criste."[18]

With typological interpretations frequently promulgated from the pulpit, medieval Christians were taught to look for congruencies between the Old and New Testaments of their faith. Thus, the interpretive skills learned in church would be enlisted when they were viewing biblical events depicted on pageant stages, and the interpretive skills learned in viewing plays would be enlisted when they were listening to sermons. Both sermons and plays can be seen as modes of performance, but sermons adopt a more explicitly didactic tone in the explication of doctrines of the faith, whereas plays, even when dramatizing doctrinal themes, allow for a wider field of audience interpretation and reaction. Moreover, the staging of typological scenes frequently shifts the dramatic tension of the biblical event upon which it is based. Rosemary Woolf notes such a transition, in her study of the mystery plays of Abraham and Isaac, in which Abraham, suffering emotional torment in the proposed sacrifice of his son, is displaced from his role as the narrative's central figure. The plays instead focus on Isaac's heroic acceptance of his fate: "It is he whose feelings are emphasized, and it is his confession of obedience to his father and to his death, which is the dramatic peak in all but one of the plays."[19] As this brief example demonstrates, the transition from page to stage allows characters to shift in their symbolic import and their dramatic function, and so it is not surprising that, in other such instances, constructions of Jewish and Christian gender and sexuality are similarly transformed.

A key corollary of many typological interpretations entails the construction of Jews as blind to Christianity's new eternal truths, and therefore Jews are enlisted to valorize a faith tradition emerging from their own, yet distinct. Recognizing the utility of Judaism for Christianity, Jeremy Cohen decodes the ways in which Christian theologians created a "hermeneutical Jew" to serve their emerging faith's doctrines: "In order to meet their particular needs, Christian theology and exegesis created a Jew of their own ... Even if, in his inception, in his function, and in his veritable power in the Christian mind-set, the hermeneutical Jew of late antique or medieval times had relatively little to do with the Jewish civilization of his day, his career certainly influenced the Christian treatment of the Jewish minority."[20] In light of these conditions, Jewish narratives were reinterpreted in congruence with Paul's assessment of Jews as blinded by an interpretive veil: "sed obtusi sunt sensus eorum, usque in hodiernum enim diem id ipsum velamen in lectione veteris testamenti manet, non revelatum quoniam in Christo evacuatur" (2 Corinthians 3:14; but their senses were made dull. For, until this present day, the selfsame veil, in the reading of the old testament, remaineth not taken away [because in Christ it is made void]).[21] Paul's very declaration of Christian truth thus entails acknowledging alternate interpretations, in that this knowledge is both veiled for some and unveiled for others. Yet as Erich Auerbach notes in his classic study *Mimesis: The Representation of Reality in Western Literature*, typological interpretations inevitably falter in the disjunction between type and antitype: "Within this frame, there is visible a constant endeavor to fill in the lacunae of the Biblical account, to supplement it by other passages from the Bible and by original considerations, to establish a continuous connection of events, and in general to give the highest measure of rational plausibility to an intrinsically irrational interpretation."[22] In staging such an "intrinsically irrational interpretation," the dramatists of the York Corpus Christi Plays continually confronted whether to stress continuity or to stress rupture between the two traditions, with surprising depictions of Jewish and Christian gender, sexuality, and eroticism thus ensuing.

Throughout the York Corpus Christi Plays the audience is reminded of Christianity's transcendence of Jewish law, for virtually all of the constituent pageants allude to typological interpretations of their intersecting faiths. In addition to the examples from Mirk's *Festial* cited previously, with Moses prefiguring Jesus, and Abraham's sacrifice of Isaac prefiguring Jesus's crucifixion, conventional typological pairings depicted in the plays include Adam, Noah, and Moses prefiguring Jesus; Eve prefiguring Mary; and Cain prefiguring Judas. In a similar vein, Jewish prophets are cited extensively throughout the pageants. Isaiah's prophecies in 7:14 are alluded to in "The Annunciation and the Visitation" – "*Propter hoc dabit dominus ipse vobis signum, et cetera*" (12.57; Therefore the Lord himself shall give you a sign) and "*Ecce uirgo concipiett, et pariet filium, et cetera*" (12.61; Behold a virgin shall conceive, and bear a son) – and are proved true in the dramatic action depicted in the cycle.[23] Indeed, prophets are occasionally cited incorrectly in the York pageants, yet such is the power of typology that even incorrect citations need not performatively detract from the pronouncement of

Christian truth. For instance, also in the pageant "The Annunciation and the Visitation," Amos is credited as saying, "*Deus pater displ[o]suit salutem fieri in medio terre, et cetera*" (12.17; God the Father will dispense salvation throughout the [middle of the] land), although as Clifford Davidson notes, this quotation has not been positively identified.[24] Similarly, Hosea's statement in 14:6, "*E[r]o quasi ros; et virgo Israell germinabit sicut lilium*" (12.88; I will be as the dew, Israel shall spring as the lily), is erroneously credited to Joel (12.85). Even if an audience member were to notice such errors, the typological message – that the Old Testament provides the foundation for the New Testament – would cohere. Arnold Williams cautions that dramatic typology must be "theatrically possible," such that "it can be communicated in an actual production designed to be seen and heard, rather than read,"[25] and throughout the York Corpus Christi Plays' texts and in their performance the typological truths of Christianity are valorized for the pleasure of their Christian audiences.

Most significant in their treatment of these themes, the York Corpus Christi Plays depict Jesus's recognition of his typological function as he fulfils biblical prophecy through his life and acts: "My fadir ordand on þis wise, / Aftir his will þat I schulde wende, / For to fulfille þe prophicye[s]" (37.25–7). In complementary contrast, when Caiaphas recognizes the significance of Jesus's resurrection, he laments, "Allas, þanne is oure lawes lorne, / For eueremare" (38.387–8), thereby acknowledging the supersessionist logic inherent to typology that views Judaic teaching as the old that gives way to the new. Further along these lines, in "The Last Supper," the playwright encodes a rejection of Jewish dietary laws when Marcelus informs Jesus, "Oure lambe is roste and redy dight, / As Moyses lawe will lely lere" (27.7–8). Jesus then declares, "Of Moyses lawes here make I an ende / In som party, but noght in all" (27.25–6), while clarifying his stance on dietary law: "But þe lambe of Pase þat here is spende, / Whilke Jewes vses grete and small, / Euere forward nowe I itt deffende / Fro Cristis folke, what so befall" (27.29–32). Jesus's words cannot help but reinforce and subvert the logic of typology, for the audiences of the pageants are confronted with the conundrum of which parts of Mosaic law are to be ended and which are to be continued within the plays' dramatic action.[26]

In this scene and others like it, the pageants latently dramatize Jesus's proclamation, "Nolite putare quoniam veni solvere legem aut prophetas, non veni solvere sed adimplere" (Matthew 5:17; Do not think that I am come to destroy the law, or the prophets. I am not come to destroy, but to fulfil). Freed from the constraints of a sermon, in which priests would guide their parishioners to a doctrinally endorsed understanding

of typology, the plays open up reasonable, if theologically question-
able, spaces for disparate interpretations, particularly as the New Testament contradicts itself on the status of Jews. Some passages describe
a sharp rupture between the two faiths, such as Matthew's quotation
of Jesus's proclamation, "Hic est enim sanguis meus novi testamenti"
(26.28; cf. Mark 14:24, Luke 22:2; This is my blood of the new testament)
and Paul's statement, "Nam si illud prius culpa vacasset, non utique
secundi locus inquireretur" (Hebrews 8:7; For if that former [covenant]
had been faultless, there should not indeed a place have been sought for
the second). In contrast, Paul envisions in his epistle to the Romans that
God will maintain, not abrogate, his covenant with the Jews: "Non rep-
pulit Deus plebem suam quam praesciit" (11:2; God hath not cast away
his people, which he foreknew), he states, proclaiming as well, "Quod si
delibatio sancta est, et massa, et si radix sancta, et rami" (11:16; see also
11:24 and 11:29; For if the first fruit be holy, so is the lump also: and if the
root be holy, so are the branches). With the New Testament vacillating in
its understanding of the Jews, performative typology could never settle
such challenging theological issues that were left unresolved within the
gospels themselves.

In witnessing performances of typology, the pageant viewers had
to distinguish between the Jewish past of their faith and its Christian
present, and so typology influenced how they perceived a range of topics, including those related to the ways in which gender and sexuality
are cross-culturally and cross-temporally constructed. Foremost, the
staging of medieval mystery plays revealed the constructed nature of
gendered difference. Katie Normington concludes that women were
not likely to have performed speaking roles in medieval drama, citing "issues of decorum, the history of performance aesthetics, and
women's public status" as the predominant reasons for their exclusion
from the theatrical sphere, although she cites evidence "that women
did participate in the mystery plays by undertaking tasks which related
to the *production* of the plays."[27] Medieval audiences likely did not see
women on the stage; they saw men and boys performing female roles,
a performative strategy that cannot help but reveal gender as staged for
public consumption. Moreover, as Robert L.A. Clark and Claire Sponsler propose, although "crossdressing was ... the standard practice" of
medieval drama, it was imbued with latent queer potential, primarily
because "transvestism is a representation which always carries with it
the possibility of an unveiling," as they further stress the inherent liminality and porousness of medieval performances.[28] Furthermore, as Lisa
Lampert notes, "not only were female figures portrayed by men or boys
in 'drag,' but the Jews represented were, of course, played by Christians

in Jews' clothing, an illusion that calls attention to the construction of Christian identity itself."[29] The performative nature of dramatic typology accentuates these issues, for supersessionist theology consolidates the plays' religious message to their audiences, while also highlighting the necessity of the Jewish past for the Christian present, even as these divisions – woman and man, Jew and Christian, "old" law and "new" law – continually collapse during performance.

What then are the boundaries of typological interpretation? In seeking correspondences between the Old Testament and the New Testament, how do Christians, whether medieval or modern, determine what define a type and its antitype? Most typological interpretations assume a gendered congruency between type and antitype: Adam, Noah, Isaac, and Moses are each viewed as anticipating Jesus and his salvific mission, but heroic women of Hebrew narrative traditions, including Rahab, Esther, and Judith, are not called upon to perform typologically within these play cycles. As much as gendered similitude stands as an unannounced but assumed foundation of much typological exegesis, the York Corpus Christi Plays complicate this assumption and stress the otherness of Jewish genders. For example, in Christian tradition, Noah is perceived as a type of Christ, predicated upon Jesus's words in the gospels:

Sicut autem in diebus Noe ita erit et adventus Filii hominis, sicut enim erant in diebus ante diluvium, comedentes et bibentes, nubentes et nuptum tradentes, usque ad eum diem quo introivit in arcam Noe. Et non cognovernunt donec venit diluvium et tulit omnes, ita erit et adventus Filii hominis. (Matthew 24:37–9)

(And as in the days of Noe, so shall also the coming of the Son of man be. For as in the days before the flood, they were eating and drinking, marrying and giving in marriage, even till that day in which Noe entered into the ark. And they knew not till the flood came, and took them all away; so also shall the coming of the Son of man be.)

Although Noah serves as a type of Jesus in the York Corpus Christi Plays, he is effeminized through the maternal and gestational imagery that describes him and his salvific mission.[30] The York dramatist envisions Noah as, in effect, giving birth to a new world order, as the character declares in "The Flood": "ix monethes here haue we bene pyned, / But when God wyll, better mon bee" (9. 217–18). Stressing the pageant's gestational imagery, Noah's third daughter-in-law confirms his words: "A twelmothe bott xij weke / Have we be houerand here" (9.251–2). In the Genesis account the rains of the flood fall for forty days and forty nights (7:12); waters cover the land for 150 days (7:24); the ark lands in the seventh month (8:4); the tops of the mountains appear on the first day of the tenth month (8:5); and Noah opens the ark forty days later (8:6). The appearance of the mountaintops occurs after a nine-month gestational period. In this dramatization of Jewish tradition, Noah's typological function as a precursor of Jesus is complicated through the emphasis on this effeminizing depiction, and he thus serves as an inverse precursor of the heroic image of Jesus depicted in the cycle's latter pageants (to be discussed in more detail later).[31] One could plausibly rebut that such an effeminization of Noah simply reflects the effeminization of Jesus in much medieval thought, yet it is nonetheless clear that Noah's gendered characterization changes between the play's biblical sources and their productions.[32] Furthermore, while the Jesus-as-mother trope was certainly key to much medieval thought, it does not circulate in the York Corpus Christi Plays themselves, and so within this cycle the effeminization of Noah contrasts with a more masculine view of Jesus, as envisioned in the martial and knightly imagery that surrounds his depictions in the cycle's later pageants.

If Noah serves as an effeminized type of Jesus in the pageants of the York cycle, what role does Noah's wife play? Indeed, Noah's wife has long stood as a mystery, mostly absent from the Old Testament but generating much interest about her identity, particularly through efforts to name this nameless figure.[33] Unlike Noah, Noah's wife worries over her friends and family who have been left to suffer the ravages of the rising waters: "Nowe certis, and we shulde skape fro skathe / And so be saffyd as ye saye here, / My commodrys and my cosynes bathe, / þam wolde I wente with vs in feere" (9.141–4). Nicole Rice and Margaret Aziza Pappano, reading this scene's parallel in the Chester plays, pointedly query, "Why is Noah generally understood as the Christ figure when Mrs. Noah is the one willing to sacrifice herself for others?"[34] As Rice and Pappano recognize, Mrs. Noah's words in the Chester cycle – "They shall not drowne, by sayncte John, / and I may save there life" – explicitly align her with a Christological function; in the York cycle her concern is tempered yet still expressed in salvific terms.[35] Towards the end of "The Flood," Noah prophesizes the earth's second destruction through fire – "For it sall ones be waste with fyre, / And never worþe to worlde agayne" (9.301–2) – to which Noah's wife responds compassionately, in her final words of the play, "A, syre, owre hertis are s[oo]re / For þes sawes that ʒe saye here, / That myscheffe mon be more" (9.303–5). It could well be asserted that the words of Noah's wife argue against her typological function as a Christ figure because she dismisses the necessity of a final cleansing of the world that is dramatically represented within the York cycle in its final pageant, "Doomsday"; however, the refusal of such a typological identification between Noah's wife and Jesus simply reveals the likely rejection of a cross-gendered typological interpretation, not its inherent implausibility. From the examples of Noah and Noah's wife, it is apparent that gender plays a pivotal role in the construction of typological truth by the York Corpus Christi Plays, with both of these figures depicted to heighten the gendered otherness of Jews and the fulfilment of the virile yet chaste masculinity represented by Jesus.

As the pageants of the York Corpus Christi cycle shift from the Christian Old Testament to its New Testament, its use of typology shifts as well. The play introducing Mary, "The Annunciation and the Visitation," repeatedly stresses her fulfilment of prophecy, thus emphasizing her role in the nascent Christian tradition rather than her Jewish identity. In the plays depicting the marriage of Mary and Joseph and Jesus's birth, the couple's marital troubles arise primarily owing to Mary's unexpected pregnancy, but secondly owing to their diverging understanding of prophecy and typology. Concerning their erotic travails, Joseph frets repeatedly over his impotence ("For I am of grete elde, / Wayke and al vnwelde" [13.5–6]), his fear of cuckoldry ("Þe childe, certis, is noght myne; / Þat reproffe dose me pyne, / And gars me fle fra hame" [13.55–7]), and his emasculated position in society ("I dare loke no man in þe face" [13.147]). Joseph's masculinity sparks a crisis in the narrative, yet this crisis can be resolved when he realizes that his masculinity and erotic identity must be secondary to the fulfilment of typological prophecies.

Concerning their views of typology, in "The Nativity" Mary recounts Balaam's prophecy in Numbers, finding confirmation of her experiences in the prophecies of the Old Testament:

For Balam tolde ful longe beforne,
How þat a sterne shulde rise full hye,
And of a maiden shulde be borne
A sonne, þat sall oure saffying be
Fro caris kene. (14.99–103)[36]

Joseph, in contrast, initially rejects the relevance of this typological prophecy to their circumstances: "But wele I wate thurgh prophicie / A maiden clene suld bere a childe, / But it is nought sho, sekirly, / Forthy I wate I am begiled" (13.61–4). In a real sense, the dramatic action of this moment of the play is whether Joseph will remain Jewish (and thus refuse the incarnation of Christ) or become a proto-Christian. Should he choose the former, Mary would face dire repercussions, as John Mirk hypothetically posits: "þe Iewes wolde han sayde þat scheo hadde ben a lecchur and so a stonod hur to deth."[37] Typology, in effect, recodes the semiotic signification of Jewish women's bodies and the ways in which Jewish men perceive those bodies: if Mary is interpreted as a Jewish woman, according to Mirk, she would be executed owing to the Jews' inability to perceive typological shifts. Upon Jesus's birth, Joseph sees that even the animals recognize Jesus as their saviour – "Forsothe, it semes wele be ther chere / þare lord þei ken" (14.125–6) – and he endorses the sort of typological prophecies that he earlier foreswore: "O, nowe is fulfillid, forsuth I see, / þat Abacuc in mynde gon mene / And prechid by prophicie" (14.136–8).[38]

Even with Joseph's belated recognition of typological truth, Jesus's birth marks Mary simultaneously as Jewish and as proto-Christian, which again demonstrates the instability of typology within the York Corpus Christi Plays as a whole. In her plans for Jesus's presentation at the temple, as depicted in "The Purification of Mary," Mary adheres to Mosaic law and aligns herself with other Jewish women:

> Ful xl days is comme and went
> Sens that my babb Jesu was borne,
> Therefore I wolde he were present
> As Moyses lawes sais hus beforne,
>
> Here in this temple, before Goddes sight,
> As other women doith in feer. (17.191–6)[39]

Joseph points out that the other women "hais conceyved with syn fleshely / To bere a chylde" (17.203–4) and therefore that Mosaic law only applies to them: "The lawe is ledgyd for theme right playn, / That they muste be puryfied agayne, / For in mans pleasoure, for certayn, / Before were they fylyd" (17.205–8). For medieval Christians such a scene would signify the impurity of not only Jewish women but also Jewish men. As Irven M. Resnick explains, "Jews, like menstruating women, were perceived to exist under a curse. After the temple's destruction, Jews were said to remain forevermore in a state of pollution, since they are without the remedies for ritual impurity prescribed in the Pentateuch … Jewish women, without temple priests to perform the requisite offerings to complete their purification after menstruation or childbirth … perpetually endure a state of defilement."[40] Christian exegetes found prophetic evidence of Jewish uncleanliness from Isaiah ("Et facti sumus ut inmundus omnes nos quasi pannus menstruatae universae iustititae nostrae" [64:6; And we are all become as one unclean, and all our justices as the rag of a menstruous woman]) and Lamentations ("facta est Hierusalem quasi polluta menstruis inter eos" [1:17; Jerusalem is as a menstruous woman among them]). Given these texts, the anti-Semitic image of Jews as unclean would likely resonate for the audiences of the York Corpus Christi Plays, yet Mary replies that she preserved her maidenhead only through God's intervention and that she nonetheless intends to fulfil the law. Joseph accepts her decision: "I will hartely consent theretyll, / Withouten dowte" (17.226–7). Although one might expect this scene to confirm typological prophecies as registered on Mary's virginal body, she instead finds community with the other Jewish women who are celebrating their children's births. That is to say, the uniqueness of Mary's body that should performatively signal her role in the new faith is undercut by her recognition of kinship with other Jewish women, thus erasing, at least momentarily, the centuries of theological assaults of Jews as somatically different from Christians.

From these examples it becomes clear that time and history cannot be effectively dramatized in the York Corpus Christi Plays, for the purported temporal logic of typology – in moving from the Old Testament to the New Testament – continually falters as these plays attempt to stage truths that should stand as transcendent. Time collapses throughout the dramatic cycle, such as in the scenes depicting the shepherds in the fields recognizing the truth of typology. In "The Shepherds" the Second Shepherd declares, "And als the texte it tellis clerly, / By witty lerned men of oure lay, / With his blissid bloode he shulde vs by" (15.17–19), and the Third Shepherd avers, "The childre of Israell shulde be made free" (15.30). The First Shepherd soon states, "Therfore yf I shulde oght aftir crave / To wirshippe hym I will begynne" (15.98–9). The Second Shepherd confirms the typological promise of the past, the Third Shepherd predicts a future event, and the First Shepherd identifies this future event as occurring at the present moment. This scene depicts a miniature vision of Christian salvation as the shepherds' opening anxiety ("What mengis my moode nowe mev[e] y[t] will I," 15.4) giving way to immediate plans of joy ("And make mirthe as we gange," 15.131). JoAnna Dutka, in her *Music in the English Mystery Plays*, proposes that the shepherds' "mirthe" indicates their singing, and so the play would thus unite its thematic transition from bleakness to bliss with a verbal transition from speech to song.[41] Past, present, and future blend together in this scene, yet the seams between these disparate temporalities cannot be hidden from view; rather, in the staging of these themes the inherent unruliness of Christian typology, as registered through earthly temporality, becomes evident.

By expanding scenes mentioned only passingly in biblical sources, the York Corpus Christi Plays create Jewish types unmoored from New Testament accounts. These expanded scenes trouble any sharp distinction between past and present ostensibly revealed by the gospels; at the same time, they subvert distinctions between Jewish and Christian gendered identities. Such is the case with "The Slaughter of the Innocents," a brief scene in the New Testament (Matthew 2:16–18) that apparently fulfils one of Jeremiah's prophecies: "vox in excelso audita est lamentationis fletus et luctus, Rachel plorantis filios suos et nolentis consolari super eis quia non sunt" (31:15; A voice was heard on high of lamentation, of mourning, and weeping, of Rachel weeping for her children, and refusing to be comforted for them, because they are not). In the typological dramatization of this scene in the York Corpus Christi Plays, Jewish women, faced with the murder of their sons, are first aligned with Mary. Worried over Jesus's potential execution, Mary frets in "The Flight into Egypt," "I ware full wille of wane / My sone and he shulde dye, / And I haue but hym allone" (18.144–6). Similarly, the Second Woman mourns, "þe knyght vppon his knyffe / Hath slayne my sone so swette, / And I hadde but hym allone" (19.212–14). These Jewish women simultaneously serve as types of Christ, declaring their salvific efforts on behalf of their lost children. The First Woman laments, "þe barne þat wee dere bought, / þus in oure sighte to see / Disputuously spill" (19.228–30). Within the context of this play, the idiom *dere bought* alludes to Jesus's suffering and crucifixion that leads to humanity's salvation. For example, in the Marian lyric "Haile be thou! Hende heven qwene," the speaker praises Mary for her role in Jesus's incarnation, prays for her intercession, and refers to Jesus's suffering: "Helpe, hende, to I am here, / þat I be his þat me dere boghte."[42] Similarly, in the lyric "Ihesu Criste, Saynte Marye sonne," the speaker seeks Jesus's divine love: "Ihesu, my saul þat þou dere boghte, / Thi lufere, mak it to bee!"[43] Of course, it should be noted that *dere bought* can also refer to Mary's suffering, such as in Geoffrey Chaucer's "An ABC," in which the speaker prays that "oure alder foo," the devil, will not overcome the human soul, which both Mary and Jesus "have bought so deere."[44] Within the typological imaginary of the York Corpus Christi plays, this Jewish woman's words prefigure Jesus's actions in her maternal sacrifice for her child, thereby dismantling standard correlations of gendered type and antitype and finding salvific promise in an identity otherwise denigrated through the pageants' collective themes.

As these examples illustrate, typology continually falters in its logic, proving correct Auerbach's assessment of it as an "intrinsically irrational interpretation." These specific examples, however, in some manner obscure the universalizing aspect of typology, which attempts to distinguish Jews from Christians in broadly gendered terms. As typology typically focuses on Jewish characters of the Old Testament prefiguring their New Testament counterparts, the traits associated with these characters then influence how the respective faiths are viewed as a whole. In this light, Adam as a type of Jesus, and Eve as a type of Mary, casts the Jews as sexual transgressors and Christians as sexually temperate, and so Jewish fecundity serves as an inverse prefiguring of Christian chastity. Notably, in "Moses and Pharaoh," Jews are depicted as a threat, in the words of Pharaoh's Second Counsellor, owing to their fertility:

> My lorde, þar are a maner of men
> That mustirs grete maistris þam emell,
> The Jewes þat wonnes here in Jessen,
> And er named the childir of Israell.
> They multyplye so faste,
> Þat suthly we suppose
> Thay are like, and they laste,
> Yowre lordshippe for to lose. (11.29–36)

The playwright of the pageant allows the Second Counsellor to ventriloquize the narration of Exodus 1:7 – "filii Israhel creverunt et quasi germinantes multiplicati sunt, ac roborati nimis impleverunt terram" (The children of Israel increased, and sprung up into multitudes, and growing exceedingly strong they filled the land). In contrast, John the Baptist, in the staging of "The Baptism," endorses chastity even between married couples, in a strikingly anti-procreative statement:

> For if we be clene in levyng,
> Oure bodis are Goddis tempyll þan,
> In the whilke he will make his dwellyng.
> Therfore be clene, bothe wiffe and man,
> Þis is my reed;
> God will make in yowe haly þan
> His wonnyng-steed. (21.36–42)

John the Baptist is often viewed as the typological fulfilment of Isaiah's prophecy – "vox clamantis in deserto parate viam Domini, rectas facite in solitidune semitas Dei nostri" (40:3; The voice of one crying in the desert: Prepare ye the way of the Lord, make straight in the wilderness the paths of our God). In Augustine's succinct phrasing, "Vox Joannes, Verbum Christus" (The voice is John, the Word is Christ).[45] As Lynn Staley Johnson observes, John's typological function is blurred: "[John the Baptist] remains a figure of the Old Law, and John is among the company that Christ leads out of Hell on Holy Saturday. Therefore, he is emblematic of the spiritual failure of the Old Law; he, in fact, stands at the nexus of the Old and New Laws."[46] Within this hermeneutic jumble, John symbolizes both old and new, both the Jewish past and the Christian future, in a temporal dramatic moment that immediately collapses in upon itself.

Yet what is most intriguing dramatically is that John the Baptist's words in this scene ventriloquize the anti-eroticism expressed in Paul's epistles. In this scene from "The Baptism," John echoes Paul's words advocating chastity rather than the payment of the marital debt:

> de quibus autem scripsistis, bonum est homini mulierem non tangere. Propter fornicationes autem unusquisque suam uxorem habeat et unaquaeque suum virum habeat. Uxori vir debitum reddat similiter autem et uxor viro. Mulier sui corporis potestatem non habet sed vir; similiter autem et vir sui corporis potestatem non habet sed mulier. (1 Corinthians 7:1–4)

> (Now concerning the things whereof you wrote to me: It is good for a man not to touch a woman. But for fear of fornication, let every man have his own wife, and let every woman have her own husband. Let the husband render the debt to his wife, and the wife also in like manner to the husband. The wife hath not power of her own body, but the husband. And in like manner the husband also hath not power of his own body, but the wife.)

Despite his pivotal role in the foundation of Christianity, Paul is not depicted in the York Corpus Christi Plays, most likely for key dramatic reasons. Epistles are not a particularly engrossing source text for re-enactment, and the more exciting episodes from his life – such as his conversion on the road to Damascus (Acts of the Apostles 9) and his escape from prison (Acts of the Apostles 16) – might prove challenging to stage.[47] Most importantly, Paul might overshadow Jesus, if the former received more stage time following the latter's crucifixion and resurrection, as well as overshadowing Mary's role in the concluding pageants. For these reasons John the Baptist must serve as a stand-in for Paul, and so his typological function is expanded so that he serves as a type not merely of Jesus but also of Paul.

Jewish sexuality is thus staged as promiscuously reproducing more Jews, whereas Christian anti-sexuality is conceived as multiplying holiness. This procreative theme underscores the troubling irony that the York Corpus Christi Plays were staged after the Edict of Expulsion in England, from which the Jews had been exiled since 1290. Moreover, in the staging of the plays in York itself, the site of the horrific Clifford's Tower massacre of 1190, the ostensible threat of Jewish sexuality in fact reflects the failure of medieval English Christians to uphold the anti-eroticism key to their faith.[48] The historical reality of late medieval York saw Christians rather than Jews reproducing, a set of circumstances that disproved the typological promise displayed on the town's pageant wagons.

As apparent in the dramatization of typology in the York Corpus Christi Plays, its inherent liminality undercuts distinctions between type and antitype, between Jewish and Christian, between man and woman, and even between past and present. In so doing, the pageants cannot inoculate Jesus himself from their queer play with theology and dramatic representation. In referring to Jesus as "hym Jesus, þat Jewe" (26.127), Judas stresses Jesus's Jewish identity, and at this critical moment the York cycle appears to deny the logic of typology, to insist on Jesus as simultaneously Jewish and proto-Christian. By unsettling constructions of gender between the Old Testament and the New Testament, and by unsteadily presenting Judaism as central to Jesus's identity and as that which all Christians must repudiate, the York Corpus Christi Plays destabilize the interpretive horizons of typology. This confusion undermines the plays' attempts to portray Jesus's identity as wholly chaste and wholly Christian, as evident in the confused deployment of the romance tradition in the latter pageants.

Jesus's Queer Romance

In transitioning typology from sermons to dramatic performances, the York Corpus Christi Plays pave the way for their depiction of Jesus's queer romance, in their joint use and subversion of this courtly genre. Given their emphasis on typology, the York Corpus Christi Plays encourage viewers to look for narrative transformations, in which type and antitype reveal a deeper Christian truth while, as we have seen, subverting the interpretive clarity promised by this transformation. This confused interplay between type and antitype is also apparent in the pageants' generic debts to romance, in which its tropes are first perverted by the villainous characters until they give way to the decorous dignity of Jesus's courtly prefiguration of salvation. In a manner similar to that between type and antitype, the conflicting visions of romance registered in the pageants can be read as mutually constitutive through their similarities and contrasts. Derek Pearsall masterfully outlines the genre: "Romance ... deals in adventure ... The hero ... chooses to go out from a secure bastion of wealth and privilege (such as the Arthurian court) to seek adventures in which the values of chivalry and service to ladies (not only being in love but 'being a lover,' a social grace as much as a private emotion) will be submitted to test and proved."[49] The New Testament scenes repeatedly signal the playwrights' thematic interest in the rarefied world of courtly romance, such as when Herod describes himself as the hero of a romance: "Dragons þat are dredfull schall derke in þer denne[s] / In wrathe when we writhe, or in wrathenesse ar wapped. / Agaynste jeauntis ongentill haue we joined with ingendis" (31.12–14).[50] Elevated and courtly phrases are used to describe Pilate: 'Hayle, sir Pilate perles, and prince of þis empire, / Haile, þe gaiest on grounde in golde þer 3e glide, / Haile, þe louffeliest lorde of lyme and of lyre' (32.338–40). Surprisingly for a play set in biblical times, the landscape is populated with castles: in "The Supper at Emmaus," which stages Luke 24:13–15, the first of the men identifies their destination as "to Emax, þis castell beside vs" (40.14) and later reiterates this point to Jesus, 'Se 3e þis castell beside her?' (40.142).[51]

As several scholars note, the cycle's courtly scenes and their echoes of romance satirically comment on the English and French courts of the day, thus underscoring the intersection of narrative and performative genres as romance merges with drama. Elza Tiner declares of the thematic relevance of these court scenes: "In the trials, Christ becomes one of the local citizens, convicted and crucified through the English judicial system, by which he redeems them all. Thus the abuses of the law by Christ's accusers become a kind of inverted mirror, instructing members of the audience to respect their own legal system and to use it justly."[52] At the same time that these scenes function as an inverted mirror, as Tiner proposes, they could also serve simply as a mirror, highlighting the injustices of the English court that, like the courts of biblical times before them, committed flagrant acts of injustice. Certainly, the courts of the York Corpus Christi Plays are dramatized to accentuate the wrongs of the past with the aristocratic customs of the present. With brazen anachronism, Caiaphas refers to his courtiers with a contemporary vocabulary of bewshers and sir knyghtis (29.1 and 23), and Pilate addresses his courtiers with a similar lexicon: "Sir knyghtis, þat are in dedis dowty, / Chosen for chiffe of cheualrye" (38.163–4). Satan employs a similarly aristocratic and French vocabulary, referring ironically to Jesus as his belamy (37.213, 338). Reflecting the classism common to romance, Jesus is disparaged with such terms as *karle* (29.32), *knafe* (29.52), and *harlotte* (29.283).

Throughout these courtroom scenes, Caiaphas, Anna, and Herod speak bombastically, in contrast to Jesus's silence, but even theatrical bombast aligns with typological thought, as recorded in a prophecy of Isaiah: "Oblatus est quia ipse voluit et non aperuit os suum, sicut ovis ad occisionem ducetur, et quasi agnus coram tondente obmutescet et non aperiet os suum" (53:7; He was offered because it was his own will, and he opened not his mouth: he shall be led as a sheep to the slaughter, and shall be dumb as a lamb before his shearer, and he shall not open his mouth). As Ruth Nisse suggests, courtly language signifies both tyranny and tyranny's threat to the incipient program of Christian salvation: "In the York plays' projection of courtly discourse, then, the exegetical arguments ... are replaced by an arbitrary method of interpretation entirely subject to political power. Counsel, ungrounded in any textual form, becomes a transparent representation of the tyrant's desire and style."[53] For salvation to be effected, Jesus must suffer the indignities of these scenes, with the earthly court inversely prefiguring the eternal one to be achieved through his resurrection.

As much as these court scenes focus on Jesus's perceived transgressions against Jewish law, they also subtly encode issues of erotic and spiritual immorality. Foremost, the tyrants desire to execute Jesus despite his innocence, but, as William Quinn points out of an unexpected encounter in "Christ before Annas and Caiaphas," Caiaphas is depicted as excessively languorous, such that he borders on the queer: "Caiaphas takes a nap in a curiously luxurious, perhaps sybaritic, perhaps sodomitic digression."[54] The scene hints at a range of taboo desires in these courts. The First Soldier offers Caiaphas wine to drink, extolling its deliciousness and rarity and urging him, "Wherfore we counsaile you this cuppe sauerly for to kisse" (29.80). Caiaphas requests this soldier to cover him with his bedclothes: "Do on dayntely, and dresse me on dees, / And hendely hille on me happing" (29.81–2). Projecting his perversions onto Jesus, Caiaphas accuses him of perversion as well, that "he pervertis oure pepull, þat proues his prechyng" (26.113). The *MED* offers as its primary definitions of *perverten* "to pervert (justice, law, truth, etc.); thwart (a judgment, cure); distort (a natural order, the meaning of Scripture)," and these scenes query the meaning of perversion within a courtly context.[55] As with type and antitype, the Jewish courtly scene will be revealed as the site of queer desire, to be purged through the insistent chastity of the Christian antitype.

As the plays shift their attention from the corrupt version of romance depicted in the trial scenes, Jesus recasts the genre's prevailing tropes,

thus demonstrating the typological potential of transitioning Jewish figures into a Christian romance. In "Mortifacacio Christi," Longeus Latus
refers to Jesus with common courtly descriptors: "O Jesu so jentill and
jente" (36.301), and Nichodemus rues that Jesus "juged was vngente"
(36.353). In recalling her love for Jesus in "The Resurrection," the First
Mary describes him in terms similar to a knight wounded on behalf
of his lady: "How might I, but I loued þat swete, / Þat for my loue
tholed woundes wete, / And sithen be grauen vndir þe grete, / Such
kyndnes kithe?" (38.282–5). Most strikingly, in an extended passage of
"Christ's Appearance to Mary Magdalene," Jesus portrays himself as a
knight, stressing the metaphorical qualities of the "armor" in which he
is costumed:

> Marie, in thyne harte þou write
> Myne armoure riche and goode:
> Myne actone couered all with white,
> Als cors of man behewede,
> With stuffe goode and parfite,
> Of maydenes flessh and bloode;
> Whan thei ganne thirle and smyte,
> Mi heede for hawberke stoode.
>
> Mi plates wer spredde all on brede,
> Þat was my body vppon a tree;
> Myne helme couered all with manhede,
> Þe strengh þerof may no man see;
> Þe croune of thorne þat garte me blede,
> Itt bemenes my dignité.
> Mi diademe sais, withouten drede,
> Þat dede schall I neuere be. (39.94–109)

Wooing Mary with his amorous words, while also calling her to "write
on her heart" his armour, and his suffering that symbolizes his perfection and his sacrifice, Jesus enacts the romance role of courtly lover. As
Rosemary Woolf established in her pioneering study, "The Theme of
Christ the Lover-Knight in Medieval English Literature," such depictions of Jesus reflected a "perfect parallelism between the theological
stress upon Christ's display of love on the Cross and the conception of
chivalric conduct in the Arthurian romances, wherein a knight by brave
endurance and heroic encounters would save the lady whom he loved
from treacherous capture, thereby hoping to gain her favour, or might
joust brilliantly in front of her, hoping by his prowess to win her love."[56]

A common motif of medieval literature, the image of Christ as a lover knight within the York Corpus Christi Plays requires not merely its citation but also its performance, with the delivery of this dialogue thus, at least potentially, escalating the romantic tension between Jesus and Mary Magdalene. Jesus must direct these words to Mary Magdalene, and it would be challenging for any staging to dampen the erotic tension of a "knight" professing his love for his "lady."

Complementing the portrayal of Jesus as a courtly knight, Mary, Jesus's mother, is depicted with the tropes of the courtly lady, such as when the apostles address her with language similar to that of knights pledging their courtly love:

> JOHANNES: Lady, youre wille in wele and woo,
>   Itt schall be wroght, ellis wirke we wrang.
> JACOBUS: Lady, we both are boune,
>   Atte youre biddyng to be. (43.219–22)

As John and James humble themselves before their lady, Mary in complementary contrast stands before Thomas in the role of courtly lady: "I schall þe schewe / A token trewe, / Full fresshe of hewe, / My girdill, loo – take þame þis tokyn" (45.166–9). The bestowal of the lady's garment, and in particular her girdle, is a standard plot point of courtly romances, as famously depicted (or more to the point, parodied) in *Sir Gawain and the Green Knight*. At the very least, this scene in the York Corpus Christi Plays, with its echoes of the interactions of courtly beloveds in romances, contrasts sharply with other depictions of this apocryphal scene, such as the one recorded in Jacobus de Voragine's *Legenda aurea*, which concerns Thomas rather than John and James: "Thomas autem cum abesset et rediens credere recusaret, subito zonam, qua corpus ejus praecinctum iuerat, ab aere recepit illaesam, ut vel sic intelligeret, quod totaliter fuisset assumta" (Thomas, however, was absent, and when he came back refused to believe. Then suddenly the girdle that had encircled her body fell intact into his hands, and he realized that the Blessed Virgin had really been assumed body and soul).[57] Legendary accounts depict the girdle falling, whereas the York Corpus Christi Plays stress that Mary grants it as a token, shifting the story's register to romance despite the anti-eroticism foundational to the new religion.

Towards the close of the York Corpus Christi Plays, Jesus and Mary are united in heaven under the familiar tropes of romance that have ostensibly been cleansed of any hints of eroticism. In "The Death of the Virgin," Gabriel outlines a vision of the heavenly court to Mary, where she will "sitte with hymselue, all solas to see, / And to be crowned for his quene and he hymselue [k]yng / In mirthe þat euere schall be newe" (44.11–13). With similarly romantic language, Jesus envisions eternal life with his mother: "Mi modir schall myldely be me / Sitte nexte þe high trinité, / And neuere in two to be twynnand" (44.180–2), and he crowns her as the queen to his king: "Ressayue þis croune, my dere darlyng, / Þer I am kyng, þou schalte be quene" (46.155–6). It would, of course, be ridiculous to argue that the playwrights of the York Corpus Christi Plays intended viewers to look upon Jesus and Mary's romance as incestuous in nature; on the contrary, it is presented as the ultimate exemplar of perfect bliss and chastity achieved in heavenly union. Yet again, however, for viewers to ponder the typology of the scene – or, shall we say, the latent but denied typology of the scene – they are asked to consider the type and antitype of Adam and Eve in contrast to Jesus and Mary. In a common exegetical interpretation Adam is seen as a type of Jesus, following Paul's words in Romans:

> Sed regnavit mors ab Adam usque ad Mosen etiam in eos qui non pec-caverunt, in similitudinem praevaricationis Adae qui est forma future … Si enim in unius delicto mors regnavit per unum, multo magis abundan-tiam gratiae et donationis et iustitiae accipienties, in vita regnabunt per unum Iesum Christum. (5:14, 17)

> (But death reigned from Adam unto Moses, even over them also who have not sinned after the similitude of the transgression of Adam, who is a fig-ure of him who was to come … For if by one man's offence death reigned through one; much more they who receive abundance of grace, and of the gift, and of justice, shall reign in life through one, Jesus Christ.)

The corresponding alignment between Eve and Mary, not explicitly stated in Pauline doctrine, arose from early Christian theologians who linked the allegorical vision of church and divinity to the Song of Songs. As Justin explains in the second century, "[Christ] became human through the virgin Mary … so that by the same way that sin, occasioned by the serpent, came into being, sin is also destroyed. For Eve, who was an uncorrupted virgin, after she had received the word of the serpent, gave birth to sin and death. The virgin Mary on the contrary was full of faith and joy when the angel Gabriel brought her the joyful news that the Spirit of the Lord would come upon her and the power of the most high overshadow her."[58] Adam is a type of Jesus, and Eve is a type of Mary, but the couples are not therefore frequently seen as conjoined types; in other words, Adam and Eve may be separately aligned with Jesus and Mary, but the former couple does not typically stand as a type of the latter. On the stage the York Corpus Christi Plays pair the opening scenes of Adam and Eve with their closing scenes of Jesus and Mary, linking type and antitype, yet with the queerly anti-erotic image of son and mother washing away the earlier vision of man and wife.

Certainly, as apparent in the pageant "Moses and Pharaoh," Jewish fecundity serves as a central theme of the Old Testament, and in the second pageant of the York Corpus Christi Plays, "The Creation," God concentrates on the earth's fecundity – "Þe erthe sall fostyr and furthe bryng / Buxsumly, as I wyle byde, / Erbys and also othyr thyng, / Well for to wax and worthe to wede" (2.65–8). He then underscores the role of the animal kingdom in propagation: "Þane fysch and foulis sere, / Kyndely I ʒow commande / To meng on ʒoure manere, / Both be se and sande" (2.145–8). He soon instructs Adam and Eve: "Looke that ye ʒem ytt wetterly; / All other creatours shall multeply, / Ylke one in tender hower" (4.21–3). In this gentle scene God encourages Adam and Eve to attend to the multiplication of their fellow creatures, that which takes place in a "tender hour," with this erotic lesson bestowed to characters presumably appearing as naked on stage. Upon realizing their fall from grace, Adam says, "For I am naked as methynke," and Eve agrees, "Allas, Adam, right so am I" (5.111–12). From contemporary evidence it is likely that the actors playing Adam and Eve would wear white leather garments to convey their nudity; this practice is documented in the Cornish miracle play *The Creacion of the World*, which includes a stage direction that *"Adam and Eva aparlet in whytt lether, in a place apoynted by the conveyour, and not to be sene tyll they be called."*[59] Reiterating the anti-erotic sentiments expressed by John the Baptist, Jesus stresses the necessity of chastity in "The Last Supper": "For þat new lawe whoso schall lere, / In harte þam bus be clene and chaste" (27.37–8). And in an apocalyptic foreshadowing of times to come, he advises the three Marys to bless the barren: "That ʒe schall giffe blissyng / To barayne bodies all, / That no barnes forthe may brynge" (34.167–9). Jewish fecundity and Christian chastity expose both the typological fault-lines between the faiths and the inherent implausibility of chastity, for Christian chastity, if fully exercised, would, of course, foreclose the possibility of future Christians. It can be safely assumed that, after witnessing the York Corpus Christi Plays, the Christians of York went home and at some point emulated Jewish fecundity rather than Christian chastity, thus aligning themselves with type rather than antitype and undoing the lesson encoded in these plays. Watching the York Corpus Christi Plays, in fact, ironically teaches its Christian audience to act like Jews.

Just as medieval typology has the potential more to obscure than to clarify the relationship between Judaism and Christianity, so too does the staging of typology in the York Corpus Christi Plays. Typology attempts to establish interpretive boundaries between Judaism and Christianity, yet it instead (simultaneously and inadvertently) emphasizes the porous borders between the two faiths and the ultimately queer relationships that surface when one attempts to distinguish between Jewish fecundity and Christian anti-eroticism. John C. Coldewey, in his reading of typology's disruptive role in medieval drama, argues that "the power of these plays ... resides precisely in their divergence from the straightforward flow of the biblical text that constitutes their superstructure and main narrative framework."[60] In the queer romance of Jesus and Mary, conscripted to serve as antitypes of Adam and Eve, the York cycle loses the imperative force of a sermon to the unwieldy theology inherent in dramatic performance. John Wyclif warned his fellow Christians against "þes pagyn [pageant] playen þei þat hiden þe treuþe of Goddis lawe,"[61] but it would perhaps be more accurate to say not that they hide the truth but that they revel in the queer contradictions of God's law and then stage them for the world to see.

Chapter Four

Excremental Desire, Queer Allegory, and the Disidentified Audience of *Mankind*

Medieval morality plays, in dramatizing the pitfalls along the path to Christian salvation, solicit their audience members to align themselves with the protagonists of their narrative action. Viewers are the Everyman of *Everyman*; they are the Mankind both of *Mankind* and of *The Castle of Perseverance*. As such, they are called to interpellate themselves into the dramatic plot by envisioning the moral choices of the protagonists as directly relevant to their own lives. Nathaniel Woodes, author of the morality play *The Conflict of Conscience*, makes this point explicit through his Prologue character as he speaks of the play's protagonist: "And so by his deservéd fault we may in time beware."[1] As David Bevington explains, medieval morality plays were "characterized primarily by the use of allegory to convey a moral lesson about religious or civil conduct, presented through the medium of abstractions or representative social characters. The most common plot of these moralities, retold in play after play, was that of an allegorical contest for the spiritual welfare of the mankind hero."[2] Given the endings of these plays, with their protagonists first falling yet then overcoming the moral snares on their road to redemption, many critics view them as theologically conservative in their ultimate message.

   Yet the journey to salvation in *Mankind* is depicted as unabashedly filthy and exuberantly queer, one that necessitates the protagonist's explorations of desires both excremental and homoerotic, and thus for viewers to undertake such a queer journey as well. Allegories depend on their surface text inviting related yet discrete interpretations, yet, in unleashing such doubled (and even multiple) meanings, they frequently invite queer readings attuned to the vagaries of erotic expression between their (putatively normative) text and their (subversive) subtext, for these structures and substructures cannot help but create hermeneutic fissures. As Angus Fletcher explains of allegory, "In the simplest terms, allegory says one thing and means another"; he then elaborates: "The whole point of allegory is that it does not *need* to be read exegetically; it often has a literal level that makes good enough sense all by itself. But somehow this literal surface suggests a peculiar doubleness of intention, and ... it becomes much richer and more interesting if given interpretation."[3] This doubled structure sparks the inherent paradox of allegory, in that its secondary semantic level often contains the potential to undermine its literal reading.[4] Within the traditions of allegorical theatre and medieval morality plays this doubling of meaning is inevitably doubled again, owing to the viewers' likely identification with the narrative's protagonist while also experiencing the disjunction between the desires expected of a fictional character and their voyeuristic desires in witnessing his moral progress. In effect, the audience members must continually oscillate within this doubling of allegorical form and its subtext, as well as within the doubling of narrative identification exemplified in the protagonist's moral journey and their personal investment with perverse plotting.

Whereas some may envision medieval allegories as inviting both textual and subtextual readings that stand consonant with Christian teaching, various exemplars of the form testify to its inherent queerness, with the surface level of narration camouflaging an erotically charged and potentially perverse subtext, as evident in such masterworks as Guillaume de Lorris and Jean de Meun's *Roman de la Rose*, William Langland's *Piers Plowman*, and the *Gawain*-Poet's *Pearl*.[5] Glenn Burger explains of literary queerness that ideologies, both those of the Middle Ages and those of today, circumscribe various constructions of desire and the self, in that culture demands "coercive performances of sexuality and identity [such] that resistance is only very provisionally enacted (never absolutely secured) within circulations of power."[6] Within such power structures, queer energies and evasions offer a critical strategy for reassessing the meaning of prevailing cultural scripts, and genre functions as just such a cultural script that regulates erotic expression, yet is simultaneously rendered susceptible to its subversion from within. Several critics have commented on the "degeneracy" evident in *Mankind*'s dramatic action, with this telling word acknowledging the play's homoerotic themes while mostly refusing to engage with the cultural meaning of such degeneracy as an unexpected path to redemption.[7] As Mankind acknowledges, his travails concern the "rebellyn of my flesch" (313), a phrase that cannot escape erotic connotations, and Mercy admonishes Mankind against his rowdy companions – "What how, Mankynde! Fle þat felyschyppe, I yow prey!" (726) – which suggests the corruptive nature of particular forms of male homosociality.[8]

Furthermore, within this dramatic landscape, characters are threatened with their imminent abasement through excrement, such as when Mischief warns his fellows: "Hens, awey fro me, or I xall beschyte yow all" (731). Male homosociality and excrement – *Mankind* revels in the humour they spark, thus creating comedy from spiritual threats and bodily corruption but also creating a conflicted site of desire and denial.

These and other such scenes of excremental humour and homoerotically charged interactions, which are staged throughout *Mankind*, demonstrate the ways in which medieval thinkers envisioned sanctified identities achieved through inverted, paradoxical, and, indeed, perverted paths, as the play compels its audience to contemplate the theological ramifications of debased desires that ironically lead to (narrative) salvation. Binary concepts of inversion and opposition undergird much of Western medieval culture, as Constance Brittain Bouchard demonstrates in her *"Every Valley Shall Be Exalted": The Discourse of Opposites in Twelfth-Century Thought.* "Historians have always recognized that scholastic arguments – organizing material into opposing categories as a first step to answering legal, philosophical, or theological questions – were fundamental in twelfth-century schools and early universities," she asserts, as she then explores the relevance of oppositional and inversionary concepts to scholasticism, narrative, religious conversion, conflict resolution, and gender.[9] Bouchard's title cites the prophet Isaiah (40:4), whose following lines envision mountains and hills made low, the crooked made straight, and the rough places made plain. Many similar biblical passages buttress concepts of inversion as a guiding principle of the Christian faith, in its foundations both in Jewish traditions and in the New Testament. The Christian Old Testament includes such passages as "qui ponit humiles in sublimi et maerentes erigit sospitate" (Job 5:11; Who setteth up the humble on high, and comforteth with health those that mourn), and "quos volebat exaltabat et quos volebat humiliabat" (Daniel 5:19; and whom he would, he set up: and whom he would, he brought down).[10] The Christian gospels likewise teach the spiritual value of inversion: "Qui invenit animam suam perdet illam, et qui perdiderit animam suam propter me inveniet eam" (Matthew 10:39; He that findeth his life, shall lose it: and he that shall lose his life for me, shall find it); and perhaps most famously, "Multi autem erunt primi novissimi et novissimi primi" (Matthew 19:30, cf. Mark 10:31; Many that are first, shall be last: and the last shall be first).

Given the prevalence of biblical sources endorsing inversion, it is hardly surprising that medieval plays feature an array of such reversals, both in their storylines and in their staging. Drama from the Middle Ages often evokes the spirit of the carnivalesque, and Mikhael Bakhtin famously describes its "peculiar logic" as "a continual shifting from top to bottom, from front to rear, of numerous parodies and travesties, humiliations, profanations, comic crownings and uncrownings."[11] Certainly, such carnivalesque humour is key to *Mankind*'s enduring popularity. David Bevington dubs it "the most indisputably popular play of the fifteenth century,"[12] and Mark Eccles affirms that it portrays "the most high-spirited fun of all the early moral plays," noting further that five of its seven characters are comic villains.[13] Surely a key part of *Mankind*'s attraction arises in the comic excess of its theologically inverted world, particularly in its bawdy excrementality and its riotously queer depiction of homosocial desires run amok. Indeed, some argue that *Mankind* is simply too inverted, too carnivalesque, too funny, to remain comfortably within the staid confines of the morality play tradition. Anthony Gash suggests that the play's exuberance, in effect, corrupts its generic identification as a spiritual allegory: "Usually treated as a morality play, [*Mankind*] is more usefully seen as compounding two genres, one official, the other unofficial, by punning between the morality play structure (the fall, repentance, and salvation of mankind) and a festive structure (the battle between the license of Christmas and the prohibitions of Lent)."[14] The generic tension that Gash identifies could be metaphorically aligned with the disjunctions among the play's contrasting images of the human body as simultaneously reflecting divine truth and earthly sinfulness, with these oppositional traditions inspiring both the play's theologically conservative message and its exuberant excess. The human body, often employed allegorically, mirrors the divine perfection of Jesus, who redeems humanity through his self-sacrifice, and the body's own imperfection as registered in humanity's excrement, which registers human corruption and the fall from heavenly grace. As the body itself signifies the impossibility of allegory and metaphor communicating transcendent Christian truths, these interpretive conundrums are multiplied when staged in an uproariously comic yet theologically conservative drama. For, as much as inversion may represent an attempt to distinguish between the high and the low, the mountain and the valley, the saved and the sinful, queer theory has demonstrated the ways in which these energies are more continuous and contiguous than disparate and disjointed, in a rhythm that Jonathan Dollimore describes as the perverse dynamic: "When the inversion of a binary reveals the proximate, it is always more than a mere reversal, more even than the utopian unity of the binary dissolved or displaced. The inversion of a binary produces not merely reversal but proximities where there was difference."[15] The carnivalesque binary that one might expect *Mankind* to uphold, from this perspective, becomes instead the unexpected lines of contiguity that prove the necessity of the profane in its many queer iterations for any meaning to cohere.

A key conundrum that then emerges is whether, within this humorous play and its carnivalesque revels, the audience is conceived as desiring the perfection of Jesus's divine body and his holy blood or the imperfection of the human body and its confrontations, daily and inevitably until the moment of death, with excrement. The audience, confronted with the oppositional force of such inversions, yet simultaneously freed from the imposition of a false critical binary, is free to opt for both; however, even this ultimate unity in *Mankind*'s tenor and vehicle testifies to the inherent queerness of allegory as a dramatic genre for expressing medieval Christian truths. Such a perspective liberates this and other such plays from the yoke of expectations of audience identification and proposes instead their disidentification with the dramatic production. As José Esteban Muñoz argues of such disidentificatory strategies, "Disidentification is a performative mode of tactical recognition that various minoritarian subjects employ in an effort to resist the oppressive and normalizing discourse of dominant ideology. Disidentification resists the interpellating call of ideology that fixes a subject with the state power apparatus. It is a reformatting of self within the social. It is a third term that resists the binary of identification and counteridentification. Counteridentification often, through the very routinized workings of its denouncement of dominant discourse, reinstates that same discourse."[16] In his theories of performativity Muñoz focuses on queers of colour, and so the application of his ideas to the audiences of medieval religious drama may appear grossly anachronistic, particularly for an environment with somewhat limited recognition of ethnic and gendered otherness. Nonetheless, Muñoz recognizes that majoritarian subjects also employ disidentificatory strategies,[17] and his model of a triangulation of identity, in which identification and counter-identification fail, and identity is fabricated in reaction to and through appropriations of mainstream culture, illuminates the cross-construction of performance and audience in such medieval dramas as *Mankind*.

On the whole, the audience can neither desire excrementality and homosexuality nor wholly repudiate the pleasures they represent, as the play fractures the tension between identification and counteridentification for a range of unexpected pleasures. As the following sections outline, the implicit allegory of the human body corrupts even the promise of divine perfection, thus demonstrating the horrific threat and inherent comic possibility of excrement. If allegory cannot hold its meaning even when considering divine perfection, its potential queerness registers even more strongly in the play's allegorical path to redemption from Mercy to the Vices and back to Mercy. The latent queerness of human desire is made manifest in the Vices' comic wrangling as they attempt to seduce Mankind into homosocial sin tinged with homoerotic desire. As Julie Paulson affirms concerning this point, "Rather than offering a distraction from the play's orthodox message, the vices' magnetism is imperative to the play's representation of Mankind's learning process."[18] *Mankind* demands that its viewers simultaneously learn its moral lesson and revel in its outrageous sin, thereby destabilizing the function of allegory and leaving queerly disidentified audience members unmoored from the comforts of aligning themselves with the protagonist.

Jesus's Perfection and *Mankind*'s Excremental Pleasures

As the comic villains Mischief, New Gyse, Nowadays, Nought, and Titivillus conspire to lure the play's eponymous protagonist into sin, *Mankind* hustles and bustles with activity, and their comic antics and scatological humour heighten its appeal. The play's dramatic and emotional climax occurs when Mercy chases off the Vices with a whip as they attempt to seduce Mankind into suicide, yet its scatological scenes imbue it with an overarching comic exuberance that counterbalances its theological message. Theology and scatology conflict with each other in ways too numerous to count, and within medieval symbolism the (male) body represents both divine perfection and humanity's fallen condition; thus humanity reflects and sullies the image of the divine because the body cannot help but act as a constant reminder of original sin. In light of this oppositional symbolism the human body itself serves as a self-negating and queering allegory, for it cannot signify a specific denotation due to its confused array of connotations, as a brief overview of its treatment by medieval philosophers and theologians reveals.

Throughout the Middle Ages many scholars posited a vertical hierarchy to the human body: the head, the *prima regio*, rules as the site of rationality, and the genital area signifies shame and humanity's fall from grace.[19] Also, owing to the discomfiting appearance of untimely erections, within much medieval thought the penis suggests the ungovernability of the male body.[20] Despite such hesitations about the corruptible human body, it is nonetheless key to the soul's moral development. Thomas Aquinas visualized the soul as immaterial and eternal, yet he also argued that it required a body for perception: "the senses operate through bodily organs, [and thus] the very condition of the soul's nature makes it appropriate for it to be united with the body."[21]

Consider also Aquinas's statement on the soul after death: "The [soul's] power of understanding and the agent and possible intellects will remain in the separated soul. For the existence of these powers is not caused in the soul by the body, although, while they exist in the soul united to the body, they do have an ordination to the body which they will not have in the separated soul."[22] The body proves its unique moral worth by housing the soul, but, in compelling the soul to reside inside a decaying form susceptible to a litany of embarrassments, the body cannot help but stand as a disputed site between the spiritual aspirations of humanity and its degraded earthly condition. *Mankind* recognizes the joint necessity of and the antagonism between the body and the soul when the protagonist introduces himself: "My name ys Mankynde. I haue my composycyon / Of a body and of a soull, of condycyon contrarye" (194–5). In a similar moment Mercy alerts Mankind to the dangers of the human body. "For þer ys euer a batell betwyx þe soull and þe body" (227), he admonishes, and later he states bluntly, "ȝour body ys ȝour enmy" (897).

Extending this moral map of the body both in medieval thought and in *Mankind*, its openings – eyes, ears, nose, mouth, anus – attest to its vulnerability to sin. The medieval homily "Estote Fortes in Bello" (Be strong in war) details the devil's stratagems for deception as he infiltrates through all bodily orifices:

Eft sone [nedre] smuȝeð derneliche swa deð þe douel ine þe monnes eȝen, if ho boð opene to bihalden idel and unnet. Ine þe eren if ho boð opene to lusten hoker and spel and leow and oðer þing þet boð to-ȝeines godes heste. Ine þe nose hwenne þe nose bið open to smelle unlofne breð. Ine þe muðe hwenne þe muð is open for to liȝen. Oðer suneȝeð on muchele ete and on ouer drinke. Et þe schape þe douel smuȝeð in derneliche hwenne hit bið ȝaru to galiche deden.

(Again, the serpent creepeth secretly; so doth the devil into the eyes of men, if they are open to behold idleness and vanity; into the ears, if they are open to listen to slander, idle stories and lies, and other things that are against God's behests; into the nose, when the nose is open to smell illicit breath (smells); in the mouth, when it is open to lie, or sinneth in excessive eating and in over-drinking; into the privy parts the devil creepeth secretly, when they are ready to (commit) lascivious deeds.)[23]

Whereas the eyes, ears, nose, and mouth are envisioned in other contexts as positive liminal spaces, such as in manuscript images depicting the soul escaping the body through the mouth at the moment of death,[24]

the anus, in contrast, was viewed primarily as a site of demonic infiltration. In her illuminating study *Sin and Filth in Medieval Culture: The Devil
in the Latrine*, Martha Bayless catalogues numerous classical and medieval accounts of demons infesting human anuses and bowels, such as
in the fourth-century *Divinae Institutiones* of Lactantius:

> Qui quoniam spiritus sunt tenues et inconprehensibiles, insinuant se cor-
> poribus hominum et occulte in uisceribus operati ualetudinem uitiant,
> morbos citant, somniis animos terrent, mentes furoribus quatiunt.

> (And since spirits are slight and not to be grasped, they insinuate them-
> selves into the bodies of men and, secretly working in their viscera, impair
> their well-being, hasten diseases, terrify their souls with dreams, harass
> their minds with turmoil.)[25]

The anus thus signifies the perils of breaches between the body's inte-
rior and exterior, and in light of the body's corruptibility, Titivillus takes
advantage of humanity's excremental needs. Seeking to distract Mankind from his divine service, Titivillus euphemistically declares "nature
compellys" (560), and Mankind states modestly, "I wyll go do þat nedys
must be don" (563). With these discreet yet telling references to the
excreting body, *Mankind* highlights how evil enters the body at the very
moment when excrement leaves it. In line with this vein of thought, the
eponymous protagonist laments the necessity that his soul must reside
in his flesh: "O thou my soull, so sotyll in thy substance, / Alasse, what
was þi fortune and þi chaunce / To be assocyat wyth my flesch, þat
stynkyng dungehyll" (202–4). Little more than a pile of excrement, the
human body is conceived as inherently inferior to the soul, such that
the inhabitation of the latter in the former stands as a defining paradox
of the human condition, which Mankind, including both the character
and the audience members called to identify with him, must overcome
on their journeys to salvation.

As much as *Mankind* laments humanity's fleshly nature, it simultaneously celebrates the perfection of Jesus's body, which cannot be defiled
even when it is debased and which showcases a perfect permeability that
contrasts with the imperfect permeability of its human counterpart. In
Mercy's description of Jesus's crucified body, the blood that flows from
his pierced side signifies redemption: "I mene Owr Sauyowr, þat was
lykynnyde to a lambe; / Ande hys sayntys be þe members þat dayly he
doth satysfye / Wyth þe precyose reuer þat runnyth from hys wombe"
(34–6). When Mercy despairs of Mankind's riotous ways, he returns to
this theme and avers, "Euery droppe of hys bloode was schede to purge

þin iniquite" (745). Jesus's wounds supersede any anxiety over the permeability of the human body, for they portend not death but eternal life. These beliefs are expressed in many theologically sanctioned pronouncements, such as those recorded by the Council of Vienne (1311–12):

> Et quod in hac assumpta natura ipsum Dei Verbum pro omnium operanda salute non solum affigi cruci et in ea mori voluit, sed etiam, emisso iam spiritu, perforari lancea sustinuit latus suum, ut exinde profluentibus undis aquae et sanguinis formaretur unica et immaculata ac virgo sancta mater ecclesia, coniunx Christi, sicut de latere primi hominis soporati Eva sibi in coniugium est formata.[26]

> (And that in this assumed nature the Word of God willed for the salvation of all not only to be nailed to the cross and to die on it, but also, having already breathed forth his spirit, permitted his side to be pierced by a lance, so that from the outflowing water and blood there might be formed the one, immaculate, and holy virginal mother Church, the bride of Christ, as from the side of the first man in his sleep Eve was fashioned as his wife.)

With this striking image of a maternal saviour, Jesus is depicted, in this moment of metaphorical childbirth, as delivering the church, which is itself envisioned in its hybrid identities of mother and bride. Such gendered imagery also aligns the bodies of Jesus and the church with those of Adam and Eve, who were themselves inspired by the divine form. On the whole, this passage depicts Jesus's body as the wellspring of the Christian Church, yet this paradoxical body, both divine and human, frequently elicits concomitant quandaries about the contrast between his divine perfection and humanity's imperfection (as prefigured in Adam and Eve's subsequent fall) – a quandary with latent comic potential, as *Mankind* so expertly exploits.

The inherent paradox of Jesus as fully human and as fully divine inevitably perplexed medieval thinkers, for the imperfection of the human body raises concerns that it might sully Christ's perfection, no matter the impossibility of the divine becoming corrupted. Certainly, any suggestions of divine dirt provoked theological anxiety in the Middle Ages. In his *Tractatus de incarnatione contra Judaeos*, Guibert of Nogent includes a mocking response to the questions, ostensibly posed by Jews, that focus jointly on the degradations of the human body and on Jesus's divinity and humanity:

> Interroga, putidissime et nequam, de Domino nostro, si spuerit, si nares emunxerit, si pituitas oculorum vel aurium digitis hauserit, et intellige

quia qua honestate superiora haec fecerit, et residua, peregerit. Aut dic mihi, ille tuus, qui Abrahae apparuit Deus, ea quae comedit in quem alium deposuit? Quomodo etiam, aut si factum est, quod consequens fuit? Contremisco dum de his disputo; sed vos, filii diaboli, me cogitis.

(Ask yourself, worst and most shameful of men, about our Lord – did he spit, did he blow his nose, did he pick at the phlegm from his eyes and ears with his fingers? And then understand with what dignity he did these things and carried through the rest of his life. Or tell me this: that man, your God who appeared to Abraham, the food that he ate – what stomach did it go into? How also, if he digested it – what happened to it then? I tremble when I argue about these things but you, you sons of the devil, you compel me!)[27]

The possibility that Jesus would experience the excremental aspects of his humanity sparked passionate debate, and as Jay Rubenstein concludes, "such were the questions the Jews raised and the defense Guibert used – that God appeared in human form in Genesis 18 and presumably was subject to the same embarrassments."[28] For Guibert, Jesus's full humanity required that he experience the ostensible degradations of excretion – a necessity that again corrupts the image of unsullied divinity.

To imagine an excreting deity requires a concomitant reimagining of the symbolism of filth and excrement, and so Christian tradition, even if apocryphal, traces Jesus's purifying effects on and through dirt. The First Gospel of the Infancy of Jesus Christ recounts the tale of a woman giving the young Jesus a bath – not that it is stated that he *needs* a bath – and discovering the curative properties of his bath-water: "On the morrow the same woman brought perfumed water to wash the Lord Jesus; and when she had washed him, she preserved the water. And there was a girl there, whose body was white with a leprosy, who being sprinkled with this water, and washed, was instantly cleansed from her leprosy."[29] This scene inverts the traditional corruptive symbolism of uncleanness and instead posits cleansing effects through dirt, as Jesus's bath-water scrubs away the signs of disease on the young girl's body. In an image that functions similarly, Mercy describes Jesus's "gloryus passyon, þat blyssyde lauatorye" (12), imagining the divine body as both bloodied in its suffering and cleansing in its spiritual function. The latent colour symbolism of this image – the red blood of Jesus's passion, and the cleansed and presumably white body of the Christian subject redeemed through it – showcases *Mankind*'s thematic interest in probing the contrasts between purity and corruption, and thus the potential of the queer dissolution of the binary that they represent.

Extending such points further, the duality of Christ's blood and body as both fully divine and fully human inevitably invites paradoxes and unintended readings in medieval literature. In one such example the poem "The Five Wounds of Christ" (from Bodleian Library MS Douce 1) envisions Jesus's body as not merely spiritually but physically nutritive: "The vertu of that precyous blode / In hongir and thurste of mortall synne / Be euer more my helfth full fode / Therby thy blisse for to wynne."[30] What becomes of Jesus's perfect blood when it becomes the poet's "helfth full fode"? Within this spiritual metaphor it is a path to everlasting salvation; yet, within its unacknowledged register as food digested by the human body, it cannot help but become contaminated by the biological processes that render nourishment into excrement. Such a belief was dubbed the Stercorian heresy, as David Grumett details: "This scatological thesis, which was promoted by critics of materialist conceptions of the Eucharist, was that if Christ's body was taken into the human body then it was also expelled from the human body."[31] Defenders of this heretical belief cited Jesus's words to the Pharisees: "non intellegitis qui omne quod in os intrat in ventrem vadit et in secessum emittitur" (Matthew 15:17; Do you not understand, that whatsoever entereth into the mouth, goeth into the belly, and is cast out into the privy?). In medieval England, Lollards were accused of the Stercorian heresy.[32] Christian theories of transubstantiation negated this possibility, of course, as Miri Rubin documents: "The question of digestion was related to the function of eating through which the eucharist was consumed; the degradations of eating, breaking, digestion, and excretion could not be allowed to work on the holy substance, not even in appearance, and this question was often raised in criticism of the eucharist."[33] Yet, as is commonly recognized in literary and linguistic theory, to deny a possibility is concomitantly to envision that very possibility, which thus raises a spectre of presence in a field in which absence is demanded. That is to say, in a play that highlights the act of excreting as it relates to issues of Christian identity, it seems likely that the audience would recognize the confused theological ramifications of the defecating Christian body.

As much as doctrines of transubstantiation insist upon the Eucharist's perfection and resistance to defilement, carnivalesque and dramatic portrayals of such spiritual concepts blasphemously literalize the Eucharist in parodic form. When taunting Mercy, Nowadays employs an inverted image of the Eucharist:

I prey yow hertyly, worschyppull clerke,
To haue þis Englysch mad in Laten:

"I haue etun a dyschfull of curdys,
Ande I haue schetun yowr mowth full of turdys."
Now opyn yowr sachell wyth Laten wordys
    Ande sey me þis in clerycall manere! (129–34)

On a weekly basis a medieval Christian mouth should receive the Eucharist and the spiritual benefits it bestows, yet in this corrupted image the consuming mouth simply fills another mouth, imagined in direct contact with Nowadays's anus. Curds are, of course, formed when milk sours, and so they metaphorically pervert the image of Christians seeking spiritual milk, as expressed in 1 Peter 2:1–2: "deponentes igitur omnem malitiam et omnem dolum et simulationes et invidias et omnes detractiones. sicut modo geniti infantes rationale sine dolo lac concupiscite ut in eo crescatis in salutem" (Wherefore laying away all malice, and all guile, and dissimulations, and envies, and all detractions, as newborn babes, desire the rational milk without guile, that thereby you may grow unto salvation). Moreover, Nowadays's words reframe Latin, the language of the church and prayer, into the tongue of excremental discourse. As Kathleen Ashley perceptively observes, "*Mankind* stages the clash of clerical discourse with anti-authoritarian speech – the preacher's high eloquence vs. popular verbal improvisation – as a performance of ideological multiplicity and conflict."[34] In pondering both what comes out of priests' mouths (words of salvation) and what priests place into their parishioners' mouths (the Eucharist), *Mankind* relies on the savage humour of the Eucharist consumed, digested, and excreted – an impossibility within Christian traditions of transubstantiation but a riotous reality in the play's demented discourse that the audience can neither accept nor reject but must hold in indissoluble and disidentified tension.

In this manner, excrement paradoxically leavens the spiritual message of *Mankind*, facilitating the spiritual growth of the audience – much like excrement itself serves a fertilizing process in agriculture. In developing this theme, the playwright alludes to the generative qualities of feces, as Nought declares: "Here xall be goode corn, he may not mysse yt; / Yf he wyll haue reyn he may ouerpysse yt; / Ande yf he wyll haue compasse [compost] he may ouerblysse yt / A lytyll wyth hys ars lyke" (372–5). In a play that thematically ponders the distinction between the corn and the chaff in numerous instances, Nought dismantles any rigid binary between them in their production, in a similar manner to the play's dissolution of the audience's ability to identify or to counter-identify with Mankind as protagonist. Excrement facilitates the growth of crops that feed the body that houses the soul, proving the intrinsic interconnection of the degraded bodily and the elevated spiritual orders. The humorously grotesque image of the act of defecation as an "overblessing" ironically reveals the fecundity inherent in excrement, for surely its use as fertilizer, within purely practical terms, is one of the greatest benefactions of humanity ever developed.

Given these oscillating conditions, virtually any food metaphor in *Mankind* opens itself to its immediate debasement, for the play continually reminds its audience of foods' excremental fate. When Mankind affirms to Mercy, "O, yowr louely wordys to my soull are swetere þen hony" (225), he employs a bodily metaphor of honey's taste to discuss the soul but one that, as the play develops its themes, cannot help but connote the path of food down and out one's digestive tract. Words are intrinsically connected to excrement throughout the play, such as when Titivillus asserts his momentary triumph – "I haue sent hym forth to schyte lesynges" (568) – comically and grotesquely uniting Mankind's words with his excrement. The apropos image of "shitting lies" bespeaks the confused condition of the sinful human body, in which the inverted world order is registered not merely in the acts of a person but also in the very structure of his body, in which excrement can emerge from the mouth and the anus. Commenting on the play's metatheatricality, Charlotte Steenbrugge observes the ways in which Titivillus "makes the audience conspirators against Mankind," thus encouraging them to enact the sins modelled by the Vice characters and indulge in the humour of excrementality that they must eventually reject.[35] Although in such moments the audience members are called to align themselves with the Vice figures, this performative tactic can never hold very long, and so disidentification – that is, the collapse of identification or counter-identification – appears a particularly apt stance for viewers to assume.

Building from these key significations, excrement thus symbolizes two conflicting desires in *Mankind*: to escape the sinfulness of the human body by rebuffing its inherent excrementality, and to indulge in and embrace the humorous pleasures afforded by such excrement. These dual significations of excrement and of excremental desire are apparent in the play as it stages riotously vulgar scenes for the ultimate enlightenment of the disidentified audience, which can neither endorse nor reject the theological issues set among the topsy-turvy truths of the dramatic stage. Through the carnivalesque force of drama and of humour, excrement presents a queer path to allegorical redemption, one that ponders the meaning of Jesus's humanity as an impossible model for the human sinner to follow. It is a richly comic *via negativa*, one that finds in excrement a means to "fertilize" the soul, but one that can never be fully embraced owing to its connection to filth and sin. As with other medieval musings on Jesus's earthly body, particularly those pondering the nature of his penis,[36] the perplexing issue of Jesus's simultaneously human and divine body illuminates an understanding of the dual functionality of the debased human body in medieval drama. As allegories call their audiences to interpellate themselves into their unfolding action, the disidentified audiences of *Mankind* must consider their relationship to excrement and to the desires – likely unanticipated – that it evokes, in the daring humour of an *imitatio Christi* that revels in the comedy of excrement for an ultimately moral lesson in divine perfection.

Mankind's Queer Allegory

As excrement plays an ultimately redemptive role in Mankind's moral journey, so too does the queerness and homoeroticism of the play's allegory. Allegory, as discussed previously, consists of a surface and a subtextual level of meaning, with additional layers of meaning as well, and queerness potentially emerging in their disunity. In teasing out the queerness of an allegory, the reader must look beneath the surface signification to acknowledge the ways in which taboo desires cannot be named but are only hazily adumbrated. Noah Guynn proposes that "allegory does not only depict the dominant order as an immutable, essential structure of being; it also plays on the instability and unpredictability of its own meaning in order to authorize more aggressive and more violent forms of social and political control,"[37] and such a realization is essential for mapping the multiple levels of allegorical meaning unleashed in *Mankind*. Within the theatrical realm, allegory's doubled structure is, at least potentially, doubled again owing to the likelihood that the surface and the subtext will function differently for the characters of an allegorical play and for its audiences. Within this doubled allegorical structure, medieval morality plays face the unbridgeable fissure between their protagonist, who ostensibly would prefer not to fall into temptation if narratively offered this opportunity, and the audience members, who enjoy seeing the protagonist suffer through the comic shenanigans of the Vice characters. Similarly to the *via negativa* of *Mankind*'s exuberantly excremental humour, the queerness of the play's allegory, in its insistent framing of unbridled homosocial desire, points to an unexpected yet apt journey to salvation.

For example, in a key irony between the salvific themes of *Mankind* and its carnivalesque pleasure, Mercy dismisses Mischief: "Why com ȝe hethyr, broþer? ȝe were not dysyryde" (53). Although Mischief's presence is hardily desirable in a spiritual sense, the disidentified audience members must desire his antics if the play is to succeed in its aspirations to entertain them. In this light, to assume a correlation between the protagonist and the audience, as so much allegorical criticism does, necessitates overlooking the disjunction between the desires of fictional characters and those of the audiences viewing their trials on stage. As Steven May rightly notes, "Mankind is (as his name suggests) an ideal representative of Fallen Man in general, not a real representative of a particular social class."[38] Within a medieval Christian perspective, every person in the audience would be figured as fallen, and thus the protagonist of a morality play represents a blank slate, a *tabula rasa*, through which viewers should evaluate their own moral perspectives. At the same time, the desires expected of a fictional character and of audience members frequently diverge because they experience the narrative under deviating conceptions of its fictional framing: no matter the fictionality of a narrative, its characters typically experience its events as real – Mankind believes his salvation is on the line – whereas no matter the realism of a narrative, its audience cannot help but experience its fictionality (the viewers recognize that Mankind is an actor assuming a fictional role, albeit one applicable to their own lives).

Soon after the play begins, the audience of *Mankind* is interpellated into its dramatic action in several scenes, with Mercy's metadramatic appeals bookending its structure. In his opening lines Mercy adjures viewers not to partake in earthly pleasures – "O ʒe souerens þat sytt and ʒe brothern þat stonde ryght wppe, / Pryke not yowr felycytes in thyngys transytorye" (29–30) – despite the fact that the entertainment unfolding before their eyes can well be construed as one of the "thyngys transytorye" that they should avoid. As Sandra Billington argues in her study of Mercy's debts to the dramatic tradition of the fool, his words often subvert his ostensible meaning: "It also appears that the further he expounds his well-known homilies, the more he undermines his message by expanding his rhetoric."[39] The audience is both enlightened and lured astray by Mercy's moralizing, and the play's allegory continually shifts in its registers, destabilizing connections between the literal and figurative meanings of his words. In a contrapuntal yet complementary moment when Mischief divulges to the audience his ludic yet serious ambition to torment Mercy – "I say, ser, I am cumme hedyr to make yow game" (69) – his words apply equally well to the audience, in that its members could metadramatically submit to his call for play and pleasure over more solemn spiritual matters. With machinations similar to those of Mischief, Titivillus alerts the audience to his plans to lead Mankind astray. Upon returning to the stage, he states, "I am here ageyn to make þis felow yrke" (556), and he cajoles the audience to support his efforts: "Not a worde, I charge yow, peyn of forty pens. / A praty game xall be scheude yow or ʒe go hens" (590–1). With the threat of financial penalty and the enticement of a "praty game," Titivillus encourages the audience to delight in Mankind's suffering, despite the play's simultaneous call for viewers to see his struggle as their own. At the play's conclusion Mercy congratulates himself on a job well done – "Wyrschepyll sofereyns, I hawe do my propirte: / Mankynd ys deliueryd by my fauerall patrocynye" (903–4) – yet he refuses to acknowledge the irony of a spiritual message encoded in a recreational diversion.

Allegory, in this manner, both solicits and corrupts efforts to align the protagonist with the audience. One could term this a *queering* of allegorical structure, in the inherent disjunction of tenor and vehicle that undermines the coherency of its message, especially because this troubling of structure coincides with contemporary denouncements of theatre that discerned the likelihood of such mixed messages. *A Tretise of Miraclis Pleyinge* rejected the possibility that one could distill a spiritual message from an earthly entertainment: "And sithen miraclis pleyinge is of the lustis of the fleyssh and mirthe of the body, no man may efectuely heeren hem and the voice of Crist at onys, as the voice of Crist and the voice of the fleysh ben of two contrarious lordis."[40] This passage also theorizes the carnal, fleshly pleasures of dramatic play, a possibility to which *Mankind* teasingly alludes in numerous passages adumbrating the homoerotic potential of sinful seduction – thus merging the queer structural prospects of allegory and its disidentified audience with latent themes of queer eroticism. Indeed, as Garrett P.J. Epp argues, "the *Tretise* treats theatrical performance and spectatorship as themselves inherently sexual activities, most dangerously so when they are centered on a representation of the actions and body of Christ."[41] For some contemporary critics, Jesus himself could not purge the medieval stage of its carnal threats, and Epp details the ways in which the actor playing Jesus would serve as a potential site of queer desire.

In line with this tension, *Mankind* establishes that, in his spiritual battle against sin and corruption, its protagonist must guard himself against the allure of sexuality, perversity, and wantonness – despite the fact that, as *A Tretise of Miraclis Pleyinge* frets, these sinful pastimes are key to medieval theatre's attraction. Furthermore, in a play without female characters, erotic sin must virtually by necessity be envisioned as including homosocial brotherhood fraught with the potential of homoerotic seduction. Mercy accuses Nought, New Gyse, and Nowadays of *wantonness* – "Þei be wanton now, but þen xall thei be sade" (181). This word is defined by the *Middle English Dictionary* as "pertaining to sexual indulgence, lewd, lascivious; of a person: given to lechery, lustful; promiscuous, of easy virtue."[42] As in its modern usage, *wanton* in the Middle Ages often pairs idiomatically with *woman* or *women* more so than with *man* or *men*, in such passages as "Wemen are wount in Wantonhede yet / With a likyng full light in loue for to falle" (from the *Gest Hystoriale of the Destruction of Troy*) and "Remembre the that the liff of courte is of the nature of folis and wanton women which ... love them more fervently that diffame them and pill them thanne suche as best louith and seruith them" (from Alan Chartier's *Treatise of Hope*).[43] At the very least, wantonness is viewed as unmasculine within medieval contexts that posit a correlation between masculinity and godliness. Given these connotations, Mercy's words potentially effeminize Nought, New Gyse, and Nowadays, whose gender identities veer between the poles of masculinity and femininity as they continually indulge in sinful behaviours. Further along these lines, the human condition is marred by carnality and perverse desire, as Mankind declares: "Euery man for hys degre I trust xall be partycypatt, / Yf we wyll mortyfye owr carnall condycyon / Ande owr voluntarye dysyres, þat euer be pervercyonatt, / To renunce þem and yelde ws wnder Godys provycyon" (190–3). Mankind acknowledges humanity's propensity for perversion as arising from one's "voluntarye dysyres," and Mercy extends Mankind's understanding of this threat as also arising from New Gyse, Nowadays, and Nought's homosocial fraternity: "To perverte yowr condycyons all þe menys xall be sowte" (296). In a passage echoing Mercy's admonition, Mankind mentions that "all þe menys xuld be sought / To perverte my condycyons and brynge me to nought" (385–6). "All the menys" would, of course, include quite literally "all the means" of such perversion, with sodomy among them.

Certainly, New Gyse, Nowadays, and Nought threaten Mankind with unbridled homosociality linked to perversity. As New Gyse approaches Mankind, he acknowledges the cold weather and the need to build a fire, alluding as well to the passages in Psalms 17:26–7 that focus on perversion and fraternal homosociality – "cum sancto sanctus eris et cum peruerso peruerteris" (324; With the holy, thou wilt be holy ... and with the perverse thou wilt be perverted). With these words, he tacitly adumbrates the possibility of homoerotic perversion.[44] Extending his immoral lesson from moral sources, New Gyse quotes Psalms 132:1: "'Ecce quam bonum et quam jocundum,' quod þe Deull to þe frerys, / 'Habitare fratres in vnum'" (325–6; Behold how good and how pleasant it is ... for brethren to dwell together in unity). This jab at friars entangles them in a web of perverse homosociality. One need only recall the friars housed in Satan's anus of Chaucer's *Summoner's Prologue*, and the accompanying tale's unctuous friar – excavating the buttocks of the ailing Thomas in the hope of finding hidden treasures – for evidence of insults of queer behaviour against the fraternal orders.[45] Nought, New Gyse, and Nowadays, in effect, serve as an inverted image of the fraternal orders, as they attempt to seduce Mankind into sin rather than to lead him to salvation, and the allegations of queerness connected to fraternal orders accelerate the play's riotous humour.

Compounding the queer tensions of these scenes, Mercy frets that Mankind will succumb to just such a sensual and perverse temptation: "To sensuall lyvynge ys reprouable, þat ys nowadays, / As be þe comprehence of þis mater yt may be specyfyede. / New Gyse, Nowadays, Nought wyth þer allectuose ways / They haue pervertyde Mankynde, my swet sun, I haue well espyede" (760–3). Mercy's lexicon of sin includes phrases of sexual transgression – the hedonism of their *sensuall lyvnge*, the seductiveness of their *allectuose ways*, and the spiritual corruption evident in his fear that they have *pervertyde* Mankind. Collectively, these anxieties point to the possibility of erotic sin leading the play's protagonist astray. Of course, not every instance of the word *perverse* and its variants denotes a homoerotic meaning, and often it simply implies sinful or unwarranted behaviour, such as when Mercy states in a soliloquy about Mankind: "Thy peruersyose ingratytude I can not rehers" (751). Nonetheless, in so many of these instances, the danger posed by New Gyse, Nowadays, and Nought is phrased with a lexicon of sin, seduction, and perversity – key indicators that these homosocial encounters flirt with homoerotic desires.

One of Nought, New Gyse, and Nowadays's chief strategies in perverting Mankind is to effeminize him, thus depriving him of the necessary masculinity, both earthly and spiritual, to resist their ministrations. Mankind worries of the potential feminization of his body: "Thys ys to me a lamentable story / To se my flesch of my soull to haue gouernance. / Wher þe goodewyff ys master, þe goodeman may be sory" (198–200). In thematically paired passages, first Mankind describes his battle with his spiritual foes as one expressly related to his masculinity – "agayn my enmys manly for to fyght" (404) – and then Mischief acknowledges the challenge of leading Mankind astray in similarly gendered terms: "He hath taught Mankynde, wyll I haue be vane, / To fyght manly ageyn hys fon" (419–20). In this battle for Mankind's soul the characters enact various grades of masculinity, with manliness envisioned as a primary weapon against perversion, despite the irony of the play's revelling in the pleasures of sinful masculinity. More so, Mankind's concern for his spiritual masculinity contrasts sharply (and comically) with his physical attacks on his enemies, particularly on New Gyse's genitals. When New Gyse, Nowadays, and Nought re-enter the stage after Mankind has struck them with his spade, New Gyse cries of the pain in his testicles, "Alasse, master, alasse, my privyte!," to which Mischief replies first compassionately, "A, wher? alake! fayer babe, ba me!" (429–30). His offer of a consolatory kiss ("ba me") is apparently made in jest, and he then demands, "Abyde! to son I xall yt se" (431). As Epp explains of this scene, "Here 'yt' can only mean one thing, which New Guise, apparently fumbling with his codpiece is about to reveal. Mischief stops him from doing so, but in the process suggests both an onstage action with homosexual overtones, and an offstage history – a past and a future – of similar actions."[46] New Gyse worries that he will be castrated, "3e xall not choppe my jewellys, and I may" (441), and Nowadays echoes this fear, fretting, "3e, Cristys crose, wyll 3e smyght my hede awey?" (442). The double entendre of *head* – in its literal meaning as the head of the human body and in its slang meaning as the top of the penis – dates back to the Middle Ages, with the *Oxford English Dictionary* documenting such usage to 1400.[47] While Nowadays may be referring to the head of his body rather than to the head of his penis, the context of his words, following so soon after New Gyse frets over his testicles, suggests that the latter interpretation is more likely than the former; it is further possible that the actor playing the role would underscore the double entendre of *head* through vulgar gestures. Richard Axton stresses the improvisational nature of *Mankind* in the tension between its status as "a preached text and a series of histrionic 'improvisations' based upon it,"[48] and, as with any dramatic presentation, a queer subtext could be emphasized during performance even if it were merely hinted at in the script. Throughout such scenes internal spiritual masculinity contrasts with external physical masculinity, demonstrating the superiority of the former over the latter while also showcasing the latter's greater comic potential.

When Mercy admonishes, "Be Jhesu Cryst þat me dere bowte / 3e betray many men," New Gyse cheekily responds: "Betray! nay, nay, ser, nay, nay! / We make them both fresch and gay" (116–19). The idiom *fresch and gay* frequently alludes to youthful and licentious sexuality, such as when Chaucer's Wife of Bath praises her fifth husband, Jankyn, because "in oure bed he was so fressh and gay" (508).[49] In complementary contrast, the portrait of Poope-Holy, or Hypocrisy, in Chaucer's *Romaunt of the Rose* accentuates how she hides licentiousness under a façade of spirituality: "Ne she was gay, ne fresh, ne jolyf, / But semede to be ful ententyf / To gode werkis and to faire, / And therto she had on an haire" (435–8). Donning a hair shirt to hide her wantonness, Hypocrisy delights in the gaiety and freshness she publicly shuns.

Of course, not all instances of the idiomatic pairing of *fresh* and *gay* imply sexuality. For example, in Chaucer's *Monk's Tale*, Dianira mistakenly sends Hercules the "sherte, fressh and gay" that murders him (2122), and Adulation says of Respublica in *Respublica*, "She is freshe and gaye *and* flourissheth" (5.5.1469),[50] so it would make little sense to argue for this phrase's universal denotation of sexuality. As always, the context of a word's usage determines not only its connotation but also its denotation, and the preponderance of evidence offered by this play, teeming as it is with imagery of excrement and illicit sexuality, invites such a queer interpretation. In a play populated only with male characters, with whom else could Mankind be "fresch and gay"? While it would be folly to argue that the word *gay* denotes homosexuality in its Middle English usage, it would be equally foolish to overlook the ways in which this word denotes unlicensed sexual play and to consider that the homosocial nature of this theatrical production, with no female roles, could only include homoerotic activities.

Similar to the erotic ambiguity surrounding *gay*, when Nowadays declares, "I myght well be callyde a foppe" (444), the play further develops its allegory of queer seduction. The *MED* defines *fop* simply as a "stupid person, fool,"[51] and the *OED* agrees that in the Middle Ages the word denotes a "foolish person, fool." Its later sense, of "one who is foolishly attentive to and vain of his appearance, dress, or manners; a dandy, an exquisite," was first registered in Thomas Otway's play *The Souldiers Fortune* (1681).[52] To assign a queer connotation to *fop* might therefore appear anachronistic by centuries, yet, at the very least, it is striking that, in line with their foppish ways, many of the attempts by New Gyse, Nowadays, and Nought to seduce Mankind revolve around homosocial issues of fashion; indeed, Epp details the ways in which "in *Mankind* the very source of corruption is effeminate fashion."[53] Mercy warns Mankind of the Vices' fashions, both in clothing and in speech – "Nyse in þer aray, in language þei be large" (295) – and, as these sinners attempt to lure Mercy into their revelries, Nought requests of Mercy, "Anon of wyth yowr clothes, yf ᵹe wyll play" (88). On the play's literal level, Nought is requesting that Mercy remove his priestly vestments so that he will be able to move more freely, thus to embrace hedonism more readily, and thus to abandon his spirituality more quickly. Claire Sponsler argues of this scene that "these unconstrained bodily movements are set up in contrast to bodies that move restrictedly and are decently clothed, bodies that willingly submit to discipline."[54] Furthermore, this scene points to an interest in men's dress (and undress) that increasingly assumes queer implications, for throughout *Mankind* the tempters are linked to new fashions and new manners and encourage Mankind to change into immodest attire by focusing on his and their "jett." Titivillus states of himself, "Euer I go invysybull, yt ys my jett" (529), and New Gyse corrupts long-standing forms of discourse, declaring to Mercy: "Ser, yt ys þe new gyse and þe new jett. / Many wordys and schortely sett, / Thys ys þe new gyse, euery-dele" (103–5). Several examples from Middle English literature testify to *jet* or *jett* denoting new fashions of speech, clothing, and behaviour, while connoting their inherent moral corruption. In his *General Prologue*, Chaucer portrays his sinful and ambiguously gendered Pardoner as fashion forward – "Hym thought he rood al of the newe jet" (682) – and similarly describes another character known for the excess of his fashion and his adulterous sexual desires: Absolon of *The Miller's Tale*, whose fashion choices are recorded as "schapen with goores in the newe get."[55] In *Mum and the Sothsegger* a "semely sage" chastises the narrator, "Hit is sum noyous nyceté of the newe jette,"[56] and in *The Castle of Perseverance* the Deadly Sin of Superbia counsels that one should indulge in new fashions: "Frende, fadyr and modyr dere, / Bowe hem not in non manere, / And hold no maner man þi pere, / And vse þese newe jettys."[57] In these and other such instances, "newe jettys" are linked to depravity of various degrees, and the connection to foppishness imbues these fashion choices with a lingering subtext of queerness.

In *Mankind* the likely moral corruption of new fashions is staged as New Gyse plans to dress the protagonist in the latest styles – "I promytt yow a fresch jakett after þe new gyse" (676) – and Nought soon returns with a "joly jakett" (718). The play's physical humour involves this fashionable jacket being repeatedly shortened to the point that the actor playing Mankind must reveal more and more of his legs, thus approaching higher and higher to his genitals and buttocks. Kathleen Ashley and Gerard NeCastro remark, "As the jesters keep shortening Mankind's coat they are both robbing him and effeminizing him."[58] W.K. Smart describes New Gyse, Nowadays, and Nought as "the young dandies of the time who pride themselves on being up to date" and documents a 1463 statute that ordered "no knight, under the estate of a lord, esquire, gentleman, nor none other person, shall use or wear from the feast of All Saints, which shall be in the year of our Lord M. cccc. Lxv., any gown, jacket, or coat, unless it be of such length that the same may cover his privy members and buttocks."[59] With his "joly jakett," the *Mankind* dramatist stages men's sinful behaviour as centring on their choices in clothes and the inherent moral dissolution found in the latest fashions, again lacing overtly homosocial scenes with undertones of homoeroticism.

In one of *Mankind*'s most daring references to homoerotic sex, the playwright extends a scatological joke into images of analingus. As Nought sings and New Gyse and Nowadays repeat his words as a chorus, the play's dramatic action momentarily ceases for bawdy and excremental pleasure:

NOUGHT: Yt ys wretyn wyth a coll, yt ys wretyn wyth a cole,
NEW GYSE and NOWADAYS: Yt ys wretyn wyth a colle, yt ys wretyn wyth a colle,
NOUGHT: He þat schytyth wyth hys hoyll, he þat schytyth wyth hys hoyll,
NEW GYSE and NOWADAYS: He þat schytyth wyth hys hoyll, he þat schytyth with his hoyll,
NOUGHT: But he wyppe hys ars clen, but he wyppe hys ars clen,
NEW GYSE and NOWADAYS: But he wype hys ars clen, but he wype hys ars clen,
NOUGHT: On hys breche yt xall be sen, on hys breche yt xall be sen.
NEW GYSE and NOWADAYS: On hys breche yt xall be sen, on hys breche yt xall be sen. (335–42)

Following these lyrics, they all sing, "Hoylyke, holyke, holyke! holyke, holyke, holyke!" (343), which, as Laura Kendrick proposes, "creates an obscene pun" because an "archaic or broad English pro-nunciation of the suffix -ly (as -lich or -lic) makes 'holy' sound like 'hole-lick.'"[60] If this reading appears to exaggerate the scatological humour of *holyke*, the insult is made more clearly in Ulpian Fulwell's *Like Will to Like*, in which Nichol Newfangle dubs Tom Colier "Tom Lick-hole."[61] More so, speech is explicitly connected to excrement in New Gyse's striking image of analingus, as he adjures Mankind: "I xall tell yow of a maryage: / I wolde yowr mowth and hys ars þat þis made / Wer maryede junctly together" (345–7). *Mankind* also refers to analingus when Nowadays taunts Nought, "Osculare fun-damentum!" (142), and refers to cunnilingus when Nought derides Mercy, "Yf ꝫe wyll putt yowr nose in hys wyffys sokett, / ꝫe xall haue forty days of pardon" (145–6). These scenes highlight the allegori-cal disruptions between Mankind as the play's protagonist and the play's construction of its disidentified audience members, who likely delight in the comic potential of sexual transgressions that they must simultaneously reject.

Although much of the erotic energies of the Vice characters appear decidedly homosocial to the point of homoerotic, it would be remiss not to mention that their wanton eroticism extends to heterosexuality as well. Both Nowadays and New Gyse are married men and admit to being henpecked husbands: Nowadays confesses that his wife Rachell stands as the victor in their marital battles (135), and New Gyse states that he has fed his wife so well that she has become his master (246). Mischief recalls raping his jailer's wife (641–5). In another moment of heterosexual transgression Mischief adjures Mankind to pursue heterosexual fornication – "3e xall goo to all þe goode felouse in þe cuntre aboute; / Onto þe goodewyff when þe goodeman ys owte" – and then requests that Mankind assent to his command: "'I wyll,' sey 3e." Mankind agrees, "I wyll, ser" (703–5). New Gyse then continues Mankind's erotic education: "There arn but sex dedly synnys, lechery ys non, / As yt may be verefyede be ws brethellys euerychon" (706–7). This homosocial exhortation to enjoy the pleasures of another man's wife is broadened to deny the possibility of sexual sin at all, which would necessarily include homosexuality, one of the key enactments of the sin of *luxuria*. As Chaucer's Parson exhorts, the "fifthe spece" of this deadly sin "is thilke abhomynable synne, of which that no man unnethe oghte speke ne write; nathelees it is openly reherced in holy writ" (909), with his words echoing Pauline injunctions:

Propterea tradidit illos Deus in passiones ignominiae, nam feminae eorum inmutaverunt naturalem usum in eum usum qui est contra naturam. Similiter autem et masculi relicto naturali usu feminae, exarserunt in desideriis suis in invicem. Masculi in masculos turpitudinem operantes, et mercedem quam oportuit erroris sui in semet ipsis recipientes. (Romans 1:26–7)

(For this cause God delivered them up to shameful affections. For their women have changed the natural use into that use which is against nature. And, in like manner, the men also, leaving the natural use of the women, have burned in their lusts one towards another, men with men working that which is filthy, and receiving in themselves the recompense which was due to their error.)

In many such medieval texts, *luxuria* extends beyond the heteroerotic to the homoerotic, and so New Gyse's words adumbrate the likelihood of erotic transgressions unfolding irrespective of the biological sex of the participants.

Complementing its treatment of excrement and queer perversion, *Mankind* portrays the proper ends of fertility and desire through its agricultural themes. Upon entering the stage Mankind is carrying seed – which is literally indicative of his agricultural ambitions and metaphorically indicative of his generative capability – as he states, "I haue brought sede here to sow wyth my londe" (542). Indeed, Mankind only falls to the homosocial enticements of Nought, New Gyse, and Nowadays after Titivillus thwarts his agriculturally reproductive ambitions by placing a board under the soil that Mankind hopes to sow, suggesting that his frustrated desires to reproduce figuratively lead him into homosocial relationships in which human procreation becomes impossible. Titivillus's actions can be interpreted as rendering Mankind impotent or sterile, yet the confused imagery that the playwright evokes of Mankind attempting to sow his seed in the earth further stresses the homoerotic activities that the play simultaneously disavows. As Kathleen Ashley proposes, Mankind's spade functions as a comic sword and "represents the power of God's word to defend the believer against the idle and tempting words of the World."[62] Mankind hits New Gyse and Nowadays in the testicles with his spade, and New Gyse cries, "Alas, my jewellys! I xall be schent of my wyff!" (381); his words suggest that she will have no use of a man who can no longer fornicate with or impregnate her. Nowadays laments more broadly, "Alasse! and I am lyke neuer for to thryue, / I haue such a buffett" (382–3). This scene indicates Mankind's emasculation of the Vices, yet in a key irony his failure to reproduce agriculturally – his sterility – betokens his kinship with these Vices whom he renders momentarily impotent.

It should also be noted that, as much as Nought, New Gyse, and Nowadays illustrate the perils of an unlicensed enactment of male homosociality, the play simultaneously depicts the moral benefits of proper male friendship. The homosocial relationship between Mercy and Mankind models the type of spiritual brotherhood prevalent in much medieval discourse: "Kysse me now, my dere darlynge. Gode schelde yow from yowr fon!" (307). This physical kiss that Mercy offers to Mankind carries no taint of homoerotic desire but instead signifies the spiritual connection between the two men. As C. Stephen Jaeger argues of medieval erotic discourses, "The extent to which all fleshly [desires] can legitimately be transubstantiated and appropriated for the spiritual is a measure of goodness, virtue, piety."[63] Homosocial desire in the spiritual and chivalric realms can be viewed positively, yet, in establishing excremental and queer attractions as sources of comic desire, the play continually reinforces the pleasure of the lower bodily order, eliciting the audience's enjoyment of scenes of riotous excess. In this manner the viewers are asked to align themselves with New Gyse, Nowadays, and Nought, potentially enacting Mankind's own perverse pleasures in their company, yet simultaneously to repulse them and the pleasures they represent. Within *Mankind*'s moral universe, the promise of Mercy saves humanity from its worst impulses, but the play's ultimately queer message reminds viewers of the bodily delights that are resurrected every time one reads or watches the play anew.

In another queer turn of the screw, Mercy, according to various medieval traditions, should be a woman, not a man, which introduces a deeper queer subtext to a play rife with erotic transgression. As G.A. Lester notes of early Christian mythography, "Justice, Truth, and Mercy are three of the daughters of God; the fourth is Peace … The male sex of Mercy in *Mankind*, and of Truth in line 840, is unusual."[64] *The Castle of Perseverance* documents this gendering of God's daughters,[65] as do the fourteenth-century poem *Cursor Mundi* and the Tudor interlude *Respublica*, which includes the four sisters in its cast of characters.[66] Recognizing the comic potential of a male actor playing a male character who traditionally should be a female character, Michael J. Preston states: "Mercy, who is represented more commonly as a woman, might in *Mankind* be seen as a priest so effeminate, considering outsiders' speculation about what went on in monasteries, that an audience might question the nature of his sexuality."[67] Furthermore, because Mercy can be doubled by the actor playing Titivillus, the audience simply cannot stake out a clear relationship to this character, leaving a dizzying sense of disidentification as the likely consequence of following a character who doubles as both male and female, Christian Mercy and an impish devil, and homosocial morality and homoerotic immorality.

In the end, *Mankind* adheres to standard medieval tropes of inversion, yet pushes them to their utmost excremental and queer limits. In a particularly striking phrase Mercy attacks human sinfulness: "Þis maner of lyuynge ys a detestabull plesure. / Vanitas vanitatum, all ys but a vanyte" (766–7). Surely the phrase "a detestabull plesure" encapsulates the frenetic fun of *Mankind*, a play that bubbles with subversive humour, while reminding its audience, in an echo of Ecclesiastes 1:2, that all of life is simply a vain pursuit. Stressing this point, Mankind says of the body and the soul, "Betwyx þem tweyn ys a grett dyvisyon; / He þat xulde be subjecte, now he hath þe victory" (196–7), and as a whole the play tracks the body's ultimate subjugation to the soul and the return to their proper spheres in relation to each other. As *Mankind* so forcefully, so exuberantly, dramatizes, however, a play's narrative action, virtually by necessity, must focus on the travails of the fallen and still falling human body rather than on the soul safe in the succours of paradise. By emphasizing the pleasures of excrementality and homoerotic perversity, *Mankind*'s queer allegory unsettles complacencies of the Christian faith, demonstrating the delights of sin on the path to salvation. Then, when the play is staged anew, it proves once again the greater pleasure of sin for its disidentified audience members, who can never be fully conscripted to side with the allegory's protagonist but must instead align with the shitty and sodomitical Vices that they must simultaneously transcend.

Chapter Five

Sodomy, Chastity, and Queer Historiography in John Bale's Interludes

A staunch advocate of the Reformation, John Bale expressed in his five extant interludes, as well as in such prose works as *The Image of Both Churches*, his fervent desire to cleanse England of corruption and, in particular, the sodomitical sins that he associated with the Catholic Church. Other than such figures as Alan of Lille (with his *Plaint of Nature*) and Peter Damian (with his *Book of Gomorrah*), few medieval and early modern authors so intently contemplated the spiritual and social ramifications of sodomy as did he, and so his works offer the opportunity to consider the sexual implications of the Reformation, particularly in relation to how such themes were staged in the private interludes of the Tudor era. Bale's dramas collectively depict the spiritual horrors of sodomy as a sign of the corrupted church and its spiritual degradation from Jesus's teachings, but in *Thre Lawes of Nature, Moses, and Christ* and *King Johan*, his recoding of England (both as a geographical landscape and as an allegorical figure) into an avatar of chastity reveals the contradictions inherent in sexual morality, especially when clerical chastity is branded as a subset of the vastly expansionary sin of sodomy. Furthermore, his effort to stage the eponymous monarch of *King Johan* as a representative of secular virtue undermines the distinctions that Bale attempts to erect between a fallen church and a reformed church, again owing to the impossibility of chastity signifying virtue in Reformation England. In the end, the queerness of Bale's plays emerges not as much in their vitriolic condemnations of sodomy, or even in their staging of Sodomismus as a character in *Thre Lawes of Nature, Moses, and Christ*, as in the impossibility of dramatically representing both England and King John as purged of sexual sin. As Cathy Shrank proposes, Bale depicts John as "a national hero, celebrated for his stand against papal interference within England's jurisdiction."[1] King John's regal and English asexuality, which should serve as the corrective to papal and

Roman sodomy, undermines the allegorical messages that Bale's plays otherwise endorse. Identified as England's first history play, *King Johan* demonstrates the ways in which allegory and historiography collide in Bale's works, with queering repercussions for the reformer's social and spiritual goals.

John Bale, the Reformation, and Anti-dramatic Interludes

Born in 1495 in Suffolk, John Bale joined the Carmelite friars at twelve years of age but broke with the Catholic Church sometime around 1533. His writings and interludes drew the admiration of Thomas Cromwell, the reformer who engineered Henry VIII's divorce from Catherine of Aragon and subsequent marriage to Anne Boleyn; he also pursued such anti-Catholic objectives as the dissolution of the monasteries. Scholars concur that Bale's acting troupe was known as Lord Cromwell's Players, and Cromwell's account books document performances by "Balle and his ffelowes."[2] During the tempestuous times of the Reformation, Bale twice fled England – first to Antwerp in 1540 until the accession of Edward VI in 1547, and then to Frankfurt and Basel when Mary gained the throne in 1553. He did not return to England until the accession of Elizabeth I in 1558. In addition to his dramatic productions, Bale penned such works as *Illustrium majoris Britanniae scriptorium, hoc est, Angliae, Cambriae, ac Scotiae summarium* (A summary of the famous writers of Britain, that is, of England, Wales, and Scotland); his anti-monastic treatise, *The Actes of Englysh Votaryes*; his proto-Protestant tracts, *The Examinations of Lord Cobham, William Thorpe, and Anne Askewe*; and his commentary on the book of Revelation, *The Image of Both Churches*. Bale died in 1563 in Canterbury, bringing to end an extraordinary literary and dramatic career as both witness to and participant in the Reformation and its refashioning of England's spiritual and sexual mores – and of its theatrical traditions as well.[3]

Only five of Bale's many interludes survive – *King Johan, The Chefe Promyses of God, Johan Baptystes Preachynge, The Temptacyon of Our Lorde*, and *Thre Lawes of Nature, Moses, and Christ* – and they collectively demonstrate Bale's interest in staging his support for the Reformation.[4] Peter Happé convincingly proposes that several of these works were conceived as part of a larger mystery cycle, declaring that "it ... seems apparent that by about 1536 Bale had begun to write a sequence of biblical plays dealing with the Apostles, the Passion, and Resurrection; and that later he expanded this incipient cycle to include the Ministry in considerable detail, followed by more details concerning the passion."[5] Bale's extant interludes are dated to 1538, although their performance history includes productions prior to their transcription in that year. Indeed, Bale describes himself as the "compiler," not the author or playwright, of *The Chefe Promyses of God, Johan Baptystes Preachynge, The Temptacyon of Our Lorde*, and *Thre Lawes of Nature, Moses, and Christ*. As John N. King explains of this term, "Bale associates himself with medieval commentary traditions that presuppose incremental accumulation and assimilation of the work of predecessors. In an age that defined rhetorical invention as the mastery of traditional commonplaces, 'compilation' was a respectable literary activity."[6] In compiling these plays, Bale sought to establish their spiritual pedigree while also enabling spiritual truths to be staged under the inherently suspect auspices of theatrical productions.

As is well known, the Tudor era was a tempestuous time in dramatic history, with civil authorities viewing suspiciously interludes and other such theatrical pastimes. Many prior plays were considered of dubious moral worth owing to their association with Catholicism, and contemporary productions also proved worrisome, as registered in a 1544 statute, issued under Henry VIII's authority, that limited dramatic performances: "His highness therefore straightly chargeth and commandeth that no manner of person or persons from henceforth ... presume or take upon him or them at any time hereafter to play or set forth, or cause to be played, any manner of interlude or common play." The statute then enumerates various exceptions to this rule, particularly for entertainments held "in the houses of noblemen."[7] Given the precarious circumstances of their composition and production, Bale faced the challenge of criticizing the Catholic Church during the transitional period of the English Reformation, which reached its zenith in 1534 with Henry VIII's declaration that he was the "Supreme Head on earth of the Church of England, called *Anglicana Ecclesia*," through the Act of Supremacy.[8] Protestants feared that Catholicism's powerful advocates might return to positions of authority, as would occur in 1553 when Mary acceded to the throne, and Bale faced an additional artistic obstacle in the fact that many of his audience members likely maintained their loyalties to Catholicism, even if they recognized the need to mute their support. Such circumstances required that Bale adopt more than a modicum of discretion in his interludes, which accounts for his frequent turn to biblical stories for source materials, particularly in *The Chefe Promyses of God, Johan Baptystes Preachynge*, and *The Temptacyon of Our Lorde*. As Seymour Baker House explains, "Because the plays were drawn largely from the Bible, reformers like Bale could present their objections to Catholic praxis while emphasizing their belief that scriptural fidelity – increasingly a literal fidelity – was the only sure guide to theological verity."[9] Sounding a similar note, Paul Christianson explains Bale's care in addressing contemporary issues through his dramatic reinterpretations of scripture: "Holy history provided the framework for his exegesis, but the mystery of unlocking the sacred tropes preserved Bale from too direct an application of specific prophecies to individual historical events."[10] Both playwrights and their audiences faced challenging political conditions with potentially lethal consequences, and thus they trod carefully into issues of spiritual commentary, which, given the times, could not help but resonate as statements of political commentary as well.

The shifting cultural tides of the Reformation are further evident in Bale's plays themselves, for in one of the defining ironies of his career Bale is a playwright hesitant over the moral valence of his artistic métier, distasteful of the potential degeneracy of his medium. Succinctly speaking to this paradox, James Simpson quips, "Bale the dramatist wants nothing more than to kill drama."[11] Numerous passages from his works record characters' suspicions of theatrical entertainments. In *King Johan*, Englande describes the immoral clergy as wandering around the countryside "lyke most dysgysed players" (*KJ*, 66); Dissymulacyon mentions that he sends his nefarious agents to mummings to lead the people astray (*KJ*, 700); and Johan denounces the Clergye for their "Latyne howres, serymonyes and popetly playes" (*KJ*, 415), deriding the Catholic Church with this dismissive pun. Philip Butterworth documents the "derogatory references inspired by the Reformation to the interplay of the *Pope* and *puppetry*," citing William Tyndale in 1528 as another example of this wordplay: "let not our most holy father make [kings] no more so drunk with vain names, with caps of maintenance and like baubles, as it were popetry for children."[12] In conceiving certain theatrical experiences as "popish," Bale carves out a creative space for a neo-Protestant theatre, yet one that is inherently conflicted by the break between old and new religious traditions. Katherine Steele Brokaw, in an analysis of the musical elements of Bale's interludes, pinpoints his theatrical ambivalence in the tension between the "antimusical stance in his early prose polemics" and the interludes themselves, in which he "creat[es] a specific and new kind of music for the Protestant Church."[13] This tension carries throughout virtually all aspects of Bale's theatrical corpus, in which he conscripts a suspect medium to deliver new moral truths to his English audience.

As much as Bale expressed hesitation about the moral purpose of the theatre, he also perceived God's intervention throughout human endeavours, and so he could envision an English theatre immoral in its past but potentially moral in its present and future. In *The Chefe Promyses of God* he accentuates this point dramatically through the words of his prologue figure, Baleus Prolocutor, who asks his audience members to ponder the possibility that transitory events – such as the interlude they are presently witnessing – can assist one's spiritual growth:

> If profyght maye growe, most Christen audyence,
> By knowlege of thynges whych are but transytorye
> And here for a tyme, of moch more congruence
> Advauntage myght sprynge by the serche of causes heavenlye,
> As those matters are that the Gospell specyfye,
> Without whose knowledge no man to the truth can fall,
> Nor ever atteyne to the lyfe perpetuall. (*CPG*, 1–7)

Eternal truths afford an incomparable advantage, but transitory experiences can also lead one to salvation. As Michelle Butler asserts of Bale's role in his interludes as Baleus Prolocutor, "Bale's anxieties about his plays' authority is part of a larger revision of medieval dramaturgy, aimed at securing a means to speak authoritatively about Protestant doctrine in a form associated with Catholicism."[14] In another such moment of metacommentary, Jesus in *The Temptacyon of Our Lorde* speaks to the audience about the moral lesson encoded in this dramatic presentation of the temptations he has withstood: "And to teache yow wayes hys myschefes to prevent / By the worde of God, whych must be your defence" (*TOL*, 47–8). Scripture, in Bale's hands, provides the moral defence every Christian needs to withstand the assaults of Satan and sin, yet it is staged through a medium tainted by the history of "popetly playes."

A guiding paradox of Bale's interludes thus arises in their attempt to justify the Reformation through a medium inherently influenced by the Catholic past. By aligning Catholicism with sodomy, Bale liberates his newly Protestant nation from the scourge of this sin, but England herself – as a geographical landscape in *Thre Lawes of Nature, Moses, and Christ* and as an allegorical figure in *King Johan* – exemplifies the challenge of erasing a sodomitical past from a redeemed present. Sodomitical traces undercut Bale's portrayal of England, even in *King Johan's* presentation of a king and a country radically reconfigured as transhistorical exemplars of sexual purity. In this light, the ascription of asexuality to England and to King John undercuts the erasure of sodomy from a nation theologically emancipated from Rome but still ensnared in the sin that, for Bale, defines the church it seeks to escape. The allegory of King John becomes entwined in an ultimately queer historiography, one that positions John as the righteous precursor of Henry VIII but also proves the fundamental instability of the dramatic medium for cleansing Reformation England from aspersions of sexual transgression.

Sodomy in Bale's Allegorical England

Bale refers directly to sodomy in his extant interludes, with the sole exception of *The Temptacyon of Our Lorde*, in order to lay the groundwork for his proto-Protestant moral agenda. In *The Chefe Promyses of God*, Pater Coelistis condemns those "vyle Sodomytes [who] lyve so unnaturallye / That their synne vengeaunce axeth contynuallye" (*CPG*, 318–19), and in *Johan Baptytstes Preachynge*, the eponymous preacher castigates the Sadducee with an opprobrious comparison: "Before God ye are no better than Sodomytes" (*JBP*, 240). In *King Johan*, sexual transgressions are explicitly linked to Sodom in Johan's words to Nobylyte, whom he upbraids for aligning himself with "the grownd and mother of whordom – / The Romych Churche I meane, more vyle than ever was Sodom, / And to say the trewth a mete spowse for the fynd" (*KJ*, 369–71). Most notably, Bale personifies Sodomismus as a character in *Thre Lawes of Nature, Moses, and Christ*, thus creating an allegorical figure who simultaneously represents and revels in the transgression. In the following passage Sodomismus explains how Catholic priests succumb to pederastic temptation:

> In Rome to me they fall,
> Both byshopp and cardynall,
> Monke, fryre, prest and all,
>   More ranke they are than antes.
> Example in Pope Julye,
> Whych sought to have in hys furye
> Two laddes, and to use them beastlye,
>   From the Cardynall of Nantes. (*ThrL*, 643–50)

From these passages it is clear that Bale frequently employs the word *sodomy* and refers to the biblical accounts of Sodom and Gomorrah to delineate the utter depravity of the Catholic Church. Correspondingly, his plays attempt to cleanse England of any residue of such sin, positing it as an inherent failing of the papacy and Catholicism.

Bale, however, does not use the term *sodomy* strictly in the sense of homoerotic and pederastic transgressions, and indeed his understanding of the word is multivalent and denotes a wide continuum of sins. In other passages of *Thre Lawes of Nature, Moses, and Christ*, Sodomismus includes within his purview adultery and promiscuity (579–82), masturbation (586–90), and bestiality (591–4, 615–19). Observing the confused denotations of the word in Tudor England, Allen Frantzen suggests that "Bale's definition of sodomy cannot be narrowed to male homosexual intercourse," noting further that the "sin is not exclusively, or even primarily, a sexual offense, but rather broadly indicates impiety, injustice, and the improper use of God's gifts." He concludes, "For Bale, the accusation of 'sodomy' encompasses both theological and sexual sins and hence serves as a powerful weapon."[15]

Furthermore, Bale perceived sodomy as intrinsically connected to idolatry, which was an issue of key concern in Reformation England, illustrated in the fact that reformers decapitated statuary in the kingdom's cathedrals to remove the spectral possibility that believers might worship representations of God the Father, Jesus, and other biblical figures rather than the spiritual essence of the Divine. In *Thre Lawes of Nature, Moses, and Christ*, Infidelitas dispatches both Sodomismus and Idololatria to overthrow Naturae Lex, which thematically establishes a tension between "unnatural" acts and actors and "natural" ones. Bale cites Paul's epistle to the Romans for linking sodomy and Sodomismus to idolatry and Idololatria, ironically putting these words in Sodomismus's mouth: "As Paule to the Romanes testyfye, / The gentyles after Idolatrye / Fell to soch bestyall Sodomye / That God ded them forsake" (*ThrL*, 603–6). Indeed, Paul limns such a connection between the two offences, bemoaning first the rise of idolatry and then the sexual transgressions that flourished as its consequence:

Et mutaverunt gloriam incorruptibilis Dei in similitudinem imaginis corruptibilis hominis et volucrum et quadrupedum et serpentium. Propter quod tradidit illos Deus in desideria cordis eorum in inmunditiam ut contumeliis adficiant corpora sua in semet ipsis. Qui commutaverunt veritatem Dei in mendacio et coluerent et servierunt creaturae potius quam creatori qui est benedictus in saecula. (Romans 1:23–5)

(And they changed the glory of the incorruptible God into the likeness of the image of a corruptible man, and of birds, and of four-footed beasts, and of creeping things. Wherefore God gave them up to the desires of their heart, unto uncleanness, to dishonour their own bodies among themselves. Who changed the truth of God into a lie; and worshipped and served the creature rather than the Creator, who is blessed for ever.)[16]

Following these words Paul addresses the people's sexual sins, as the women turn away from men, and the men turn away from women. Sodomismus soon reiterates the connection between idolatry and lust:

"I wyll corrupt Gods Image / With most unlawfull usage, / And brynge hym into dottage, / Of all concupyscence" (*ThrL*, 683–6). Bale links idolatry to sodomy in additional passages in other interludes, such as *The Chefe Promyses of God* (315–21 and 682–95). In Elena Levy-Navarro's words, sodomy represents for Bale "a moral state of damnation," one that bears the possibility for "all of humanity [to] become 'sodomites' when God withdraws his grace from them because all of humanity is, then, given over to their irresistible depraved natures."[17]

As much as sodomy denoted a range of sexual and spiritual transgressions during the Tudor era, it was a topic of increased interest at Henry VIII's court, specifically in regard to homosexual activity. Long under the purview of ecclesiastical courts, sodomy was criminalized in 1533 by the so-called Buggery Act, with this statute first lamenting, "Forasmuch as there is not yet sufficient and condign punishment appointed and limited by the due course of the laws of this realm, for the detestable and abominable vice of buggery committed with mankind or beast," and then affirming that the offence was now a felony punishable by death and loss of property.[18] The Acte for the Punishment of the Vice of Buggerie sparked controversy and debate over the ensuing decades, and as Montgomery Hyde records, "during the next twenty years the Act was repealed twice and re-enacted four times, after which it was to remain undisturbed on the statute book for upwards of three centuries."[19] Given these shifting conditions, it appears that Bale did not see sodomy as solely the equivalent of buggery, yet it simultaneously appears likely that he perceived buggery as a particularly egregious subset of sodomy. Certainly, homoeroticism emerges as a key element in Bale's denouncing of sin, such as when, in *The Chefe Promyses of God*, Pater Coelistis castigates humanity's sinfulness: "My children with mennis so carnallye consent / That their vayne workynge is unto me moche grevaunce. / Mankynde is but fleshe in hys whole dallyaunce" (*CPG*, 192–4).[20]

In an irony arising from his thematic concern with sodomy and male homosociality, however, Bale introduces few female characters in his interludes – other than Englande in *King Johan* and Idololatria in *Thre Lawes of Nature, Moses, and Christ* – who might dissipate their homosocial energy, and so sodomy circulates primarily around male sexual transgressions, even when certain acts – bestiality and masturbation, for instance – can be engaged in by women. Women are notably absent from *The Chefe Promyses of God*, in which Bale refrains from including Eve in the first act, which depicts God's punishment of Adam and humanity's fall. It is similarly notable that Bale refrains from depicting Noah's wife in the second act of this interlude, considering her scene-stealing roles in several mystery cycles, including those of York and Chester. With a company of male actors, Bale may have deemed that performances of his plays would benefit from male actors playing male roles, with the aforementioned exceptions of Englande and Idololatria pointing to the variability of gender, but Bale's condemnation of female sexuality should not be discounted in this regard. In several passages he denounces women as vigorously as he denounces sodomites, such as when he speaks disparagingly of the Catholic Church through metaphors of womanhood. In *The Image of Both Churches*, Bale employs an eroticized image of women – notably the Whore of Babylon in Revelations – to condemn the practices of the Catholic Church: "They know ... that over a gorgeous glittering whore every fleshly man is inordinately wanton, fierce, and greedy. Following his ways therefore, they have always for lucre's sake gloriously garnished their holy mother, the madam of mischief and proud synagogue of Satan, with gold, silver, pearl, precious stone, velvets, silks, mitres, copes, crosses, cruets, ceremonies, censings, blessings, babblings, brawlings, processions, puppets, and such other mad masteries (whereof the church that Christ left here behind him know not one jot), to provoke the carnal idiots to her whoredom in spirit."[21] What is perhaps most interesting about this passage, and most relevant to the interludes' consideration of gender and sodomy, is that Bale evades a potential binary between male sodomy and heterosexuality in his condemnation of Catholicism. Instead, both are envisioned as dangerously sinful, and these denigrations of sexuality, and others like them, ironically circumscribe his ability to describe England and King John as avatars of sexual morality in his interludes.

Furthermore, because chastity stands as the assumed model of Catholic priestly sexuality, no matter the failing of individual clergy to uphold this virtue, it similarly registers as a sinful archaism of the "prior faith." And so, as much as modern readers of Bale's works might assume a binary opposition between sodomy and chastity, in actuality Bale views chastity as an offshoot of sodomy. Prior to and throughout the Reformation the erotic and marital practices of the clergy were long a matter of debate in the church, and the prohibition against clerical marriages was still a relatively recent development in ecclesiastical practice. In 1074 Pope Gregory VII forcefully advocated that ordained priests should pledge celibacy; in 1123 Pope Callixtus II, presiding over the First Lateran Council, invalidated clerical marriages; and in 1139 the Second Lateran Council, under the leadership of Pope Innocent II, confirmed this decree. In *The Examination of Lord Cobham*, Bale fulminates against priestly chastity: "Unspeakable filthiness of all fleshly occupying was then called priests' chastity, as it is yet, and will be till it come to the highest, that God may take full vengeance."²² In similar passages from *The Image of Both Churches*, he excoriates "blind papists" for "their wiveless chastity," denouncing the "prodigious beastliness in lecherous living under the colour of chastity."²³ With two phrases bordering on the oxymoronic in today's parlance but impeccably logical in his own, Bale rails against "sodomitical chastity" and "whorish chastity," as well as denouncing "stinking chastity" and "Romish chastity."²⁴ In Bale's wideranging disquisitions on the pleasures of sin, as depicted in *Thre Lawes of Nature, Moses, and Christ*, Sodomismus testifies that the transgression he represents is a consequence of Catholic priests who are compelled to forgo marriage, which bespeaks the dangers of chastity:

> I dwelt amonge the Sodomytes,
> The Benjamytes and Madyanytes
> And now the popysh hypocrytes
>   Embrace me every where.
> I am now become all spyrytuall,
> For the clergye at Rome and over all
> For want of wyves, to me doth fall,
>   To God they have no feare. (*ThrL*, 571–8)

According to Sodomismus, priests succumb to a range of erotic transgressions because they have no wives with whom to engage in theologically approved sexual relationships. These unmarried men fail to uphold the virtue expected of their religious vocation and instead indulge in various prohibited eroticisms, thus demonstrating the inherent immorality of priestly chastity.

Consider also this exchange between Infidelitas and Evangelium in *Thre Lawes of Nature, Moses, and Christ*, in which the former accuses the latter of forsaking the church:

> INFIDELITAS: Marry, so they saye, ye fellawes of the newe lernynge
>   Forsake holy church, and now fall fast to wyvynge.
> EVANGELIUM: Naye, they forsake whoredome with other dampnable
>   usage,
> And lyve with their wyves in lawfull marryage
> Whyls the Popes oyled swarme raigne styll in their olde buggerage.
> (*ThrL*, 1383–7)

"Lawfull marryage" stands as the proper corrective to the sodomitical sins of the past, yet Donald Mager notices the sharp irony of this

passage at the moment of its staging, proposing that Bale's audience would be encouraged to "kindly overlook the inference that
the reformed English priests, including Bale himself and his closet
confederates, needed to forsake 'whoredome' when they took wives
under the 'newe lerynynge,' and therefore gave up their own 'olde
buggerage.'"[25] In light of sodomy's multiple meanings, chastity
devolves into an inherently conflicted state, particularly given the
play's staging in England, in which many members of the audience
would presumably be reformed sodomites within Bale's wide-ranging definition of the sin.

One of the chief tensions in allegories arises from the disjunction
between the universality of their themes and the specificities of their
plots. As Pamela King notes of the use of allegorical forms in morality plays, "they are set in no time, or outside historical time, though
their lack of historical specificity is generally exploited by strategically
collapsing the eternal with the contemporary."[26] King's insight bears
relevance to Bale's depictions of England and sexual sin in that the
allegorical message of a Christian playwright should ostensibly speak
to all members of the faith, yet the details of a particular play – the
location of its staging, the nationality of its actors, the allusions to
regional geography and topography – could demarcate its audience
to a subset of the religion. A key allegorical register of *Thre Lawes of
Nature, Moses, and Christ* envisions its theological message as relevant
throughout Christendom and as especially relevant to its political
leaders, such as when Naturae Lex urges, "Ye Christen rulers, se yow
for thys a waye: / Be not illuded by false hypocresye" (*ThrL*, 773–4).
As the interlude concludes, Fides Christiana similarly envisions the
play's message as pertaining to Christians throughout the world:
"Now wyll I forewarde to all the christen nacyons, / And se in effect
these lawes observed all" (*ThrL*, 1988–9). Fides Christiana soon reiterates this point, with phrasing that would apply beyond the borders of
England: "Have a due respect unto your contreye natyve, / Whych
hath brought ye up and geven ye norryshment" (2008–9). With such
lines Bale imagines an international audience of Christian believers,
despite the likelihood that his interludes were performed throughout
the English countryside by the touring company of Lord Cromwell's
Players.

Counterbalancing these universal themes, Bale portrays England in
Thre Lawes of Nature, Moses, and Christ as infiltrated by the type of sexual transgression that his Vice characters represent, and thus he brings
immediacy and pertinence to the interlude's staging in the newly Protestant land. In one such scene initially devoid of geographical specificity,

Infidelitas envisions sexual relationships between friars and nuns as a sign of the degraded times:

> A symple probleme of bytcherye.
> Whan the fryre begonne, afore the nonne,
>   To synge of precyouse stones,
> "From my youth," sayt she, "they have confort me," –
> As it had bene for the nones. (*ThrL*, 821–5)

As Brokaw notes, the phrase *precious stones* – in Latin, *lapides preciosi* – "comes from the *Breviarum Romanum*'s prayer for the dedication of a church,"[27] the phrase having been inspired by Revelations 21:19: "fundamenta muri civitatis omni lapide pretioso ornata" (And the foundations of the wall of the city were adorned with all manner of precious stones). The "precious stones" that form the foundation of the church and of church buildings are humorously reconceived as a friar's testicles, in a vulgar devolution of a Christian ideal. One could well imagine this type of invective, in its blanket indictment of Catholicism, as applying to the religion in all of its geographical reach, but the interlude's next lines tie these transgressions specifically to England, as Infidelitas continues his mirthful attack on Moseh Lex:

> With us was it merye
> Whan we went to Berye,
>   And to Our Lady of Grace,
> To the bloude of Hayles,
> Where no good chere fayles,
>   And other holye place. (*ThrL*, 830–5)

In three consecutive lines Infidelitas locates sexual transgressions in English sites: the abbey of St. Edmund at Bury, Suffolk; the Rood of Grace at Boxley, Kent;[28] and Hailes Abbey in Gloucestershire. Additional moments that undermine the interlude's geographic universality include Idololatria's mention of such sites as "Quene hythe" (*ThrL*, 538, cf. 1305) and Infidelitas's mention of "Yngham Trynyte" (*ThrL*, 957). Furthermore, Ambitio celebrates the priests "in Englande that moch rather wolde to dwell / Whores in their dyoceses than the readers of Christes Gospell" (*ThreL*, 1212–13). Allegory often teeters between the universal and the specific, and in this instance Bale's play imagines the universal failings of the church as stretching across England's borders from east to west. Such a depiction of a sin-infested England is, on the one hand, hardly surprising: Bale must depict the Catholic threat to the island if he is to argue for the religion's removal and its replacement with the Anglican Church.

On the other hand, however, Bale's emphasis on England's corrupted state cannot solely be constrained to the historical past, and in her transition from a geographical landscape in *Thre Lawes of Nature, Moses, and Christ* to an allegorical figure in *King Johan*, this multivalent figure – simultaneously allegorical character, historical kingdom, geographical location, widow, and mother – cannot escape the taint of sodomitical chastity, whether she proclaims her desires in eroticized terms or, in complementary contrast, in wholly asexual terms. In one such instance Englande rebuffs the Cardinal's words and imagines rape as preferable to allowing the return of the Catholic clergy:

> For me pore Ynglond ye have done sore amys;
> Of a fre woman ye have now mad a bonde mayd.
> Yowre self and heyres ye have for ever decayd.
> Alas, I had rether be underneth the Turke
> Than under the wynges of soch a thefe to lurke. (*KJ*, 1766–70)

Here Englande employs the tropes of Western crusading literature, in which Muslims (or, as they were frequently termed, Saracens) are depicted as sexually voracious, but she tweaks this paradigm in her preference for being "underneth" a Turk than for being degraded by the dissolute Catholic Church.[29] "Underneth" might imply the political dominion of England by external forces, yet the image also carries a sexual colouring that implies rape. In many ways this passage inverts Bale's image of priests lusting over "a gorgeous glittering whore" in *The Image of Both Churches* (discussed previously), with virtuous England rejecting the lascivious priesthood – who should ostensibly be chaste – and finding rape by a non-Christian man preferable to spiritual degradation by Christian men.

It is not surprising that, in representing Bale's world-view, Englande articulates pro-Reformation tenets, but she frequently does so with eroticized imagery that undermines the chastity she ostensibly models. In a striking paradox, Englande, a widow, explains that she is God's spouse:

ENGLANDE: Thes vyle popych swine hath clene exyled my hosband.
KING JOHAN: Who ys thy husband? Tel me, good gentyll Yngland.
ENGLANDE: For soth, God hym selfe, the spowse of every sort
   That seke hym in fayth to ther sowlys helth and confort.
SEDICYON: He ys scant honest that so many wyfes wyll have. (*KJ*, 107–11)

Sedicyon's deft jibe at a polyamorous deity simply makes apparent the erotic imagery just barely cloaked beneath the metaphor of nuns as brides of Christ. Along these lines, Bale portrays Englande as multiply and conflictingly widowed. The pope has ostensibly exiled God from the land, but Bale refuses then to imagine God as dead, although Englande is portrayed simultaneously as his spouse and as his widow. On a secular level, Englande can be viewed as a widow owing to Richard the Lionheart's absence, but again, Bale envisions a potential husband as absent rather than dead. Most critically, the relationship between Englande and Johan cannot be envisioned as a marriage, despite the allegorically erotic potential in the relationship between a feminized representation of the nation and her temporal monarch. Englande must be conceived as chaste within the play's erotic logic, but the prime familial relationships that she allegorizes as widow and as mother must admit the possibility of an Englande who cannot enact chastity, and if she were able to emblematize chastity, she would represent sodomy anyway, given its conflicted and contradictory meanings.

Pursuing this line of reasoning further, chaste religious women – that is to say, nuns – can figure equally as sodomitical figures within Bale's world-view. Given these conditions, his portrayal of Englande as God's widow – the stage directions describe her as *"Ynglond Vidua"* (following *KJ*, 22) – cannot help but cast her within the terms of Catholicism's female religious orders, in which nuns are envisioned as brides of Christ. For Bale, however, nuns are as sexually problematic as priests. Several passages of *The Image of Both Churches* lambaste nuns for their erotic transgressions and condemn both male and female Catholic religious figures as sodomites, such as when Bale includes nuns among the "innumerable swarm of Sodomites" and berates the "Monks, nuns, canons and friars [who] have fled into monasteries, convents, and houses ... for in all voluptuous pleasures have they there lived."[30] In conjoining his attacks of nuns with those of other purported Catholic sodomites, Bale does not envision lesbianism as clearly as he envisions male homosexuality, yet the inclusion of women under the rubric of sodomites aligns them with similar sexual transgressions of men, even when these offences can only be imagined as parallel but not identical. A chaste nun, in this paradigm, is a sodomitical one, and from this perspective a chaste England envisioned as God's widow cannot be preserved from aspersions of sodomy even when she is refuting an eroticized image of her rape by Catholicism, for the image of a woman married to God has always already been conceived within a rubric that simultaneously avows and disavows a romantic connection to the Divine.

Whether England is envisioned as wife, mother, or widow, her allegorical identification as female is essential to Bale's depiction of the land as fruitfully proceeding from heterosexual generation. In contrast, the lineage of the play's Catholic male characters focuses exclusively on homosocial reproduction, in which the Pope as Antichrist fathers Infidelitas, who sires Falsehood and Prevy Treason, who respectively sire Dissymulacyon and Sedicyon; Dissymulacyon then fathers Privat Welth, who fathers Usurpid Powre. Such an allegorically homosocial lineage builds the anti-Catholic and anti-sodomitical themes of the play, construing these characters as the progeny of exclusively male lines. Even when John mistakenly assumes that Sedicyon is the child of Englande, Sedicyon claims that he was born "under the Pope in the holy cyte of Rome" (*KJ*, 183). Sedicyon's words do not quite make the claim that the pope is his father, but he clearly aligns himself with Catholicism and its homosocial traditions. Contrasted with this exclusively male line, Englande's presence frees her land from the taint of sodomitical – that is, same-sex – reproduction. Yet, at the same time, given the confused status of her allegorical positions as God's widow and Johan's mother (*KJ*, 1573), she blurs the border between illicit and licit sexual relationships that she should ostensibly uphold, both in *Thre Lawes of Nature, Moses, and Christ* and *King Johan*, for the proclamation of her conflicting roles allows the spectre of sexual activity to undercut her virtuous image. Dramatic performances invite numerous ironies in the practice of double casting, and it is surely ironic that the performer playing Englande also plays the role of the dissolute Clergye, as indicated in the stage direction "*Go owt Ynglond and drese for Clargy*" (following *KJ*, 154). The doubling of actors, in this instance, simply makes manifest what the play's confused allegory about sexuality, sodomy, chastity, and gender attempts to obfuscate – that Englande and Clergye share more than Bale intends in their relation to sodomy.

Emerging from these erotic paradoxes and contradictions, it becomes clear that in *Thre Lawes of Nature, Moses, and Christ* and *King Johan* Bale highlights, rather than muffles, the conflicted state of England in his geographic and erotic imaginary. It is a land tainted by a history of Catholic sodomy, menaced by a future of sodomy – yet, given the present circumstances of defending Henry VIII and the erotic excess of his multiple marriages, one that cannot be envisioned as cleansed by chastity, asexuality, or simply sexual purity. In fundamental terms, Bale cannot vindicate an uxorial and maternal England from aspersions of queerness (in terms of sodomy and chastity). This queer spectre likewise emerges in *King Johan* in his depiction of the eponymous monarch as a foreshadowing of Henry VIII, particularly given Bale's interest in rewriting England's historical past during the critical juncture of the Reformation.

Allegorical Kingship and Bale's Queer Historiography

Dramatic historiography requires a backward gaze on past events and then their reconstitution in the present, often for the explicit purposes of better understanding the present and influencing the future. In this manner, present concerns often take precedence over historical veracity, and as numerous scholars have explicated, medieval and Renaissance chroniclers and historians viewed their work as testifying to eternal truths rather than accurately attending to the details of bygone events. Paul Strohm, in considering medieval narrative and historiography, states that "a text can be powerful without being true," investigating the ways in which "fictive elements teem within historical narratives, trial depositions and indictments, coroner's rolls, and other officially sanctioned accounts."[31] Similarly commenting on the historians of the Tudor and Stuart eras, Herschel Baker discerns their predilection for "partial truths, and even the distortions and evasions, of church or state or party. ... Their work acquired the function of persuasion and instruction, and on occasion it became the tool of propaganda."[32] Plays dramatizing historical personages and events implemented a similarly didactic function: to allow their audiences to contemplate the meaning of the past for its relevance to the present. Certainly, Bale criticized some historians for the veracity of their claims, thus establishing himself as a writer of truths: "In the firste part of thys boke, maye men breuelye beholde how and by whom thys realme was first inhabyted, whiche thynge hath bene hytherto in all Englysh Chronicles, doubt-fullye, vnagreablye, yea, and vntrulye treated, vpon coniecturs, fantasyes, and lyes onlye, by reason of ignoraunce in the scripturs and moste auctorysed hystoryes."[33] As the author of England's first history play, Bale merges history's didactic and moral purposes to advocate for the Reformation, basing these claims on truths otherwise untold or unknown; yet he does so with ultimately, and surely unintended, queering consequences.

History writing, in its various modes and rhetorical approaches, cannot entirely sidestep issues of gender and sexuality, even when presenting seemingly straightforward accounts of yesteryear. Indeed, sexuality constitutes a key means to consider the meaning of the past in the moment of its present reconstitution. As Stephen Guy-Bray, Vin Nardizzi, and Will Stockton propose in their formulation of a queer historiography, looking back at history entails reconceiving the ways in which sexuality was constructed in multiple eras, particularly those of the past and present: "the literal backward gaze that ends the hetero-sexual relation becomes at once the metaphorical backward gaze that demonstrates the connection of past literature to the present ... and the sheer variety of the forms of sexuality."[34] In other words, while one may assume a congruency between the sexual practices and identities of the present and the past, to look to the past is always to face the inherent disjunction of then and now, and also to enjoy the freedom to reconceptualize the meaning or experience of historical sexualities for the purposes – whether they be archival, cultural, polemical, or theatri-cal, among many other such motivations – prompting this endeavour. Queer historiographies employ eroticism for ideological purposes, thus highlighting the functionality of sexuality for the author's objectives while also, at least tacitly, revealing its inherent malleability.

In *Thre Lawes of Nature, Moses, and Christ*, Bale deploys such a queer historiography in his account of Danish invasions of England, which foreshadow the nation's current "occupation" by the Catholic Church. Infidelitas avows, "The same Danes are they men prophecy of playne, / Whych shuld over ronne thys realme yet ones agayne" (*ThrL*, 1335–6). Evangelium requests that he clarify his meaning, and Infidelitas further explains: "Dane Johan, Dane Robert, Dane Thomas, and Dane Harrye; / These same are those Danes that laye with other mennys wyves, / And occupyed their lands to the detryment of their lyves" (*ThrL*, 1338–40). As Peter Happé observes of Bale's wordplay, "*Dane* is a pun for *Don/ Dom*, the title for the religious."[35] The invasions that England has endured, if we may term the presence of Catholicism as such, do not register simply as historical, political, or theological events but as erotic ones as well, and Bale envisions these invaders, if not precisely as rap-ists, then as seducers and adulterers, those who cuckold the island's men and leave them queered from their masculine and matrimonial prerogatives. Although Bale does not explicitly address this possibility in these lines, given his frequent focus on the sodomitical tendencies of Catholic priests, it seems equally likely that these allegorically invading churchmen qua Danes would set their lascivious sights on England's menfolk. In a similar yet contrasting fashion in *The Actes of Englysh Votaryes*, Bale employs yesteryear's Danish invasions to undercut the morality and masculinity of Catholic monks: "After that entered the Danes so fast (sayth Ranulphe) at euerye porte, that no where was the Englyshe nacyon able to withstande them. And the monkes to helpe the matter wele forewarde, by counsell of their Archebyshop Siricius, gaue them .x. thousand pounde to begynne with, that they myght lyue in rest and not be hyndered. For lytle cared they what became of the reest, so their precyouse bodyes were safe."[36] Here again we see the queerness of history writing, in the traitorous monks forsaking the English people to enjoy the pleasures of their sybaritic lifestyle.

As these brief examples of the Danish invasions attest, historiography unleashes queer undercurrents as writers ponder the relevance of the past to the present, and these tensions erupt in Bale's portrayal of King John and his erotic biography. Some simple historical facts will assist in setting the stage for the ensuing analysis: England's King John, who reigned from 1177 to 1216 and is most famous for signing the Magna Carta, married twice, first to Isabella, Countess of Gloucester, in 1189, and then to Isabella, Countess of Angoulême, in 1200. The marriage to Isabella of Gloucester was annulled in 1199 on grounds of consanguinity, in that they were both great-grandchildren of Henry I. Pope Clement III had allowed the marriage, providing a dispensation to the interdict of Archbishop Baldwin of Canterbury, but forbad sexual relations between the two.[37] During this marriage John fathered two illegitimate children: Richard FitzRoy and Joan, Lady of Wales. Isabella of Angoulême was merely twelve years old when she married John, and historians have long debated whether their relationship was romantic and heartfelt or calculated and passionless.[38] John's second marriage lasted until his death, and the couple engendered five children: Henry III, the future King of England; Richard, Earl of Cornwall; Joan, Queen of Scotland; Isabella, Holy Roman Empress; and Eleanor, Countess of Pembroke and Leicester. With a first marriage of enforced chastity ending in annulment yet witnessing the birth of two children, and a second marriage producing five offspring, John's erotic biography would appear to provide fascinating source materials for later dramatic adaptations of his life. Certainly, given Bale's active endorsement of the Reformation, the parallels between John and Henry VIII, in their multiple marriages, children both legitimate and illegitimate, and their fractious relationships with the Catholic Church, would appear productive conduits for developing the themes of Bale's play. In the interplay between history and history writing, however, queer undercurrents destabilize his attempt to portray John as an erotically blameless monarch undone by a corrupt clergy.

In *King Johan* Bale repeatedly stresses his use of historical chronicles to demonstrate the play's veracity over any propagandistic ambitions, but this transparent rhetorical ploy soon falls to its own contradictions in depicting the king's sexual biography. In the interlude's opening, Johan identifies himself as "Johan, Kyng of Ynglond, the cronyclys doth me call" (*KJ*, 9). Historical chronicles, however, signify erratically in the play, with characters respectively denouncing and praising their accuracy. Nobylyte sees historical documents as inherently biased accounts because they are written by the ecclesiastical orders: "Yow pristes are the cawse that Chronycles doth defame / So many prynces and men of notable name, / For yow take upon yow to wryght them evermore" (*KJ*, 585–7). Veritas, in contrast, extols the authors of various chronicles, ostensibly for praising Johan: "For hys valeauntnesse many excellent writers make, / As Sigebertus, Vincentius and also Nauclerus; / Giraldus and Mathu Parys with hys noble vertues take – / Yea, Paulus Phrigio, Johan Major and Hector Boethius" (*KJ*, 2200–3). Of course, these chroniclers do not uniformly present the historical John in a positive light, thus demonstrating the pliability of Bale's source materials and the inherent paradoxes of his historiographical ethos. For example, in detailing John's struggles with the English clergy, Matthew Paris writes, "Thus was the abbot compelled, in that year, to pay out 1,000 marks to the ever-demanding, ever-grasping King John, to the greatest harm of this church." He also dubs John "a greater tyrant than whom has never appeared among those born of women," detailing how the monarch "truculently extorted" funds for his endeavours.[39] In *The Topography of Ireland*, Gerald of Wales describes John disparagingly as one "led away by the fervor of youth and ensnared by its passions, [who] is prone to vice, and rude to his monitors; [who lends] himself to the seductions of his time of life, instead of resisting the impulses of nature."[40] Gerald later sounded a different note, dedicating *The History of the Conquest of Ireland* to John and celebrating his fecundity: "It has pleased God and your good fortune to send you several sons, both natural and legitimate, and you may have more hereafter."[41] John receives no rebuke for his "natural," which is to say illegitimate, offspring, in a clear sign that Gerald now overlooks transgressions that he might have censured under other circumstances. From these examples it is clear that Bale employed the chronicles to justify his portrayal of King John and simply overlooked information unsympathetic to his cause, particularly those facts that would complicate his portrayal of the king's erotic virtue.

Bale's historiographical efforts are further troubled by his debts to the allegory tradition, in that several characters of *King Johan* are dual figures representing both allegorical and historical figures: Sedicyon is also recognized as Stephen Langton, the Archbishop of Canterbury; Usurpid Powre represents the pope symbolically, while also representing the historic Innocent III; and Privat Welth symbolizes Cardinal Pandolphus. Moreover, while allegories are frequently unmoored from history, occurring in an "any time" appropriate for the consideration of moral issues, the imaginary events of *King Johan* can be dated to approximately 1208, the year that Innocent III placed England under interdict. At the very least, Sedicyon declares, "Fyrst, to begynne with we shall interdyte the land" (*KJ*, 1205). In addition to these dual levels of history and allegory, Bale introduces what we might term *political typology* into his plays, identifying English kings as fulfilling the same roles as figures from the Christian Old Testament did. For example, the audience learns that "thys noble kynge Johan as a faythfull Moyses / Withstode proude Pharao for hys poore Israel" (*KJ*, 1107–8). Likewise, Johan's father, Henry II, is likened to Joshua – "that duke Josue whych was our late kynge Henrye" – and is praised because he "clerely brought us in to the lande of mylke and honye" (*KJ*, 1112–13). Such political typology in *King Johan* coincides with Bale's wider efforts in the Reformation, as evident in his typological figuration of Henry VIII in *The Examination of Lord Cobham*: "King Henry the eighth, now living, after the most godly example of king Josias visited the temples of his realm, he perceived the sinful shrine of this Becket to be unto his people a most pernicious evil, and therefore in the word of the Lord he utterly among other destroyed it."[42] Josiah, the reforming king as depicted in 2 Kings 22–3 and 2 Chronicles 34–5, serves as an apt figure for Bale to employ, given the interest of both kings in quashing idolatry. The connection between Henry VIII and Josiah is also affirmed in *Thre Lawes of Nature, Moses, and Christ* when Moseh Lex affirms, "Who hath restored these same thre lawes agayne / But your late Josias and valeaunt Kynge Henrye?" (*ThrL*, 2021–2). Throughout Bale's corpus and particularly in his interludes, the intersections of allegory, history, and political typology illustrate his attempts to delineate sharply between his protagonists and antagonists, but these sharp divisions ironically admit queer subversions of the moral figures he intends to uphold.

As much as *King Johan* foregrounds Bale's interest in the tension between a corrupt clergy and an honourable monarch who defends his land and faith from its assaults, this storyline is doubled by an erotic biography that must queerly reimagine the meaning of royal sexuality. For instance, Bale details King John's lineage in both historical and allegorical terms, with Johan citing his line of descent: "My granfather was an emperowre excelent, / My fathere a kyng by successyon lyneall, / A kyng my brother lyke as to hym ded fall – / Rychard Curdelyon they callyd hym in Fraunce" (10–14). From these lines the audience is reminded of John's royal stock, including his grandfather, Henry V, the Holy Roman Emperor; his father, Henry II, the English king; and his legendary brother, Richard the Lionheart. Notably, these men's formidable wives are not mentioned as part of John's ancestry, including Henry V's wife Matilda, who controlled England for several months in

1141 during the Anarchy; and Henry II's wife and John's mother, Eleanor of Aquitaine. On the one hand, such an erasure is to be expected, given both the patriarchal lineages recorded in the Old and New Testaments and the typical topics portrayed in early English drama, particularly the psychomachia's focus on a protagonist tempted by sin and Vice figures but corrected by goodness and Virtues. On the other hand, these omissions complicate the interlude's presentation of Johan by ironically endowing him with an entirely homosocial lineage – much like that of his Catholic antagonists (as discussed previously). The omission of Eleanor of Aquitaine ironically underscores the play's interest in Johan's maternity in its allegorical register, with Englande claiming Johan as her son (*KJ*. 1572), which at least implicitly links Johan to God because Englande declares that her spouse is God (*KJ*, 1572–3; cf. 109). The conjoint offspring of male historical forebears, an allegorical figure of his nation, and of divinity, Johan is envisioned both as the product of human sexual reproduction and as purged of this lineage through the chaste reimagining of the marriage of England and God. In the tension between allegory and history, Bale prioritizes allegorizing King Johan rather than historicizing him, but in withholding the historical facts of the women in his lineage, the playwright misses the opportunity to model the type of procreative heterosexual marriage that would bolster the Reformation's agenda, particularly in its condemnation of Catholic chastity.

With his wives and children excised from this dramatic presentation of his life, and whether he is the scion of human or divine reproduction, Johan stands as a chaste exemplar of monarchy who condemns the sodomitical sins aligned with the Catholic Church. Although *King Johan* is not as overtly concerned with themes of sodomy as is *The Image of Both Churches* or *Thre Lawes of Nature, Moses, and Christ*, the play frequently returns to the issue of the monastic orders and their return to England, thus thematically envisioning the corruption of the land by men tainted by erotic transgressions. As Dissymulacyon predicts, Usurpid Powre "wyll also create the orders monastycall, / Monkes, chanons and fryers with gaye coates and shaven crownes, / And buylde them places to corrupt cyties and townes" (*KJ*, 993–5). Given Bale's invective against the monastic orders, along with Dissymulacyon's warning of their plan to "corrupt" cities and towns, it seems likely that Dissymulacyon foresees a vast range of transgressions arising throughout England – a corruptive infiltration of the land. Other scenes in the play directly refer to the biblical account of Sodom, such as when Cyvyle Order, momentarily accepting Johan's assessment, agrees to avoid the sinful tendencies of the church: "With the wyffe of Loth we wyll not backeward locke / Nor

turne from owre oth, but ever obeye yowre grace" (*KJ*, 522–3). Furthermore, given Bale's interest in the concept of natural law, those characters disparaged as unnatural assume queer inflections. King Johan
denounces Sedicyon for his "un naturall" qualities and as "worse than
a best brutall" (*KJ*, 177–8). Nobylyte, reckoning with the implications of
the unfolding events, muses, "Yt is clene agenst the nature of Nobelyte /
To subdew his kyng with owt Godes autoryte" (*KJ*, 1176–7). Englande
describes the clergy as "bastardes they are, unnaturall by the rood!" (*KJ*,
69), and Veritas states, "All manhode shameth to see your unnaturall
doynge" (*KJ*, 2266). With a sharp swipe, Englande stresses the priesthood's swinish qualities, calling the pope "the bore of Rome" (*KJ*, 75)
and stating that the priesthood "to such bestlynes inclyne" (*KJ*, 78, cf.
107). In Christian iconography, pigs and boars are typically indicative
of lust and anti-Semitism. As Lucia Impelluso documents, swine are frequently illustrated "at the feet of saints, to underscore how the holy person managed to overcome the sin of lust. As a symbol of lust [pigs] may
also appear at the feet of the personification of Chastity, who tramples it
in disdain."[43] Given the sodomitical threats to the land, Johan's asexuality stands as a regal prescriptive to right clerical wrongs. The paper-thin
line between asexuality and chastity, however, ultimately cannot hold,
and so the taint of chastity – a subset of sodomy – inevitably bleeds
upon the virtuous king.

Following this line of reasoning, Johan's chastity undermines his masculinity as the play unfolds, as he aligns himself with feminine models
of forbearance that situate him as the object of homoerotic desire. For
example, in defending himself against Clergy, Johan likens his position
to that of the biblical Susanna:

> Ye speke of defylyng, but ye are corrupted all
> With pestylent doctryne or leven pharesayycall.
> Good [and] faythfull Susan sayd that yt was moche bettere
> To fall in daunger of men than do the gretter,
> As to leve Godes lawe whych ys his word most pure. (*KJ*, 1458–62)

In the apocryphal story of Susanna – included in Daniel 13 of the
Vulgate – two elders lust over the beautiful heroine and threaten to
accuse her of adultery if she does not succumb to their rapacious
desires. At the very least, Susanna's narrative thematizes the abuse of
religious, spiritual, and social laws by the elders designated to protect
and enforce them, and so Johan tacitly allegorizes himself into an object
of queer desire, with Clergye unethically pursuing him in a perversion
of his (and their) duties.

As Johan's chief antagonist, Sedicyon manifests much of the play's sideways engagement with issues of sodomy and homoeroticism. In his first appearance on stage, Sedicyon enters as a Vice figure of the morality play tradition, devilishly declaring, "I wyll tell tales, by Jesus!," to which the pious King Johan responds, "Avoyd, lewde person, for thy wordes are ungodlye" (*KJ*, 43, 45). As is common with Vice figures, Sedicyon introduces bawdy and excremental humour in the play, frequently with fart jokes (*KJ*, 166, cf. 1757) and the occasional scatological threat: "I wyll beshyte yow all yf ye sett me not downe softe" (*KJ*, 804). Such vulgar humour heightens the play's homoerotic themes, such as when Sedicyon says to Privat Welth, "I wold thow haddyst kyst his ars for that is holy" (*KJ*, 893). When Privat Welth wonders how Sedicyon can prove the holiness of one's rear end, the latter replies: "For yt hath an hole evyn fytt for the nose of yow" (*KJ*, 895). The corruption of the Catholic Church is further captured with excremental and bodily images, such as the relics that Sedicyon calls upon for absolution, as part of the play's thematic treatment of the perversion of penance. Sedicyon mentions, among the many relics cited, "a dram of the tord of swete Seynt Barnabe" (*KJ*, 1216), as well as "a scabbe of Saynt Job, a nayle of Adams too, / A maggott of Moyses, with a fart of Saynt Fandigo" (*KJ*, 1221–2). Ironically developing the theme of chastity further, Sedicyon absolves Clergye of his sin and encourages him to reproduce – "Ye are now as clene as that day ye were borne, / And lyke to have increase of chylderne, catell and corne" (*KJ*, 1234–5) – but Cyvyle Order replies, "Chyldryn? He can have non, for he ys not of that loade" (*KJ*, 1236). A corrupt, chaste, and sodomitical clergy cannot reproduce, and within the play's logic Johan himself cannot be shown as either the scion or the progenitor of his historical family.

Bale's depiction of King John on the blurry border between history and allegory destabilizes the monarch's moral authority, a condition all the more ironic in light of the play's introduction of Imperyall Majestie. With this allegorical figure, Bale envisions kingship as transcending the bodies and lives of the men who reigned throughout English history, as Thea Cervone explains: "[Bale] refuses to locate Imperyall Majestie in the body of either King John or Henry VIII and thereby doubly asserts that Imperyall Majestie is timeless, that he exists via the Divine Right of Kings and the Royal Supremacy."[44] In deus ex machina style, Imperyall Majestie appears towards the play's conclusion, declaring the success of Cyvyle Order and the reformed Clergy in their efforts to cleanse the kingdom:

Thus I trust we shall seclude all maner of vyce,
And after we have establyshed our kyngedome

In peace of the Lorde and in hys godly fredome,
We wyll confirme it with wholesom lawes and decrees,
To the full suppressynge of Antichristes vanytees. (*KJ*, 2641–5)

It is a triumphant end for the play, with pro-Reformation sentiments firmly expressed and apparently entrenched throughout the land, but here again the conflict between allegory and history undermines Bale's message, simply for the fact that even the apparently all-powerful figure of Imperyall Majestie lives inside the play's allegorical register but outside of its historical register and thus could never stem the tide of past historical events. In short, even the barest knowledge of history proves Bale's allegory to be a falsehood that strips John's erotic history from his dramatic depiction, recasting a twice-married man of seven children as a chaste figure, despite the inherent contradiction of chastity as a marker of sodomy in anti-Catholic thought.

In the end, Bale's attempts to merge allegory and historiography founder over the issue of England's and King John's apparently blameless sexualities. Indeed, a brief history of John's appearance in theatre and film documents his stock utility as an antagonist, often a villain, of ambiguous sexuality, such as in the legends of Robin Hood, when he inadvertently pursues romance with his mother, Eleanor of Aquitaine, who is disguised as Marian, in Anthony Munday's *Downfall of Robert, Earle of Huntington*.[45] In George Peele's *Troublesome Reign of John, King of England* (c. 1589), he is frequently overshadowed by his mother, asking for her advice – "Mother, what shall I do?" (1.4.163) – and being chided by her – "Son John, follow this motion, as thou lovest thy mother" (1.4.99), and other characters deride him as "Eleanor's damnèd brat" (1.4.214, cf. 1.10.30).[46] In William Shakespeare's *Life and Death of King John*, Eleanor similarly dwarfs her son in key scenes, such as when she declares, "I am a soldier, and now bound to France" (1.1.150); when John frets over her absence, "Where is my mother's care?" (4.2.117); and when he fails to cut an impressive figure in battle, complaining of his sickness rather than dispatching his foes (5.3.3–4, 5.3.16–17).[47] King Philip describes his friendship with John in homosocial flourishes that echo marriage rituals, declaring, "This royal hand and mine are newly knit, / And the conjunction of our inward souls / Married in league, coupled, and link'd together / With all religious strength of sacred vows" (3.1.226–9), which ironically highlights the absence of John's wife in the play. Bounding several centuries ahead, in James Goldman's *Lion in Winter*, Eleanor favours Richard over John in their battles of succession, dismissing John as "wee Johnny" and infantilizing him: "Johnny, you're so clean and neat. Henry takes good care of you." Richard dismisses him as a "walking pustule," and John, while conspiring to kill his father, whimpers, "You kill him; I'll watch."[48] Or consider Peter Ustinov's simpering vocal performance as John in the animated Disney film *Robin Hood* (1973), in which the character's queerness registers even in the purportedly child-friendly fare of the Disney catalogue. In Bale's presentation of a perfectly chaste king, we see the unlikely beginnings of his queer trajectory through dramatic and then cinematic culture, demonstrating the ways in which staging history, while raging against sodomy and chastity, can introduce unexpected erotic undercurrents into one's work.

Chapter Six

Camp and the Hermaphroditic Gaze in Sir David Lyndsay's *Ane Satyre of the Thrie Estaitis*

As is apparent to even the most distracted of its audience members, Sir David Lyndsay's mid-sixteenth-century *Ane Satyre of the Thrie Estaitis* revels in carnivalesque and crude humour.[1] With lines such as "Thow hes ane cunt lyke ane quaw-myre [quagmire]" (835) and "Bischops ar blist [blessed], howbeit that thay be waryit [cursed], / For thay may fuck thair fill and be unmaryit [unmarried]!" (1370–1), its humour is broad, vulgar, and farcical.[2] Moreover, its characters acknowledge the play's crudity, such as when Diligence, in his closing lines, summarizes its offensiveness: "Becaus we have bene sum part tedious, / With mater rude, denude of eloquence, / Likewyse, perchance, to sum men odious" (4653–5). Such vulgarity bears obvious debts to the riotous traditions of medieval carnivals, yet Lyndsay's obscene humour also exploits the humorous performative possibilities of drama, as he pays close attention to the metadramatic staging of his characters' bodies and the drag genders that his actors must perform. In many ways Lyndsay's play can be understood as both a descendant of the medieval carnivalesque and as an early-modern precursor to camp, because several actors are called on to highlight the disjunction between their male bodies and their female roles, particularly by emphasizing the contrasting genitalia expected of each. By compelling his audience members to question their gazes, to continually confront the simultaneity of male actors and female characters demanded by early Scottish theatre, Lyndsay creates a corporeal allegory that corrupts any pretension of erotic coherency and fosters in viewers a hermaphroditic gaze that must continually question the genders performed.

Writing during the years of the Scottish Reformation, Lyndsay assumes notably different tones as a poet and as a playwright. His poems address many of the same themes as does *Ane Satyre of the Thrie Estaitis*, yet the sharp modification in voice – from sincere yet restrained condemnation in the former to riotous and vulgar humour in the latter – highlights the ways in which he took advantage of emergent stage conventions to reconfigure its gendered traditions. Certainly, *Ane Satyre of the Thrie Estaitis* defies simple generic categorization. It adheres to British traditions of medieval allegory and the carnivalesque, but it simultaneously transcends these sources, particularly in light of the play's debts to continental traditions. Anna Mill identifies strong French influences on its structure, viewing it as a "morality-farce-*sottie*," in which the play's part 1 consists of "a complete morality of the temptation and repentance of a human soul," which is followed by "the farce-interlude of the Pardoner and the Pauper"; part 2, she proposes, "is really a *sottie* in which the fools disguised as Spirituality are on trial."[3] As the descendant of dramatic traditions on both sides of the English Channel, *Ane Satyre of the Thrie Estaitis* stands as a sui generis work, a rare surviving work of early Scots drama and one that bridges disparate Western performative traditions.

The first section of this chapter places Lyndsay's poetry and *Ane Satyre of the Thrie Estaitis* within the cultural context of the Scottish Reformation, highlighting their shared themes in addressing a variety of contemporary concerns related to religion and sexuality. The second section explores the challenges of corporealizing allegory on the stage, in the performative obstacles of bringing abstract concepts to life, and demonstrates how Lyndsay often relies on conceptually carnivalesque humour to depict the female body and its riotous exess. In its third section, this chapter analyses the ways in which, through its excessive and riotous humour and its exaggerated display of gender's constructed nature, *Ane Satyre of the Thrie Estaitis* simultaneously evolves and devolves into spectacle, unmooring the satire from its foundational ethical seriousness into the apolitical realm of camp. Camp humour, which exaggerates the performance of gender to undo its cultural hegemony, frequently focuses on the superficiality of façades, and this strategy demands that the audience see both male and female simultaneously in order to demolish gender's cultural weight. As Susan Sontag muses in her classic essay "Notes on 'Camp,'" "Camp is the triumph of the epicene style. (The convertibility of 'man' and 'woman,' 'person' and 'thing.') But all style, that is, artifice, is ultimately epicene."[4] Furthermore, in its exuberant condemnation of and staging of sexual sin, Lyndsay's satire fractures the frame of the theatrical experience and implicates the viewers as one of its key targets through his creation of their hermaphroditic gaze. A camp reading of *Ane Satyre of the Thrie Estaitis*, one that accentuates the ways in which Lyndsay builds an allegory thematizing the hidden truths of his actors' bodies, illuminates the play's investment in infusing dramatic protocols with a parodically embodied sensibility, with its political message of reform curiously irrelevant to its deeper theatrical interests.

The Sexual Politics of the Scottish Reformation

Sir David Lyndsay was born circa 1486, and evidence, circumstantial yet compelling, suggests that he attended St. Salvator's College of the University of St. Andrews.[5] Throughout his adult years he lived among Scotland's aristocratic elite, acting as a courtier in the royal household and employed in various occupations therein, including an early position as "ischar [usher, doorkeeper] to the Prince."[6] Administrative documents record that Lyndsay complemented his courtly duties with his theatrical pastimes, as evident in a 1511 expenditure for "ij½ elnis blew taffatis and vj quartaris yallow taffatis to be ane play coit to David Lindesay for the play playt in the King and Quenis presence in the Abbay."[7] Lyndsay's poems likewise attest to the union of his courtly career with his literary pursuits, such as when he recounts, in *The Dreme of Schir David Lyndesay*, his experiences playing with the young king James V: "Sumtyme, in dansing, feiralie [nimbly] I flang [leapt]; / And, sumtyme, playand fairsis [farces, short plays] on the flure [floor]" (12–13).[8] His poetic career flourished in the 1520s and 1530s, a period during which he produced such major works as *The Dreme of Schir David Lyndesay*, *The Complaynt of Schir David Lindesay*, and *The Testament and Complaynt of Our Soverane Lordis Papyngo*. By 1530 Lyndsay had become a court herald,[9] and he undertook a series of diplomatic missions in the 1530s and early 1540s to negotiate trade agreements and to find an appropriate queen for James V.[10] Lyndsay wrote *Ane Satyre of the Thrie Estaitis* in the early 1540s, and it was performed publicly at least twice in his lifetime: in Cupar on 7 June 1552, and in Edinburgh on 12 August 1554.[11] As his poems contain autobiographical elements that illuminate the contours of his courtly career, so too does *Ane Satyre of the Thrie Estaitis* carry light touches of historical allegory. John MacQueen notes that King Humanitie likely represents James V; Lady Sensualitie "is to some degree a satiric portrait of the king's divorced mistress, Margaret Erskine, Lady Lochleven, by whom he had a son, the future Regent Moray, in 1531"; and Lyndsay appears to have cast himself in the role of Diligence.[12] A poet and a playwright whose work documents his avocational and vocational pursuits and the political and religious issues of his day, Lyndsay died circa 1555.

As an artist of the Reformation, Lyndsay grappled with the social and spiritual shifts of his day, and he treats several related religious themes both in his poetry and in *Ane Satyre of the Thrie Estaitis*. For example, Lyndsay endorses the translation of the Christian Bible in *Ane Dialog betwixt Experience and ane Courteour, Off the Miserabyll Estait of the World*, stating "Thocht euery Commoun may nocht be one Clerk, / Nor hes no Leid [language] except thare toung maternall, / Quhy suld of god the maruellous heuinly werk / Be hid frome thame?" (552–5). In *Ane Satyre of the Thrie Estaitis*, Flatterie righteously condemns the translation of the New Testament – "this is the New Testament, / In Englisch toung, and prentit in England! / Herisie, herisie!" (1153–5) – yet the character's allegorical register condemns his words as misguided. In another such point of congruency, *The Dreme of Schir David Lyndesay* features as one of its subplots "The Complaynt of the Comovn Weill of Scotland" (918–1036), which recounts such moments as Comoun Weill seeking refuge from Law and lamenting that "Liberalitie and Lawte, boith, ar loste" (989), and that "knychtlie curage, turnit in brag and boste" (991); these moments are echoed in Common Weill's appearances in *Ane Satyre of the Thrie Estaitis*. Allegorical battles between Sensuality and Chastity appear in many of Lyndsay's works: in *The Dreme of Schir David Lyndesay*, "Sensuale plesour hes baneist Chaistitie" (983), and in *The Complaynt of Schir David Lindesay*, the "lusty lady Chaistitie / Hes baneist Sensualitie" (391–2). Lyndsay depicts another such battle between this virtue and this vice in *The Testament of the Papyngo* (864–954), and in *Ane Satyre of the Thrie Estaitis*. *The Complaynt of Schir David Lindesay* features such allegorical figures as Dissimulance ("Dissimulance dar nocht schaw hir face" [399]) and Foly ("Foly is fled out of the toun" [401]), with these actions mirrored in his dramatic masterpiece.[13]

Further evident from both his poetry and *Ane Satyre of the Thrie Estaitis* is that Lyndsay supported the goals of the Reformation primarily from a monarchist viewpoint. As David Reid explains, "In Lindsay the supernatural kingship of Christ is not a charter to reform the country ... It is rather a charter for the king to reform the clergy."[14] In *The Tragedie of the Cardinall*, Lyndsay ventriloquizes the spirit of David Beaton, the last Scottish cardinal before the Reformation, who was murdered by reformers in 1546. Beaton admits his political errors – "I causit all that trybulatioun" (110) – and in the section of the poem addressed "To the Prelatis" he advises his fellow clergymen to mend their ways: "My deir brether, do nocht as ʒe war wount; / Amend ʒour lyfe now, quhill ʒour day Induris" (302–3). Lyndsay similarly encodes pro-Reformation sentiments in *Ane Satyre of the Thrie Estaitis* when Dissait frets, "Brother, heir ye yon proclamatioun? / I dreid full sair of reformatioun" (1516–17), expressing his unease over impending religious reforms. In complementary contrast, Pauper desires the realm's rehabilitation: "War I ane

king, be Coks deir passioun, / I sould richt sone mak reformatioun!"
(2961–2). Gude Counsall perceives the king's role in reforming the land:
"My worthy Lords, sen ye have taine on hand / Sum reformatioun to
mak into this land, / And als ye knaw it is the King[s] mynd, / Quha till
the Common-weill hes ay bene kynd" (2556–9). As Sarah Carpenter proposes of his politics, Lyndsay "is clearly not a writer committed to the
Reformation; he advocates change from within rather than a rejection of
the system itself"; she further comments, "Lindsay does not see the spiritual as separate from the political, and his solutions for both the king
and the government look to God."[15] Carol Edington, reading a variety
of Lyndsay's works, declares that "he articulates a basically humanist
critique of the sixteenth-century Church, railing at abuses but accepting the essential tenets of the Catholic faith."[16] Drawing firm conclusions about Lyndsay's religious beliefs nonetheless remains challenging,
and Kevin McGinley rightly cautions that it would be "overly simplistic
to align Lyndsay neatly with either Reform Catholicism or evangelical
Protestantism."[17] As did many other writers of this era, Lyndsay criticized corrupt practices of the Catholic clergy and endorsed the necessity
of reform, even if he remained ambiguous in his writings about whether
such reform should be achieved through a clean break with the church.

Lyndsay's critique of the Catholic Church, both in his poetry and in
Ane Satyre of the Thrie Estaitis, focuses frequently on issues of sexual
impropriety, and many of his satirical jabs at eroticism are framed to
improve Scottish society morally while not directly advocating the
Protestant cause. As R. James Goldstein notes, "From his earliest court
poetry to the three major works of his final years, Lindsay is conspicu-
ously preoccupied by proper definitions of gender and the regulation of
sexual desire."[18] Along these lines, Lyndsay evinces an abiding thematic
interest in moral probity, such as in *The Dreme of Schir David Lyndesay*,
his Scottish variation on the themes and structure of Dante's *Divine
Comedy*, in which he contemplates the consequences of regal sexual
immoderation and proposes an appropriate solution:

Als, I beseik thy Maiestie serene,
Frome Lychorie thow keip thy body clene:
Taist neuer that Intoxicat poysoun:
Frome that vnhappy sensuall syn abstene,
Tyll that thow get ane lusty, plesand Quene. (1091–5)

In advocating a viable solution to the problem of monarchical sexual
transgression, Lyndsay identifies erotic practices as a source of concern
for the Scottish people and attempts to instigate reform from the top of

the social order. Here Lyndsay's advice alludes to the medieval concept of marital chastity, and contemporary Scottish theologians such as John Hamilton, the Archbishop of St. Andrews, advocated various enactments of chastity to counteract the rampant immorality they believed to be sullying the land. Hamilton outlines the "thre degreis" of chastity, urging parishioners married and unmarried to cleave to this virtue:

> Now thairfor ye sall understand that thair is thre degreis of chastitie. The first is kepit amang gud maryit men and wemen that leivis ane chast lyfe in the stait of matrimonie, kepand thame self alwais within the bondis of that sacrament ... The secund degre of chastite is mair perfit than the first, and is kepit amang thame that levis ane chast lyfe in the stait of wedohede ... The thrid degre of chastitie is mair perfit than the first and secund, and is kepit amang thame quhilk liffis ane chast lyfe in the stait of virginitie.[19]

For Hamilton, chastity will reform a fallen Scottish society, one whose moral failings cross boundaries of class, gender, and social status.

In line with Hamilton's thesis and applying it to the priesthood, Lyndsay advocates marital chastity frequently in his poetry, yet given the comic vulgarity of so much of *Ane Satyre of the Thrie Estaitis*, it is striking that many of these passages addressing sexuality are rather restrained and seem tonally aligned with his poems. In an early scene of the play Wantonnes denies that lechery should be considered sinful, citing the Catholic Church to bolster his claims:

> Beleive ye, Sir, that lecherie be sin?
> Na, trow nocht that! This is my ressoun quhy:
> First at the Romane [court] will ye begin,
> Quhilk is the lemand [shining] lamp of lechery,
> Quhair Cardinals and Bischops generally
> To luif ladies thay think ane pleasand sport,
> And out of Rome hes baneist [banished] Chastity,
> Quha with our Prelats can get na resort. (235–42)

Rome stands as the "lemand lamp of lechery," but the passage refrains from any crude imagery and instead concentrates on Chastitie's banishment. Later in the play Divine Correctioun proposes that the curative for excessive sexuality is marital chastity, again stressing Chastitie's role in proper sexuality:

> Sen ye are quyte of Sensualitie,
> Resave into your service Gude Counsall,

And richt sa this fair Ladie Chastitie,
Till ye mary sum queene of blude royall:
Observe then chastitie matrimoniall. (1753–7)

Following the rejection of Sensualitie, Chastitie is embraced, both before and after marriage. As the play closes, Divine Correctioun announces the "nobill Act[i]s of our Parliament" (3819), and in the fourteenth of the fifteen acts proposed to reform Scottish society Lyndsay endorses marital celibacy for priests: "We grant them licence and frie libertie / That thay may have fair virgins to thair wyfis, / And sa keip matrimoniall chastitie, / And nocht in huirdome [whoredom] for to leid thair lyfis" (3954–7). One of the play's chief themes as embodied in this character, Chastitie guides the drama from its central conflict to its resolution, with sexually sinful characters harassing virtuous ones until order is restored in its conclusion.

As the proponents and detractors of the Scottish Reformation discussed the virtues of chastity, so too did they ponder the moral consequences of sodomy – a particularly wide-ranging and amorphous cluster of sexual transgressions throughout the Reformation.[20] Hamilton addresses sodomy several times in his catechism, linking the biblical story of Sodom and Gomorrah to a range of other sins. He berates it as the "abhominabil unclennes of lichorie [lechery]" and as "the syn of the flesche abhominabil and nocht to be spokin," which he further associates with people's "pryde, thair gluttony and thair ydilnes."[21] In a similar fashion, Lyndsay condemns sodomy repeatedly, yet briefly, and then passes on to other topics, such as in the following lines from Ane Dialog betuix Experience and ane Courteour: "For that self Syn of Sodomye, / And most abhominabyll bewgrye [buggery], / That vyce at lenth for tyll declare / I thynk it is nocht necessare" (3472–5). This poem's speaker mentions as well "this foule Syn of Sodomye" (3526, cf. 5812–17) and envisions "ane systerne [cistern] full of Sodomye" but refrains from speculating over the topic in greater detail: "Quhose vyce in speciall gyf I wald declair, / It wer aneuch for tyll perturbe the air" (4950–2). Likewise in Ane Satyre of the Thrie Estaitis, Lyndsay addresses sodomy in passing, such as in Divine Correctioun's account of the biblical story of Sodom and Gomorrah:

Remember how, into the tyme of Noy,
For the foull stinck and sin of lechery
God be my wande did al the warld destroy:
Sodome and Gomore richt sa full rigorously
For that vyld sin war brunt maist cruelly. (1709–13)

As these excerpts collectively suggest, Lyndsay's treatment of sexual transgressions and sodomy is restrained in his poetry, with such restraint also apparent in numerous scenes of *Ane Satyre of the Thrie Estaitis*. He acknowledges sin and condemns it but resists vituperation and contumely, instead urging individuals to concede their moral failings and to rehabilitate themselves. Much of Lyndsay's humour in *Ane Satyre of the Thrie Estaitis* depicts male characters envisioning, rather than enacting, carnivalesquely riotous female bodies, and so these moments remain abstract, although they simultaneously point to the riotous camp excess elsewhere in his masterwork.

Corporeal Allegory and Conceptually Carnivalesque Women

Embodiment plays a key role in most dramatic experiences, in that the actors corporealize a playwright's characters and perform the actions assigned to them. Such a foundational aspect of the theatre, often overlooked or simply assumed, calls into question the ways in which actors undertake the challenge of adapting their bodies to perform a play in congruence with the playwright's, the director's, and their own visions. As Collette Conroy perceptively avers, "In theatre bodies have to both exist and not exist," suggesting as well that such theatrical bodies "seem to have shifting boundaries."[22] Actors must adjust their bodies to fit the abstraction of a character on a page, and so the actor's body must exist while simultaneously cloaking its existence and inhabiting a fictional construction; in so doing, it continually builds and demolishes the boundaries between these two performative poles. Beyond the fundamental issue of embodying characters, actors must also engender their roles, as they are called upon to inhabit genders not wholly parallel to their own, even when male actors play male roles and female actors play female roles. Within a given performance, the gender that actors perform will frequently metamorphose, in line with the play's plot and its characters' narrative arcs, and these transformations register on the actors' bodies.

Certainly, the gendered body is malleable in *Ane Satyre of the Thrie Estaitis*, as one of its key plot lines involves the effeminizing and subsequent masculinizing of Rex Humanitas. After he performs his opening lines, the stage directions indicate, "*Heir sall the King pass to royall sait and sit with ane grave countenance till Wantones cum*" (following line 101), and he declares his intention to model proper regal morality for his people: "Considering ye knaw that my intent / Is for till be to God obedient, / Quhilk dois forbid men to be lecherous" (217–19). Identified as a virgin by Wantonnes ("For quhy, yon king ... / Kennis [knows] na mair of ane cunt / Nor dois the noveis [novice] of ane freir" [461–3]),[23] the upstanding monarch devolves into a bumbling lover, admitting his erotic naïveté: "Quhat sall I do, quhen sho cums heir? / For I knaw nocht the craft perqueir [by heart, thoroughly] / Of luifers gyn [stratagems]" (484–6). Rex Humanitas succumbs to the pleasures of erotic transgression, and his masculinity alters as a result, with Persone observing: "Ye se the King is yit effeminate / And gydit be Dame Sensualitie" (1121–2). From these passages it is apparent that Lyndsay envisions a transformation in Rex Humanitas's gendered performance, from regal monarch to sexual naïf and feminized sinner and then back to masculine ruler of the people, and that the male actor playing the role must register these gendered shifts by suitably embodying them in performance.

As much as a play's performance requires its characters and their genders to be corporealized, bodies can also be introduced as thematic elements without the necessity of performance. Through dialogue, description, and exposition, playwrights in numerous instances call their audiences to envision the human body, allowing it to remain an imaginary abstraction rather than a dramatic embodiment, and much of Lyndsay's gendered satire is more conceptually carnivalesque than performatively camp (as discussed in the following section). As a genre, allegory is predicated upon such an emphasis on the abstract and the conceptual, as Joanne Spencer Kantrowitz argues in her reading of *Ane Satyre of the Thrie Estaitis*: "In this very special world [of allegorical theatre] ... [t]he narrator's interest is not in the character of these figures, but in their *qualities*, since they are what they represent: concepts."[24] Lyndsay imbues many of these characters with the satirical humour of inversion and erotic excess, such as when Spiritualitie admits his predilection for prostitutes – "Howbeit I dar nocht plainlie spouse ane wyfe, / Yit concubeins I have had four or fyfe" – and also mentions his many children born from these liaisons: "And to my sons I have givin rich rewairds, / And all my dochters maryit upon lairds" (3387–90). The Abbot similarly boasts, "My paramours is baith als fat and fair / As ony wench into the toun of Air" (3433–4), and he then details his care for his illicit progeny (3435–8). In these and other such passages the audience is invited to envision, but not to witness, the sexual transgressions of religious men.

Further along these lines, male characters describe women's bodies in conceptually carnivalesque terms in several of the most riotous passages of *Ane Satyre of the Thrie Estaitis*. Even before the play begins, its "Proclamatioun Maid in Cowpar of Fyffe" envisions female audience members as excessively leaky: "And ye ladyis, that hes na skent [scarcity, dearth] of leddir [genitalia, pudenda], / Or ye cum thair faill nocht to teme [empty] your bleddir; / I dreid, or we haif had done with our wark, / That some of yow sall mak ane richt wait [wet] sark [under-shirt]!" (274–7). In an extended vulgar passage towards the play's conclusion, Foly exponentially multiplies such crude humour and catalogues the female body's explosive excrementality:

Allace, I trow scho be forfairne [undone, near death]:
Scho sobbit and scho fell in sown,
And then thay rubbit hir up and doun;
Scho riftit [belched], routit [belched, *or* bellowed] and made sic stends [leaps];
Scho yeild and gaid at baith the ends
Till scho had castin ane cuppill of quarts,
Syne all turnit to ane rickill [succession, stream] of farts;
Scho blubert [blubbered], bockit [belched] and braikit [farted] still,
Hir arsse gaid even lyke ane wind-mill;
Scho stumblit and stutterit with sic stends
That scho recantit at baith the ends;
Sik dismell drogs [excrement] fra hir scho schot
Quhill scho maid all the fluir on flot;
Of hir hurdies [buttocks] scho had na hauld
Quhill scho had tumed [emptied] her monyfauld [many times]! (4379–93)

Carnivalesque visions of the female body spark much of the outrageous humour of *Ane Satyre of the Thrie Estaitis*, yet because these images are reported yet not enacted, imagined yet not embodied, they lack a performative dimension that could effectively heighten their gendered humour. Allowing an actor to corporealize such an explosively excremental female body would present technical challenges to this very day, but Lyndsay's attention to it highlights its comic possibilities, while still remaining unable to exploit the campy disjunction between male actors and female roles for even more riotous effect.

Similarly evoking the play's conceptual delineation of female bodies, Lyndsay's characters often describe female sexuality as unconstrained when it must nonetheless remain unembodied in performance. Falset reports, "My wyfe, with preists scho [did] me greit onricht, / And maid me nine tymes cuckald on ane nicht" (4268–9); with this exaggerated vision of female sexuality, he conceives of women as erotically voracious, if not insatiable. Sounding a similar note, Solace recounts his mother's promiscuity:

Thay callit my mother Bonie Besse,
That dwelte betwene the Bowis.

Of twelf yeir auld sho learnit to swyfe,
Thankit be the great God on lyve!
Scho maid me fatheris four or five;
. . . .
Scho is baith wyse, worthie and wicht [robust, bold],
For scho spairis nouther kuik [cook] nor knycht:
Yea, four and twentie on ane nicht,
And ay thair eyne scho bleirit [bleared]. (160–4, 170–3)

Bonie Besse's erotic history – fornicating at twelve years, marrying four
or five men in quick succession, copulating with twenty-four men in
a given evening – testifies to the comically obscene vision of female
sexuality central to *Ane Satyre of the Thrie Estaitis*. Privileging narration
over performance in this and other such scenes, Lindsay at times aligns
his play more with the fabliau tradition of medieval narrative than with
the performative traditions of medieval farce. When it is described, the
female body remains conceptual and abstract, even in the comic excess
of such abstraction, whereas when it is performed, the female body
must become embodied and thus attain a contrasting level of signification. As Janet Hadley Williams notes, various scholars have criticized
Lyndsay for his apparent "contempt of women"; she counter-argues
that, although Lyndsay "was conservative in his attitudes," he was
"also aware that female agency and perspectives were valid in a variety
of contexts and would well serve his themes."[25] The contrast between
women as conceptual images (that is, the ways in which male characters talk about women) and women as embodied characters (the ways
in which male actors perform as female characters) highlights Lyndsay's use of women to advance his reformational and comic themes,
yet in both formulations women are notably absent. In moving from
poetic page to dramatic stage, the embodied nature of performance
facilitates mild critiques of sexual vice to metamorphose into riotous
acts of camp excess. Camp unleashes the humour of the actor's performances in ways beyond the standard vulgarity of the carnivalesque
and the fabliau because this queer brand of humour focuses fixedly on
the secrets purportedly hidden by costumes and the necessity for the
audience members to question their gaze.

Camp and the Hermaphroditic Gaze

In recognizing these points about women's conceptual presence but
embodied absence in many scenes of *Ane Satyre of the Thrie Estaitis*, one
must also acknowledge that most medieval and early modern plays do

not stress the disjunction between their actors and the gendered characters they perform, presuming instead that the audience will suspend its disbelief and accept the dramatic unreality of the ostensible congruence between the actor and his role. Early British plays with female parts in their casts of characters must confront the dramatic challenges of men corporealizing female roles, and the degree to which they cloak or emphasize the discrepancy between actor and role bears the likely potential of de-escalating or escalating their humour. Certainly, for a work of the late medieval and early Renaissance era, *Ane Satyre of the Thrie Estaitis* features an extraordinarily large number of female characters, including Sensualitie, Hamelines, Danger, Fund-Jonet, Veritie, Priores, Abbasse, Chastitie, Jennie (the Taylour's daughter), Taylours Wyfe, Sowtars Wyfe, and Foly's daughter Glaiks, as well as the Cotters Wyfe and Bessie in the play's proclamation, with this fact alone escalating its camp potential. More female roles require more male actors to play them, each of whom could then exploit the humour of the disjunction between his body and his character. Males of a variety of ages, ranging from boys to adolescents to men, would play female roles, and adolescent males, with higher voices and less-developed frames, would be better suited to play leading female roles of younger women. Richard Rastall states of the myriad challenges of embodying and engendering performance during this era: "The first possibility is to face the real problem and make an effort to overcome the expression of his masculinity as best he can, persuading us by vocal manipulation and other means that he is not really a male … The actor's alternative is to use his masculinity for positive ends, playing the role as a deliberately transvestite performance in which the masculinity is at comic odds with the stated background femininity."[26] In many instances throughout *Ane Satyre of the Thrie Estaitis*, Lyndsay embraces the second of Rastall's options, devising his drama to exploit rather than subdue the humour of men performing female roles.

This key distinction between *Ane Satyre of the Thrie Estaitis* as either an abstract or a corporeal allegory highlights the transition in its comic registers: the grotesquely carnivalesque depictions of women remain in the abstract, as the audience members must envision them for themselves, whereas the embodied depictions of female characters allow the play's camp humour to flourish. To look at one such example, Lyndsay's depiction of Fund-Jonet obscures her gender, as she straddles the borders between masculine and feminine. Danger invites her to sing, and Fund-Jonet replies:

Sister, howbeit that I am hais [hoarse],
I am content to beir a bais [bass].

Ye twa sould luif mee as your lyfe:
You knaw I [leird] [taught] yow baith to swyfe [fuck]
In my chalmer, ye wait [watched] weill qhuair. (315–19)

With her bass voice, Fund-Jonet unsettles typical expectations of gendered performance. Although she ascribes her pitch to her hoarse throat,
hoarseness typically renders one's voice huskier than notably deeper, and
as Roderick Lyall explains of her gendered instability, "Fund-Jonet (literally 'foundling Janet') has proved something of a problem to editors.
[Douglas] Hamer suggests, presumably because the character takes the
bass part and has instructed the ladies in sexual matters, that Fund-Jonet
must be male; Jonet, however, is unmistakably a female name, and there
really was a woman known by this nickname at the court of Mary of Guise
in 1544–45."[27] Garrett P.J. Epp proposes that Fund-Jonet "allows a dual
reading: the old crone who teaches younger women how to gain sovereignty over men; and the over-sexualised, effeminate man, who hands his
sovereignty over to women in his pursuit of sexual experience."[28] Lyndsay does not describe Fund-Jonet's physical characteristics, and so any
conjecture concerning her appearance – whether she be young, middle
aged, or old; feminine, effeminate, or masculine – must be extrapolated
from the text. All we can be sure of is that the character bears a female
name but is performed by a male, but by stressing her bass voice, Lyndsay
introduces a deeper level of gender ambiguity than the character would
otherwise impart. The key crux for interpreting this scene centres on the
actor's intonation of the bass voice: does he pitch his lines to suggest a
woman's hoarse throat (to minimize the gender difference between male
actor and female role) or to suggest a man's bass coming from a woman's
mouth (to maximize the gender difference for comic effect)? The lower the
bass, the more humorous the performance, and in this play that revels in
comic excess it appears congruent with Lyndsay's objectives to opt for the
more humorous theatrical mode, particularly as it would then deepen the
humour of Rex Humanitas's erotic interest being piqued by Fund-Jonet's
song: "Up, Wantonnes! Thow sleipis to lang! / Me thocht I hard ane mirrie
sang" (327–8). Moreover, Fund-Jonet's bass contrasts with Solace's treble –
"I have sic plesour at my hart / That garris me sing the [tribill] pairt," he
proclaims (146–7) – and these characters jointly indicate Lyndsay's staging of the camp humour available from female and male characters who
sound as if they were male and female characters respectively.

If this perspective is granted, that the performers of *Ane Satyre of the
Thrie Estaitis* in the past (as well as in modern day) should exaggerate
and lean into its gender-bending comedy, its camp foundations come into
sharper focus. Certainly, as Wayne R. Dynes posits, camp is an inherently

performative mode: "Camp is not grounded in speech or writing as much as it is in gesture, performance, and public display. When it is verbal, it is expressed less through the discursive means of direct statement than through implication, innuendo, and intonation."[29] The line between a comic play and a camp one is often ambiguous, but in each instance a campy performance should enhance any latent humour of the characters' dialogue to exaggerate its parodic play with embodied gender. Moreover, the camp elements in *Ane Satyre of the Thrie Estaitis* signal the ways in which medieval dramatic practices metamorphosed, and thus to posit a teetering between the carnivalesque and campiness is simply to recognize that, as cultural modes age, they invite subsequent artists to refurbish and revitalize their tropes. As Andrew Ross explains, "The camp effect, then, is created not simply by a change in the mode of cultural production (and the contradictions attendant on that change), but rather when the products ... of a much earlier mode of production, which has lost its power to produce and dominate cultural meanings, become available, in the present, for redefinition according to contemporary codes of taste."[30] Within the mores of early British drama the medieval carnivalesque, notwithstanding its raucous and delightfully obscene humour, was growing over-familiar, and camp infused its codes with a necessary update for a new age. Greg Walker proposes that Lyndsay seems to chafe against the restrictions of allegorical form throughout *Ane Satyre of the Thrie Estaitis* and sought ways to invigorate this tradition: "it is as if Lyndsay were trying to find ... a new grammar and architecture for political drama, one that would draw from, but finally transcend the mechanisms of personification allegory and moral counsel." He concludes further that the allegorical form might provoke "frustrations ... in a playwright wishing to do something more than chart a familiar didactic course."[31] In many ways the play's didactic and reformatory aims are overshadowed by its innovations of allegory and dramatic form, which exploit the conceptual humour of the carnivalesque to advance its comedy into enacted camp.

Although the term *drag queen* is anachronistic for considering the staging of sixteenth-century Scottish drama – as are such terms as *homosexual*, *heterosexual*, and *queer* – it captures the gendered excess recognizable as a standard enactment of camp. "In the sense of a concealed nature informing a flagrant appearance, drag is the essence of camp," writes Philip Core, as he also connects this performative mode to medieval practices: "The jokes of drag queens, as well as their pardonable antics in disguise (like those of the mediaeval jester) ... express desires and facts that are socially unacceptable in a format which society has elected to accept as whimsy."[32] In playing such roles as Fund-Jonet, Sensualitie, Taylours Wyfe, and Sowtars Wyfe, Lyndsay's male actors must conceal and reveal their false genders;

they must heighten and exaggerate their façade of femininity for its inherent comic potential. Building on this performative element, the play repeatedly stages the disjunction between characters' exterior appearances and their hidden desires, such as when the Prioress is disrobed: "*Heir sall thay spuilye* [strip, divest] *the Priores and scho sall have ane kirtill [gown] of silk under hir habite*" (following line 3682). The comedy of the scene hinges on the contrast between the Prioress's façade and the revelation of her sexual desires, with the First Sergeant proclaiming of her transformation, "This halie Priores / Is turnit in ane cowclink [courtesan, whore]" (3686). Still, as much as this scene focuses on the Prioress's doubled costume – her habit cloaking a silk gown – it need not necessarily draw the audience's attention to the male actor playing the role, for Dissait, Flattrie, and Falset similarly change their costumes – "*Heir sall they cast away thair conterfit clais*" (following line 1559) – with Gude Counsall soon noting their deception and subsequent arrest (1639–54). In the scenes in which the disjunction between female characters and their male performers is stressed, as will soon be explored, their camp potential would be difficult to quell.

In staging the contrast between male actors and female roles, Lyndsay confronts his audience with the necessity of a hermaphroditic gaze, one that recognizes the confusion of ostensibly rigid gender categories when they are staged through camp modes. It should be noted that the hermaphroditism theorized in this discussion is metaphorical, theatrical, and based on late medieval reception of classical literature; it is not biological, real, and based on current medical and psychological understanding of intersex individuals. In recent parlance the term *hermaphrodite* has fallen out of favour, and *intersex* is now preferred as, according to the Intersex Society of North America, "a general term used for a variety of conditions in which a person is born with a reproductive or sexual anatomy that doesn't seem to fit the typical definitions of female or male."[33] *Hermaphrodite* is thus an archaic term but one that captures the ways in which medieval and early modern commentators theorized individuals, both real and fictional, who corporeally challenged the binary between male and female. Throughout the classical era and the Middle Ages, commentators pondered the meaning of hermaphroditism and the confusion it evoked in those viewing intersex bodies, as evident in Ovid's etiological account in his *Metamorphoses*, in which the water nymph Salmacis desperately loves Hermaphroditus, the son of Hermes and Aphrodite. Hermaphroditus rejects her advances, Salmacis prays to the gods to join them forever, and the gods grant her wish:

velut, si quis conducat cortice ramos,
crescendo iungi pariterque adolescere cernit,

sic ubi conplexu coieruent membra tenaci,
nec duo sunt et forma duplex, nec femina dici
nec puer ut possit, neutrumque et utrumque videntur.

(As when one grafts a twig on some tree, he sees the branches grow one,
and with common life come to maturity, so were these two bodies knit
in close embrace: they were no longer two, nor such as to be called, one,
woman, and one, man. They seemed neither, and yet both.)[34]

Appearing neither male nor female, yet simultaneously male and female,
the hermaphroditic body demands interpretation, for it confuses those
eyes accustomed to clear divisions between the sexes. Augustine, in
The City of God against the Pagans, outlines the challenges of decoding a
hermaphroditic body:

Androgyni, quos etiam Hermaphroditos nuncupant, quamvis admo-
dum rari sint, difficile est tamen ut temporibus desint, in quibus sic
uterque sexus apparet, ut ex quo potius debeant accipere nomen incer-
tum sit.

(Although androgyni, whom men also call hermaphrodites, are very rare,
yet it is difficult to find periods when they do not occur. In them the marks
of both sexes appear together in such a way that it is uncertain from which
they should properly receive their name).[35]

Notwithstanding the interpretive dilemmas of intersex bodies, Augustine sees any divergences from an assumed corporeal norm as part of
God's creation, extolling a shared humanity and a common descent:

Sicut ergo haec ex illo uno negari non possunt originem ducere, ita quae-
cumque gentes in diversitatibus corporum ab usitato naturae cursu quem
plures et prope omnes tenent velut exorbitasse traduntur, si definitione
illa includuntur, ut rationalia animali sint atque mortalia, ab eodem ipso
uno primo patre omnium stirpem trahere confitendum est.

(Therefore, since we cannot deny that these are descended from that one
man, such is the case also with any races whatsoever that are reported
to have deserted, as it were, by their divergent physical types, the nor-
mal path of nature that the majority and, in fact, nearly all men follow. If
these peoples are classified among rational and mortal animals, then we
must admit that their stock is descended from that same single father of
all mankind.)[36]

At the same time that early commentators viewed hermaphrodites as bordering between the sexes, many also credited an inherent superiority to masculinity over femininity. Augustine declares, "A meliore tamen, hoc est a masculino, ut appellarentur loquendi consuetudo praevaluit. Nam nemo umquam Androgynaecas aut Hermphroditas nuncupavit" (However, our established manner of speaking has given them the gender of the better sex, calling them masculine. For no one ever called them in the feminine *androgynaecae* or *hermaphroditae*).[37] Pseudo-Albertus Magnus's *De secretis mulierum* expresses a similar view: "The question arises whether a hermaphrodite ought to be called a man or a woman. One might answer that he can be called by either name because he has either sex, but this is incorrect; he should be called by the name of a man alone. The reason for this is that when a determination must be made about something, the worthier alternative should be chosen."[38] The long-standing sexism of the Middle Ages explains the preference for the masculine in these treatises on hermaphroditism, yet it is also revealing about the expectations of gender during this period: when gender is in doubt, the masculine serves as the default expectation. A similar dynamic occurs on the early British stage: even when a play confuses the gender presentation of a character, masculinity must remain the default expectation, for the audience knows that the actor playing the role is a man.

Given these conditions and the interpretive conundrums elicited by bodies evading strict assignments of sex and gender, audiences of medieval and early modern drama must repeatedly question what precisely is being communicated on stage. One could certainly argue that all early English plays with male actors playing female roles summon the viewer's hermaphroditic gaze. Lyndsay's play demands this response from viewers, whereas most other works attempt to camouflage the discrepancy between the actor's and his character's sexed bodies. For example, in the proclamation of the play's performance in Cupar, the Auld Man requests, "Bessy my hairt, first let me lok thy cunt, / Syne lat me keip the key, as I was wount" (144–5). Bessy readily assents, and the stage directions state, "*Heir sall he lok hir cunt and lay the key under his heid: he sall sleip and scho sall sit besyd him*" (following line 147). In locking Bessy's chastity belt, the Auld Man reveals and conceals the camp nature of gendered performance, drawing attention to the disjunction between female role and male actor and tacitly reminding viewers that the sexual tension of this scene is heteroerotic on its surface but homoerotic beneath. With the Auld Man so fixated on his wife's genitalia and so fearful of his imminent cuckoldry, the staging of the scene's dramatic action – the locking of a chastity belt that protects not a vagina but a penis – requires the audience to see both a female character and a male actor and to hold this hermaphroditic vision in tension. Bessy asks the Fule – and the audience as well – "Se ye not how my cunt is lokkit?" (167), and so their eyes are drawn, theatrically and metatheatrically, to the lock that might hide but cannot oversignify the actor's penis.

In another such moment ripe for camp performance, Sensualitie insists that the gaze be directed towards her, escalating the scene's humour owing to the conflicting significations of her body. On one level, she speaks to such male characters as Rex Humanitas, Solace, and Placebo, encouraging them to luxuriate in her beauty; on another level, her words extend beyond the stage's "fourth wall" to summon the audience members both to gaze upon her beauty and to see beneath the feminine façade before them:

> Behauld my heid, behauld my gay attyre,
> Behauld my hales [neck], lusum [lovely] and lilie-quhite;
> Behauld my visage, flammand as the fyre;
> Behault my papis of portratour perfyte.
> To luke on mee luiffers hes greit delyte. (279–83)[39]

In this dramatization of a poetic blazon cataloguing the female beloved's beauty, Sensualitie insists that the audience indulge in the scopophilic pleasures available through her head, neck, and face, stressing the beauty of her white skin and red complexion. In a poetic blazon, the lyric speaker's male voice praises his beloved's beauty, and frequently he attests to her strong moral character as well. In this scene, however, the female character accentuates her own beauty, which highlights her narcissistic pride and the likelihood that the lines would be delivered with flagrant excess. Sensualitie's emphasis on her breasts cannot help but remind the viewer of the disjunction between actor and role, and it is certainly within the realm of plausible stagings that the actor would campily stress this disjunction to enhance the scene's humour.

Certainly, these breasts stand in marked contrast to those more often dramatized on medieval stages. In *Christ's Burial*, Mary repeatedly refers to Jesus's nursing: "Yit suffer me to hold yow her on my lape, / Which sumtym gafe yow mylk of my pape!" (745–6).[40] These lines are repeated with minor variations in the following two stanzas, and in the third stanza she adjures Jesus, "Remembere, my awn son, þat ȝe sowket my breste!" (773). In Thomas Garter's *Virtuous and Godly Susanna*, Susanna's mother bewails her daughter's jeopardy:"These brests my Spouse, with tender milke, proceeding from my hart / Did giue her suck, did nourish her, alas moste greeuous smart" (834–5),[41] and in John Philip's *Pacient and Meeke Grissell*, Grissell cries over her daughter who has been taken from her, purportedly to be executed: "My Daughter reft from tender Paps, alas my wofull paine" (1176).[42] Despite these repeated references to breasts, the actors performing Mary, Susanna's mother, and Grissell would be unlikely to employ gestures in a manner to fracture the performative illusion of femininity and would focus on the pathos of a mother's compassion and sorrow for her child. Obviously, few plays could be further in sense or sensibility than *Christ's Burial*, *Virtuous and Godly Susanna*, and *Pacient and Meeke Grissell* from *Ane Satyre of the Thrie Estaitis*, yet each of these plays requires actors to consider the most appropriate way to corporealize women's breasts in their performances.

In the moment that Sensualitie draws attention to her breasts, her attire must almost by necessity metamorphose from a theatrical costume to drag, for the illusion is both highlighted and punctured at its most vulnerable point. Sensualitie's attention to her breasts would also build the scene's humour, for as Terry Goldie wryly comments, "drag is always to some degree ridiculous."[43] Judith Butler further explains of drag's dynamics: "embodying the excess of that production, the queen will out-woman women, and in the process confuse and seduce an audience whose gaze must to some degree be structured through these hegemonies, an audience who, through the hyperbolic staging of the scene, will be drawn into the abjection it wants both to resist and to overcome."[44] It behoves the actor playing Sensualitie to "out-woman women" and, by doing so, to reorient the audience's gaze from the presumed certainties of embodied gender to its hermaphroditic repositioning that recognizes such a performative undoing. Moreover, Sensualitie then adds: "Rycht sa hes all the kinges of Christindome: / To thame I haif done pleasouris infinite, / And speciallie unto the Court of Rome" (284–6). With these words, and in line with Lyndsay's critique of a sexually immoderate clergy, Sensualitie adumbrates dual senses of sodomy and its confused categories of sexual transgression: as a female character, she alludes to the abrogation of heteroerotic chastity, yet as a male actor concurrently dissolving the illusion of femininity, he hints at the homoerotic dalliances alleged against the clergy. Within this dual framing of the female body, the audience is called to see the hermaphroditic nature of performance and thus to witness the eradication of gender as a stable conduit of theatrical and thematic meaning that multiplies – or at least doubles – its satirical targets.

Lyndsay employs stage directions, in addition to his exaggerated female characters, to heighten the camp potential of encounters between them. In a scene with potentially queer undertones the actors are instructed: *"Heir sal the Bischops, Abbots and Persons kis the Ladies"* (following line 1752). With male characters kissing men playing female roles, the sodomitic insinuations levelled at the Catholic clergy are tacitly adumbrated, with the humour depending in large part on the campiness of the kiss. In contrast, the stage directions focusing on the virtuous (or, perhaps more accurately, the non-Vice) characters describe embraces rather than kisses, which lessens the potential for exaggeratedly corporeal humour. Concerning Rex Humanitas, Lyndsay's stage directions state: *"Heir sall the King resave [Gude] Counsell, Veritie and Chastitie"* (following line 1760), and *"The King imbraces Correction with a humbil countenance"* (following line 1785). In his gendered evolution away from sin, Rex Humanitas "receives" Gude Counsell, Veritie, and Chastitie and "embraces" Correction but refrains from kissing both the male and the female characters. In a similar moment that quells any erotic tension, the stage directions record: *"Heir sall the Temporal staits, to wit, the Lords and Merchands, imbreasse Johne the Common-weill"* (following line 2721). In comparing these embraces with the kisses between the ladies and the bishops, abbots, and parsons, it appears that Lyndsay allows for deeper physical intimacy to be expressed when male actors playing sexually transgressive male characters embrace male actors playing female characters, including the immodest and unrestrained Sensualitie, thus exploiting and exposing the camp potential of the scene.

The frequent spats between male and female characters function similarly, in that the female characters, in belittling and battling their husbands, assert their dominance through an exaggerated and comic performance of female strength. The stage directions stress the women's physical domination of their husbands – *"Heir sall they speik to thair gudemen, and ding [beat with heavy blows] them"* and *"Heir sall thay ding thair gudemen with silence"* (following lines 1355 and 1365) – with the Sowtars Wyfe stating contentedly, "Of our cairls we have the victorie" (1376). The dramatization of these scenes elicits the exaggeration of gender for comic effect, with the actors likely enacting a tyrannical vision of femininity that leaves male characters quivering in their wake.

Furthermore, several of the female characters of *Ane Satyre of the Thrie Estaitis* are introduced in pairs, including Veritie and Chastitie, Taylours Wyfe and Sowtars Wyfe, and Hameliness and Danger, who enter trailing Sensualitie. (The stage directions state, *"Heir sall entir Dame Sensualitie with hir madynnis Hamelines and Denger"* [following line 270]). Each of these pairings doubles the comic potential of men playing female roles, and as Sara Murphy explores, the pairing of female characters underscores the inconsequentiality of male characters, while escalating the play's sexual humour:

> The two female pairs [the Taylours Wyfe and the Sowtars Wyfe, Veritie and Chastitie] ... portray Scotland's potential future as a world where men have transitioned from irresponsible members of the social polity to irrelevant ones, leaving women with no other choice than to create alliances amongst themselves. They reveal two different kinds of disorder, sexual and criminal: there is the homoerotic behavior between Taylours Wyfe and Sowtars Wyfe, which implies that frustrated women will fulfill their sexual needs with each other if necessary, and there is the criminalization of Veritie and Chastitie that results in their side-by-side placement in the public stocks, subversively chained together and publicly shamed.[45]

In this fictional world where men have abdicated their responsibilities, the female characters bond together to advance their aims – as Murphy notes, sexual objectives for Taylours Wyfe and Sowtars Wyfe, justice for Veritie and Chastitie. The stagings of these homosocial pairs unleash camp potential in their gendered embodiment of allegory. In this scene in which men are uninterested in or unable to engage in sex, an erotic tension simmers as the female characters speak openly of their unmet desires: Taylours Wyfe laments, "For it is half ane yeir almaist / Sen ever that loun [ruffian] laborde my ledder [pudenda]" (1331–2); and Sowtars Wyfe similarly complains, "I mervell nocht, sa mot I lyfe, / Howbeit that swingeour [ruffian] can not swyfe" (2168–9). Yet again, such camp potential requires the viewers to question their hermaphroditic gaze: in other words, do they see a lesbian subtext to these pairings, do they look beyond the surface of costuming to see a gay male subtext, do they see both at once, or do they see none at all? Women helping one another to dress and undress need not carry any erotic meaning in itself, even with the sexual nature of these character's conversations.

At the same time, the friendship of Taylours Wyfe and Sowtars Wyfe has the potential to accelerate the erotic and campy humour of *Ane Satyre of the Thrie Estaitis*, particularly when these women narrate their intention to disrobe each other. Sowtars Wyfe requests Taylours Wyfe to undress her, and it is critical to consider precisely what the audience does or does not see in this encounter. "Cummer, will ye draw aff my hois and schone [shoes]; / To fyll the quart I sall rin to the toun" (1380–1), Sowtars Wyfe requests. Taylours Wyfe readily agrees:

> That sal I do, be Him that made the mone,
> With all my hart: thairfoir, cummer, sit doun.

Kilt up your claithis abone your waist,
And speid yow hame againe in haist,
And I sall provyde for ane paist [meal],
Our corsses [bodies] to comfort. (1382–7)

Murphy declares, "As the Sowtars Wyfe exposes to her female companion and the audience the genitalia that her husband has not seen for forty days, the cross-dressed male playing her part creates a comic yet unsettling transgendered moment."[46] Epp similarly observes of these characters in performance: "Staging the wives of the Sowtar and the Taylour explicitly as cross-dressed men ... could arguably not only signify the excessive masculinization of these monstrous women, and the relative feminisation of their husbands, but also allow Woman to vanish as an effective threat."[47] More so, this unsettling moment continues in the stage directions, which command the actor: "*Sho lifts up hir clais above hir waist and enters in the water*" (following line 1391). In both of these instances, how high does the Sowtars Wyfe lift her clothes above her waist? Whether modestly or immodestly, whether with light humour or broad farce, the audience is compelled to envision the disjunction between what should be seen – the vulva – and what would be seen – a penis. Much like Sensualitie's command that the characters and audience alike should "behault my papis of portratour perfyte," these scenes with Sowtars Wyfe allow, even if they do not require, a camp performance, with the campier humour appearing more congruent with the play's comic ambitions that persistently challenge the audience's gaze.

With a comic sensibility congruent to this scene, Lyndsay frequently portrays his characters shedding their clothes, which again opens the opportunity for carnivalesque humour to transform into campiness. When the Pardoner divorces the Sowtar and his wife, he commands them to kiss each other's buttocks in a parody of the marital kiss:

To part sen ye ar baith content,
I sall yow part incontinent [immediately],
Bot ye mon do command.
My will and finall sentence is:
Ilk ane of yow uthers arss[is] kis.
Slip doun your hois. Me thinkis the carle is glaikit [foolish]!
Set thou not be, howbeit scho kisse and slaik [lick] it!
Heir sall scho kis his arsse with silence.
Lift up hir clais; kis hir hoill with your hart. (2174–81)

Following these words, the Sowtar interjects, "I pray yow, Sir, forbid hir for to fart!," and the stage direction states, "*Heir sall the Carle kis hir arsse with silence*" (following line 2181). Such excremental and anal humour, as discussed in chapter 2, is featured frequently in early British drama, but in most instances it is represented only verbally, not visually. Surely the actors must follow the Pardoner's orders to "slip doun your hoise" and "lift up hir clais," and so once again the audience's gaze is focused on their nether regions. In carnivalesque fashion, the *osculare fundamentum* trope inverts the wedding kiss, yet in a camp staging, the character of Sowtars Wyfe has two holes (an anus and the opening to the vagina), whereas the actor playing her has only one (an anus), and so much of the humour of this encounter, whether latently or exaggeratedly staged, hinges on the semiotic instability of what the Sowtar finds when he lifts up his wife's clothes. In a similar moment Wantonnes propositions Hamelines, "Quhat rak thocht ye and I / Go junne our justing lumis [tools, equipment]?" (544–5),[48] with this double entendre reminding the audience that both actors have "jousting tools" – penises. Indeed, this line could be viewed as simply an entendre – not a double entendre – for the *Dictionary of the Scots Language* documents the additional meaning of *lume* as "the male sexual parts. *Sing.*, the penis."[49] It should be noted as well that *lume, lome,* and its variants also include meanings with yonic connotations such as "an open vessel or receptacle,"[50] but even with this possibility of a heteroerotic resonance to Wantonnes's words, the audience's hermaphroditic gaze must interpret the doubled erotic possibilities of the encounter.

As much as *Ane Satyre of the Thrie Estaitis* campily highlights the dissonance between male actors and female roles, Lyndsay also reminds his audience of the comic challenges of male actors staging male desire. In contrast to the long-standing denigration of the female body as leaky (as evident in Folly's excursus on his wife), the male body is often construed as hard and impermeable, and these stereotypes are connected to the genitalia of the respective bodies: the penetrated and lubricious vagina, and the penetrating and ejaculating penis. By focusing on the erections of Rex Humanitas and Foly, Lyndsay characterizes the male body as unrestrained and unrestrainable. Solace warns Rex Humanitas of Sensualitie's attractions: "Scho is wantoun and scho is wyse, / And cled scho is on the new gyse: / It wald gar all your flesche up ryse / To luik upon hir face!" (202–5). As Solace's words are framed in the subjunctive – suggesting that the sight of Sensualitie would give Rex Humanitas an erection – the allegory remains abstract rather than embodied. In a similar moment that humorously asks the audience to envision erections, Pauper regrets that, in comparison to the unrestrained sex lives of bishops, he cannot divorce his wife and find a more beautiful woman: "Bot thay lyke rams rudlie [roughly] in thair rage / Unpysalt [with an erection] rinnis among the sillie yowis [ewes], / Sa lange as kynde of Nature in them growis" (2769–71).[51] In contrast, when Foly contemplates the unruliness of his penis, the spectacle calls for it to be staged:

> Me think my pillok [penis] will nocht ly doun –
> Hald doun your head, ye lurdon loun [rascally ruffian]!
> Yon fair las with the sating [satin] goun
> Gars [causes] yow thus bek [to bow] and bend.[52] (4438–41)

Does Foly direct his head toward his "flamboyant penis" (in Greg Walker's memorable phrasing) while speaking these lines?[53] Is some sort of stage phallus employed to indicate his erection? Presumably a prominent codpiece would be employed for this scene rather than a simulated penis, but the dialogue nonetheless calls for the audience to envision what it cannot see. Certainly, Foly is speaking to his penis because it is moving, and its actions cause him to respond in kind. Although the previous scenes of men discussing male genitalia remain conceptual, Foly's reaction to his penis requires the performance to be embodied, even if hidden underneath his costume. As a male actor plays a male role here, the scene need not evoke a camp register in its performance, but it nonetheless testifies to Lyndsay's enduring interest in demanding that his audience ponder the genitalia of his actors. That is to say, the audience's hermaphroditic gaze becomes conditioned to question the congruency of actor and genitalia, even when they align.

In this camp confusion that arises between actors and their bodies, Lyndsay introduces a series of epistemological crises in his play, but ones that are built firmly on foundations of humour. Thematizing this issue, he dramatizes the possibility that ignorant and sinful men will not comprehend his allegory. When the Doctour (of Divinity) preaches of the two steps on the ladder to salvation as necessitating the love of God and of one's neighbour (3526–30), the Abbot states, "And I beleif that cruikit men and blinde / Sall never get up upon sa hich ane ledder," as he also wonders, "Quhat and I fal? Than I will break my bledder!" (3552–3, 3556). The Parson similarly frets, "Thy words war nather corne nor caiff [chaff]" (3562), pointing to the potential for words to lose their mooring in meaning. If the hermaphroditic gaze cannot effectively distinguish between bodies and is instead caught in a visually equivalent conundrum of seeing neither corn nor chaff, the audience is left with the uncertainty of the body against the pleasure of its continual and exaggerated masking or unmasking. That is to say, as much as *Ane Satyre of the Thrie Estaitis* urges the reformation of Scottish society, it also implicates the audience members in its satire, calling into question their ability to parse the events unfolding on stage.

As is common in medieval narrative and drama, including such famous examples as Andreas Capellanus's *De amore* and Geoffrey Chaucer's *Canterbury Tales*, *Ane Satyre of the Thrie Estaitis* urges its audience to overlook its comic transgressions, thereby defanging the satire of any venom but not of its humour. Cementing this theme, Diligence admonishes the audience to view the comic shenanigans on stage as play: "Prudent peopill, I pray yow all, / Tak na man greif in speciall, / For wee sall speik in generall, / For pastyme and for play" (70–3). In such moments, carnivalesque narratives and festive performances apologize for their uproarious fun, adumbrating a return to the prevailing ideological order. Terry Eagleton declares of this tension that "carnival, after all, is a *licensed* affair in every sense, a permissible rupture of hegemony, a contained popular blow-off as disturbing and relatively ineffectual as a revolutionary work of art."[54] In bridging the carnivalesque and camp through performances of gender and sexuality, Lyndsay created an innovative work of art that challenged many of the mores of the British stage and presaged Renaissance masterworks with their own camp elements,[55] yet camp suffers from political pitfalls similar to those of the carnivalesque. As Moe Meyer observes, "This piggy-backing upon the dominant order's monopoly on the authority of signification explains why Camp appears, on the one hand, to offer a transgressive vehicle yet, on the other, simultaneously involves the specter of dominant ideology within its practice, appearing, in many instances, to actually reinforce the dominant order."[56] Women's bodies serve as fodder for men's laughter, but because the women's bodies are really men's, the hermaphroditic gaze of the audience is compelled to deconstruct that which is staged before it. Through the camp excess of *Ane Satyre of the Thrie Estaitis*, Lyndsay calls for social and sexual reform while undoing any sense of gendered coherency for this reformatory project, reminding his audience that men's desires for women are sometimes better understood as men's desires for men, and that a play so interested in themes relevant to the Scottish Reformation reveals its deeper interest to be the queer and corporeal comedy latent in staging allegory.

Terrence Mcnally's
Corpus Christi and the Queer
Legacy of Early English Drama

Queerness, as the previous chapters have argued, contributes much to the pleasure of early English drama, even if it mostly arises from textual margins, performative possibilities, and other locations of subjunctive potential. In the othering of Jewish genders (which also subverts Christian pieties) in the York Corpus Christi Plays, in the frenetic homosocial seductions of *Mankind* that fracture the presumed identification between audience and protagonist, in the impossibility of chastity signifying virtue in John Bale's *King Johan*, and in the campy gender humour of Sir David Lyndsay's *Ane Satyre of the Thrie Estaitis*, queerness coexists with, and possibly subverts, performances aligned with theologically and ideologically sanctioned interpretations. With the exception of such intriguing works as *Dux Moraud* and *Gammer Gurton's Needle*, most early English plays, particularly those belonging to mystery and morality traditions, instil in their viewers a salvific lesson of a sinner lost and then redeemed, with queerness highlighting the challenges of imparting even a simple moral lesson within the framework of play and performance.

In the modern theatre the medieval past is alive and well and thus provides an intriguing opportunity to consider the shifting dynamics of queerness from the past to the present. At its simplest, *medievalism* refers to the creation of post-medieval artefacts that are set in or obviously influenced by the medieval past.[1] With the passing of the Middle Ages, medieval plays now straddle the border between past and present, inviting their audiences to enjoy a centuries-old narrative tradition that must be reconceived by modern directors and actors whenever they are staged anew. In this way, dramatic medievalisms upend a standard dichotomy inherent in the field as a whole: the distinction between cultural artefacts that arose during the Middle Ages and those that arose afterwards. In *The Cambridge Companion to Medievalism,*

Louise D'Arcens identifies two primary modes of medievalism as the "found" and the "made" Middle Ages: the former "emerge[s] through contact with, and interpretation of, the 'found' or material remains of the medieval past surviving into the post-medieval era," and the latter "encompasses texts, objects, performances, and practices that are not only post-medieval in their provenance but imaginative in their impulse and founded on ideas of 'the medieval' as a conceptual rather than a historical category."[2] The modern-day staging of medieval plays bridges any divide between the found and the made Middle Ages, for a script may be found from the archives of the past, but the performance must be made in the present. Further along these lines, the reconstruction of a medieval play in the present could entail a staging that aims either for free-floating anachronistic whimsy or for detailed historical accuracy; yet, even this latter option could not escape the necessity of anachronism in its casting of modern actors who seek to entertain modern audiences. The Middle Ages, as in so many other instances, exists as a palimpsest upon which the past can be written over to accommodate new desires and identities, all the while remaining grounded in a vision of a lost era of courtly manners, barbaric violence, or any other such construction of the past. Nostalgia motivates many playwrights and performers in their re-creation of early English works in modern times, as Claire Sponsler posits in her study of medieval plays produced in the United States of America: "placing their faith in a hermeneutics of reconstitution, reenactments of medieval plays position performance as a form of nostalgic recuperation, by desire and necessity kept separate from contamination by modern life."[3] Whatever the motivation of a company staging medieval plays in the present, these productions testify to the vibrancy of early English drama in the present, no matter the debunked evolutionary view that dismissed them as inherently inferior to the later works of the Renaissance.

As with the cinematic world and its continual return to the Middle Ages, the theatrical realm appears unlikely ever to tire of mining the medieval past for new stories and subject matter (even if previously told), and so it offers another venue for considering the impact of wholly made medievalisms on contemporary culture.[4] Artistic directors of theatre companies can choose from a wide range of subfields within the corpus of made medievalist plays, including dramas (James Goldman's *The Lion in Winter*, Howard Brenton's *In Extremis: The Story of Abelard and Heloise*); comedies (Christopher Fry's *The Lady's Not for Burning*, Michael Hollinger's *Incorruptibles*); and many musicals (*Once Upon a Mattress, Camelot, Pippin, Spamalot*). History plays include such subdivisions as Thomas Becket plays (Jean Anouilh's *Becket*, T.S. Eliot's

Murder in the Cathedral), Joan of Arc plays (George Bernard Shaw's *Saint Joan*, Jules Feiffer's *Knock Knock*), and Shakespeare's medievalist plays (*Richard II; Henry IV, Parts 1* and *2*). In addition to Shakespeare, Shaw, and Eliot, a variety of canonical authors have penned dramas set in the Middle Ages: for example, Pierre Corneille's *Le Cid*, Alexander Pushkin's *Boris Gudonov*, and Alfred, Lord Tennyson's *The Foresters: Robin Hood and Marian*. These plays and others of their ilk exemplify a variety of relationships to the medieval past that collectively reflect the three primary discourses of medievalism outlined by David Matthews: "The Middle Ages 'as it was,' [in which] the Middle Ages is depicted as if realistically"; "the Middle Ages 'as it might have been,' [in which] the Middle Ages is depicted through or as legend"; and "the Middle Ages 'as it never was,' [in which] a quasi-, pre-, parallel or non-Middle Ages is depicted, using medieval motifs which create a medieval appearance."[5] Each of these discourses of medievalism can be found throughout the vast variety of the theatrical Middle Ages, with directors and actors regularly re-creating the past in the present across the globe.

In another twist of the screw, a third type of theatrical medievalism, which could be designated as the meta-medieval, comes into focus: modern plays directly inspired not simply by the Middle Ages but by the era's mystery and morality plays, including such works as Tony Harrison's *The Mysteries*, Sarah Ruhl's *Passion Play*, and Jordan Harrison's *The Amateurs*, as well as the related subgenre of plays dramatizing biblical events that are at least somewhat influenced by the traditions of the mystery plays, including Stephen Adly Guirgis's *The Last Days of Judas Iscariot* and Paul Rudnick's *The Most Fabulous Story Ever Told*, as well as biblically inspired musicals such as *Joseph and the Amazing Technicolor Dreamcoat, Godspell*, and *Jesus Christ Superstar*. Novels and films such as Clive Sansom's *Passion Play* and Denys Arcand's *Jesus of Montreal* contemplate the meaning of medieval ritual in the past and thematize its relevance to modern lives. In this miniscule subfield of modern literature and cinema that depicts a group of performers putting on a medieval mystery or morality play, sexual transgressions inevitably structure the plot. Barry Unsworth's *Morality Play* portrays a priest joining an acting troupe and solving a murder while contemplating the surprising similarities between his former vocation and his new employment. As evident from these three intersecting traditions of theatrical medievalisms – found medieval plays staged in the present, made medievalist plays, and meta-medieval plays – the Middle Ages remain a vibrant source of inspiration for the artists and patrons of today's theatre and beyond.

As with the early English dramas examined in the preceding chapters of this volume, any and all of these plays could be analysed for their potential queerness, in the ways in which queer scopophilia, queer dialogue, queer characters, and queer performances continue to disrupt any blanket assumption of heteronormativity within the theatrical sphere – an assumption that, given modern theatre's long-standing support of queer rights, may no longer be held in the first place. Queer expression has flourished in twentieth- and twenty-first-century British and American theatre with the works of such gay and lesbian playwrights as Tennessee Williams, Lorraine Hansberry, Edward Albee, Joe Orton, Caryl Churchill, Tony Kushner, Michael R. Jackson, Brandon Jacob-Jenkins, and Patricia Ione Lloyd.[6] Rather than simply instituting a closeted or uncloseted view of medieval drama versus modern drama, in which the subterranean queerness of the early English theatre contrasts with the candid queerness of the present moment, it is always more fruitful to consider the ways in which queerness functions within its specific cultural moment in a given narrative and performative text. John Bale's Sodomismus in *Thre Lawes of Nature, Moses, and Christ* and Tennessee Williams's Brick in *Cat on a Hot Tin Roof*, despite their numerous thematic differences and their separation by more than five hundred years, stand as particularly compelling characters precisely because their queerness evades simple definitions.

Among these disparate specimens of theatrical medievalisms, Terrence McNally's *Corpus Christi* stands out in its attempt to unite the practices of medieval drama with a modern theme of queer universality. In his play's preface McNally explains its narrative roots: "*Corpus Christi* is a passion play. The life of Joshua, a young man from south Texas, is told in the theatrical tradition of medieval morality plays" (vi), although he cautions, "I'm a playwright, not a theologian" (v).[7] McNally succinctly explicates his understanding of this tradition: "Men play all the roles. There is no suspense. There is no scenery" (vi). Within this format *Corpus Christi* explores the following themes: "The purpose of the play is that we begin again the familiar dialogue with ourselves: Do I love my neighbor? Am I contributing good to the society in which I operate or nil? Do I, in fact, matter?" (vi–vii). By recasting the passion play as an explicitly queer narrative with Jesus and his disciples reconceived as gay men, McNally tackles themes of deep spiritual and social relevance, asking his audience members to consider the possibility of a queer saviour and his suffering on their behalf.

Certainly, one could quibble with McNally's assessment of early English theatre and its traditions. He conflates the tropes of passion plays and of morality plays, and *Corpus Christi*, in dramatizing the life and crucifixion of a Christ figure, adheres more closely to the structures of the former than to those of the latter. That is to say, Joshua represents a Christ figure more than an allegorical Everyman figure who is seduced into sin but then repents and finds redemption. Also, although one might argue that a mystery cycle lacks suspense owing to the fact that its outcome is preordained, this is not the case with morality plays such as *Everyman*, in which the salvation of the protagonist's soul, while narratively likely, cannot be deemed such a foregone conclusion that the audience would experience no tension in its climax. To suggest that early English plays were staged without scenery also grossly oversimplifies the visuality of their production.[8] Evaluating McNally's understanding of medieval theatre illuminates key aspects of *Corpus Christi* and its debts to prior traditions, yet such a perspective should not concomitantly be constrained by a frequent limitation in the study of medievalisms: a niggling presumption that the playwright should maintain absolute fidelity to medieval sources. Just as McNally readily admits that he is not a theologian, he would likely also admit that he is not – and likely does not desire to be – a scholar of medieval drama, and so his play should not be assessed according to the historically documented practices of early English theatre as much as according to the ways in which he reimagined them for his artistic purposes in the late twentieth century.

In applying the structures and themes of medieval plays to address the bigotry targeted at queer people in the late twentieth century, McNally aims for a spartan simplicity to direct the audience's attention squarely on the narrative and its characters. The stage directions indicate that this simplicity is nonetheless highly stylized, such as in his efforts to homogenize the appearance of the actors: "*The other ACTORS join in as they begin to undress and change into the 'uniform' of the play: white shirt, khaki trousers, and bare feet*" (1).[9] In repeated dialogue, John introduces the play's characters: "I bless you, [full name of the actor]. I baptize you and recognize your divinity as a human being. I adore you, [first name of the actor]. I christen you, (name of the character)" (2–8).[10] These words, ritualistically recited as each actor and his character are addressed, establish the divinity of these human roles, not simply or even centrally Joshua's. In this key revisioning of the thematic traditions of early English theatre, redemption does not stand as the protagonist's narrative goal for divinity but is already established as the precondition of the human, available to all. Original sin is washed away.

Key to McNally's vision of human divinity is the redemption of sex and eroticism, and to this end he stresses Joshua's humanity, seeking to overcome any reticence among his audience about pondering Jesus's sexuality: "Very few Christians are willing to consider that their Lord and Savior was a real man with real appetites, especially sexual ones" (v). Jesus's status as fully human and fully divine stands as perhaps the defining paradox of the Christian faith, and McNally demands that his audience engage with the repercussions of this tenet, envisioning a saviour erotically attracted to the humans around him. He further asks his audience to consider the sexual implications of the virgin birth, staging this pre-eminent miracle of the Christian tradition in a humorous motel scene, with the accompanying stage direction "*MARY gives birth and takes a doll out from under her skirt*" (12). In an adjacent room the Woman Next Door (James) cries out, "Fuck me, fuck me, fuck me," as the Man Next Door (Andrew) replies, "That's what I'm doing, you damn woman. I'm fucking you, I'm fucking you, I'm fucking you" (14). By contrasting the virgin birth with human intercourse, McNally establishes them as parallel in their spiritual power: the Woman Next Door and the Man Next Door may not be conceiving the next saviour of humanity, but the very banality of their intercourse, staged alongside Jesus's or Joshua's birth, symbolizes its sublime potential. Moreover, the sexual encounter between the Woman Next Door and the Man Next Door erodes any distinction between heterosexuality and homosexuality, for this overheard encounter transpires simultaneously with a heterosexual couple (Woman Next Door and Man Next Door) and with a gay couple (James and Andrew) because the actors assigned the primary roles of James and Andrew respectively double as Woman Next Door and Man Next Door. Within McNally's *Corpus Christi*, sexuality permits transcendence if one has the courage to pursue it.

For the most part, McNally characterizes Joshua and his disciples as queer through recognizable stereotypes: during his high school years Joshua despises football and instead enjoys musical theatre, even rehearsing "(I'm in Love with) A Wonderful Guy" from *South Pacific*. His graduating class votes him "Most Likely to Take It Up the Hershey Highway" (30). A queer, adolescent Jesus sparks some of the play's richest comic moments, such as when Peggy Powell reflects on dating Joshua: "You don't decorate your high school gym for your senior prom or edit the yearbook with someone you think is the Messiah. He wasn't boyfriend material, that's for certain" (39). Joshua's disciples are similarly identified as gay: Thaddeus is a hairdresser, and Philip is an HIV-positive "go-go boy" with "bells on his feet" (53–5). Judas takes hits of poppers in the disco scene (53), and James and Bartholomew marry each other, with Joshua blessing their union: "May the first face you see each morning and the last at night always be his. I bless this marriage in Your name, Father" (62). Judas, in a statement of disproportionate value for some gay men, announces, "I've got a big dick" (8). By employing such stereotypes, McNally flattens his characters into types rather than developing them into personalities, in a move that aligns well with the practices of early English theatre. More significantly, these gay stereotypes contrapuntally highlight the relative banality of Jesus's disciples in the gospel accounts, whose narrative arcs are determined more by the relationships of the disciples with Jesus than by their individualized personalities.

Following Joshua's birth and adolescence, *Corpus Christi* adheres to the basic narrative contours of the gospel accounts of Jesus's life and death: James Dean, replacing Satan, tempts Joshua in the desert, offering him "all the pleasures of His earthly kingdom" (46). Joshua miraculously multiplies fish (48–9), with the miracle of the loaves and fishes following (64). He cures a man possessed by a demon (50–1), and he heals the centurion's wife, whose husband repeats his dialogue from Matthew 8:8: "You have only to say the word and she will be cured" (60). Judas's surrender of Joshua is envisioned both as a tragic betrayal and as a romantic break-up, Joshua having predicted Judas's perfidy and obliquely identified him to the others: "One who has lain with Me. One who has said he loves Me and knows that I love him" (69). When Judas identifies Joshua to the Soldier with a kiss, the stage directions indicate that "*JOSHUA kisses him back, hard*" (72), thus giving visibility to queer desire. The crucifixion soon follows, and McNally accentuates the grotesque violence of this moment; the stage directions instruct: "*For the first time we see how horribly JOSHUA has been battered. Blood runs down His face and body. His eyes are half-swollen shut. It should be hard to look at Him*" (79). Like Jesus in the gospels, Joshua suffers to save humanity, with the violent visuality of his sacrifice metaphorically representing the torment inflicted on gay people for much of Western history. In penning *Corpus Christi*, McNally was grimly inspired by the recent murder of Matthew Shepard, whose death he compares to Christ's: "Beaten senseless and tied to a split-rail fence in near-zero weather, arms akimbo in a grotesque crucifixion, he died as agonizing a death as another young man who had been tortured and nailed to a wooden cross at a desolate spot outside Jerusalem known as Golgotha, some 1,990 years earlier" (vi). By aligning the murder of Matthew Shepard with the crucifixion of Joshua (and thus Jesus), McNally condemns the long-standing bigotries of Western ideology and exalts all those who have suffered for their queerness.

As the familiar events of the gospels unfold, it becomes evident that, despite all the hubbub and the predictable jeremiads of fundamentalists that surrounded the initial staging of *Corpus Christi*, its queerness is less revolutionary than simply normalizing. In an early moment of metadiscourse Thomas discusses the theatrical experience and exhorts the audience: "It's called the willing suspension of disbelief – or in certain cases the *un*willing suspension of disbelief. … We want to take you someplace beautiful, someplace thrilling, someplace maybe you've never been before. Come with us. At least meet us halfway" (4). But any members of the audience with a fundamental – not fundamentalist – understanding of Christianity have "been here before," and McNally's adaptation of the gospels into a modern morality play does not alter the contours of the story beyond the surface transition of a presumably straight Jesus into a recognizably gay Joshua. The High Priest reveals the necessity of sin for a corrupted vision of religion: "The son of God is a cocksucker? I don't think so. We need sinners" (65). Replacing Pilate's query in the gospels, "Are you the King of the Jews?," McNally's Pilate instead queries, "Art thou a queer then?" (75). Joshua replies with Jesus's words: "Thou sayest I am" (75; cf. Luke 23:3). For Joshua and his disciples, queer sexuality serves as a key means to transcendence, despite the casual cruelty of their society. Theologically, God's statement that "all men are divine" (20) could be viewed as a more radical challenge to central tenets of Christianity than the depiction of a gay Jesus figure. For the most part, *Corpus Christi*, as a passion play with gay male characters, simply reiterates the gospels' call to love one's neighbour, a demand that appears to be both relatively banal to envision and unutterably impossible to achieve.

Contemporary reviews of *Corpus Christi* mostly ranged from tepid endorsements to flippant denouncements. Robert Brustein compares it unfavourably to other modern works of gay theatre, including the plays of Paul Rudnick, Tony Kushner, and Larry Kramer – "*Corpus Christi* contains all the soft flaws of those canonical gay works with none of their brittle virtues" – and cheekily dubs it a "modern misery play."[11] Several critics agreed that the play's queer retelling of Jesus's passion registered as little more than a promotional ploy: Jameson Currier describes *Corpus Christi* as "an ecumenical folk mass … that uses homosexuality as a gimmick."[12] Thomas Fish writes that the play "would not be considered radical in its approach to gay identity politics,"[13] and Clive Barnes jibes, "Blasphemy is one thing. Boredom is entirely another. I can't judge the blasphemy content, but as for boredom, *Corpus Christi* exemplifies it."[14] Sharon Green's review captures both the play's limitations and its promise:

> At the beginning of the performance, one actor declared the play's intention to take its audience somewhere "thrilling." *Corpus Christi* is ulti-

mately disappointing for its failure to do so and its lack of originality and provocation, making the vehemence of the protests against its content come more sharply into focus as displaced homophobic anxiety. I wished McNally had told a bolder, more interesting story. And yet, there is also something powerful and moving in McNally's intention to reclaim this "old and familiar" story and the sheer presence of these bodies onstage trying to make it their own. In the context of recent debates over decency in artwork, the importance of this staging of *Corpus Christi* extends beyond the play's literary significance.[15]

Apparent in these critical responses to *Corpus Christi* is the accusation that the play is too obvious in its queerness and that the substitution of recognizably gay characters for presumably straight ones requires little imagination on the part of the playwright or little rumination on the part of the audience.

Corpus Christi demonstrates the potential for a queer theatre to reconceive the meaning and depiction of sexuality on stage, while also showing the limitations of simply replacing a "straight" storyline – if the gospels can be so narrowly conceived – with a "queer" one. Moreover, queer theatre has long been criticized for its tendency to "preach to the converted" – to direct its messages to sympathetic audiences and thus not to challenge the status quo effectively. Yet, as Tim Miller and David Román argue, this allegation holds queer theatre to an impossible and paradoxical double standard:

Mainstream reviewers who employ the phrase [*preaching to the converted*] position queer people as needing to be preached *to*, while queer people who employ the phrase position queer audiences as defiantly against being preached *at*. Regardless of how the phrase is employed – whether it be to insist that queer artists are propagandists and queer audiences infantile, or to insist that queer artists are didactic and queer audiences bored with it all – lesbian and gay theatre that supposedly preaches to the converted is never understood as a valuable, or even viable, activity.[16]

Miller and Román discern value in theatrical experiences that preach to the converted, in plays and performances that cannot be quarantined from charges of propaganda and didacticism but instead merit and embrace such designations. After centuries of homosexuality being mostly left in the margins and the performative subjunctive of the theatrical realm, visible queerness can rarely escape being denounced as propaganda by homophobes and as didacticism by queer people who are rightly convinced of our full legitimacy as human beings.

In many ways, the charge of preaching to the converted appears latent in dramatic criticism that is dismissive of early English theatre: the plays are Christian propaganda, they are excessively didactic in their spiritual posturing, and they rehash similar plot lines over and over. The evolutionary theory of English drama proposes that the simplicity of medieval and early Renaissance plays ceded to the greater sophistication and depth of such talents as Marlowe, Shakespeare, Beaumont, Fletcher, and Jonson. If we reconfigure our perspective on these plays, however, viewing their tendency to preach to the converted as an appropriate, if not preferred, rhetorical circumstance during their period of production and thus as, if not precisely an advantage, not a detriment, their unique contributions come into sharper focus. Early English drama and twentieth- and twenty-first-century queer theatre share little in common, yet in the tendency of some critics to dismiss their achievements simply because of their interest in building either a Christian or a queer (or queer-friendly) community through didactic narrative frameworks, their place in theatrical history is blurred, at times beyond recognition. Worst still, the inherent pleasure of witnessing their performances is presumed to be blanched by didacticism, thus denying the simple fact that there would not have been audiences for these plays, in the past or in the present, if no one enjoyed them.

At the same time that McNally viewed medieval passion and morality plays as his inspiring genre for *Corpus Christi*, he also compared plays to rituals and stressed that his play adhered more to the traditions of the latter than to those of the former: "The play is more a religious ritual than a play. A play teaches us a new insight into the human condition. A ritual is an action we perform over and over because we *have* to. Otherwise, we are in danger of forgetting the meaning of that ritual, in this case that we must love one another or die" (vii). In this defence of his play McNally limns the importance of repeating stories from the past, no matter the limitations of this strategy, for the repetition reminds – or at least attempts to remind – audiences of lessons that must be continually learned and relearned. As with many playwrights and artists, McNally perhaps puts too much faith in theatre and ritual, for humanity seems determined not to learn this vital lesson. The fiercest advocates of theatre believe in its revolutionary potential, but narratives rarely achieve the goals to which they aspire: to state the obvious, *Lysistrata* did not end war, *A Raisin in the Sun* did not end racism, and *Corpus Christi* did not end homophobia. Pre-Reformation plays did not instil a uniform understanding of Christianity in its audience, nor did Reformation drama end subsequent controversies about the very nature of faith and theology. The power of representation should be neither overestimated nor underestimated.

From these converging perspectives, McNally's *Corpus Christi* exposes the paradoxical limitations of queer representation in the theatre: as important as it is to tell stories that are representative of a diversity of identities and experiences, the substitution of one identity for another, within the framework of a familiar narrative, need not alter the standard trajectories of the story and its interpretation. *Corpus Christi* illuminates through counter-example some of the power of queerness in early English drama. Precisely because it is unexpected, precisely because it must remain in the shadows, in the moments that it does become recognizable, its inherent force is realized, if only momentarily, if only in happenstance and ephemeral circumstances. Yet, if McNally is correct that a ritualized theatre reminds viewers of eternal truths that must continually be learned and relearned in each generation, the queerness of the dramatic past serves as an essential reminder that this message has long been more ecumenical than some might imagine.

Notes

Introduction

1 For a brief overview of Western theatre in the early Middle Ages, see Ogilvy, "Mimi, Scurrae, Histriones," 604–19, esp. 606–10. See also Clopper, *Drama, Play, and Game,* esp. 1–24.

2 The Roman martyrology identifies the three Marys as Mary Magdalene, Mary of Cleopas, and Mary Salome, but the relevant gospel passages (John 20:1, Matthew 28:1, and Luke 24:10) offer conflicting accounts. On the ways in which such scenes were staged, see Ogden, *The Staging of Drama.*

3 McGee, "The Role of the *Quem quaeritis* Dialogue," 189.

4 Concerning the geographical distribution of *Quem quaeritis* dialogues, see Bjork, "On the Dissemination of *Quem quaeritis,*" 46–69.

5 Davril, "Johann Drumbl," 66–7.

6 Kobialka "The *Quem Quaeritis,*" 50. See also Norton, *Liturgical Drama,* in which he discusses the challenges of defining the term *liturgical drama* (1–18).

7 Johnston, "An Introduction to Medieval English Theatre," 1–2.

8 The Latin text is taken from Young, *The Drama of the Medieval Church,* 1:249–50; the translation is from Fitzgerald and Sebastian, *The Broadview Anthology of Medieval Drama,* 21–2.

9 *The Resurrection of Our Lord,* in Chadwyck-Healey Database; *Christ's Resurrection,* in *The Late Medieval Religious Plays,* ed. Donald Baker, Murphy, and Hall, 169–93. *The Resurrection of Our Lord* includes four Marys in its cast of characters: Marie Madalene, Marie Solome, Marie Iacobi, and Marie Iose. Unless otherwise noted, all text references throughout are to lines of the stated edition.

10 Richard Axton, "Popular Modes," 39.

11 *A New Theatrical Dictionary,* 384; cited in Kelley, *Flamboyant Drama,* xi.

12 Symonds, *Shakespere's Predecessors*, 14–15.
13 See, for example, the foundational work of Jonathan Goldberg, including *Sodometries* and his edited collection, *Queering the Renaissance*. Additional key studies include DiGangi, *The Homoerotics of Early Modern Drama*; Walen, *Constructions of Female Homoeroticism*; and Masten, *Queer Philologies*. Many titles could be added to this list, as well as to any bibliography of queer studies of Renaissance drama.
14 Key studies of Shakespearean queerness include Sanchez, *Shakespeare and Queer Theory*; Stanivukovic, *Queer Shakespeare*; and Menon, *Shakesqueer*.
15 To the best of my knowledge, this present volume is the first to examine the queerness of medieval drama as it relates to sexuality and its staging, and few scholars, other than Garrett P.J. Epp, have tackled the surprising expressions of erotic desire on the medieval stage. Epp's work is cited frequently, and admiringly, throughout this study. Sturges, in *The Circulation of Power*, explores the queer temporality of medieval drama.
16 Greenblatt, *The Swerve*. Greenblatt identifies Poggio Bracciolini's fifteenth-century rediscovery of Lucretius's *De rerum natura* as the decisive turning point in Western intellectual history. For pointed critiques of Greenblatt's oversimplification of the transition from the medieval to the early modern, see "Book Review Forum: *The Swerve*," 313–70.
17 See such studies as Ryan, "Marlowe's *Edward II*," 465–95; and Donaldson, *The Swan at the Well*.
18 Davidson, *Deliver Us from Evil*, 20.
19 For a history of anti-theatrical critiques, see Barish, *The Antitheatrical Prejudice*; and Clopper, *Drama, Play, and Game*, esp. 32–107.
20 Augustine, *Confessions: Books 1–8*, 92–3.
21 Davidson, *A Tretise of Miraclis Pleyinge*, 109.
22 Gosson, *Markets of Bawdrie*, 175.
23 Sheingorn, "The Bodily Embrace," 80.
24 Spector, *The N-Town Play*. Text references are to the play and line numbers.
25 Lumiansky and Mills, *The Chester Mystery Cycle*. Text references are to the play and line numbers.
26 *Wisdom*, in Eccles, *The Macro Plays*, 113–52.
27 *Jacke Jugeler*, in *Three Tudor Classical Interludes*, ed. Marie Axton, 64–93.
28 *Horestes*, in *Three Tudor Classical Interludes*, ed. Marie Axton, 94–138.
29 Thomas Inglelend, *The Disobedient Child*, in *The Dramatic Writings of Richard Wever and Thomas Inglelend*, ed. John Farmer, 72.
30 Epp, *The Towneley Plays*.
31 Thomas Preston, *Cambises*, in *Tudor Plays*, ed. Creeth, 443–503. On incest in early drama see Boehrer, *Monarchy and Incest*; and Luis-Martinez, *In Words and Deeds*.

32 Thomas Garter, *Virtuous and Godly Susanna*, in Chadwyck-Healey Database.
33 Lancashire, *Two Tudor Interludes*, 157–238.
34 *Candlemes Day and the Kyllyng of þe Children of Israelle*, in Donald Baker, Murphy, and Hall, *The Late Medieval Religious Plays*, 96–115.
35 *Solace* simply means "joy, pleasure, happiness," with the *Middle English Dictionary* also testifying to its usage as "sexual intercourse," as in Nicholas and Alison's adulterous encounter: "And thus lith Alison and Nicholas, / In bisynesse of myrthe and of solas" (1.3653–4), in Chaucer, *The Riverside Chaucer*. See also *Middle English Dictionary*, s.v. "solace," 1 (a).
36 *A Play of Love*, in Heywood, *The Plays of John Heywood*, 143–81.
37 Salvato, *Uncloseting Drama*, 9; italics in the original.
38 Savran, *A Queer Sort of Materialism*, 59.
39 Grantley, *English Dramatic Interludes*, 1.
40 On the relationship between Scots and English, see Jones, *Edinburgh History of the Scots Language*, with the quotation appearing on p. vii.
41 Croxton *Play of the Sacrament*, in *Non-cycle Plays and Fragments*, ed. Davis, 58–89, following line 228.
42 Mr. S., *Gammer Gurton's Needle*, ed. Whitworth, xi and 1.
43 Butterworth, *Staging Conventions*, 19–21.
44 Warning, *Ambivalences of Medieval Religious Drama*, 22.
45 As discussed more fully in chapter 6, *hermaphrodite* and its variant forms are now considered archaic terminology for describing intersex people. At the same time, these words retain their utility for discussing the constructions of gender and bodily morphology during the medieval and early modern eras, precisely because they cover a range of possibilities, including mythic ones, beyond a strict definition of *intersex*.

1 A Subjunctive Theory of Dramatic Queerness

1 Sackville and Norton, *Gorboduc*, in *Two Tudor Tragedies*, ed. William Tydeman, 53.
2 Stern, *Making Shakespeare*. For Stern, a "stage-to-page" approach involves "combining theatre history and book history" to understand better the "multiple contexts rather than authorial intention" behind the creation of a play (5).
3 Folse, *The Grammar Answer Key*, 164.
4 Victor Turner, "Liminality and the Performative Genres," 20–1.
5 Schechner, *Between Theater and Anthropology*, 36.
6 Roach, "Culture and Performance," 46.
7 Walsh, "Touching, Feeling, Cross-Dressing," 55.
8 *Damon and Pythias*, in Edwards, *The Works of Richard Edwards*, 108–84.

9 Woodruff, *The Necessity of Theater*; see esp. 185–7 on pleasure and beauty.
10 Rodosthenous, "Staring at the Forbidden," 3, 8. For additional studies of the logistics of theatrical viewing, see Bleeker, *Visuality in the Theatre*; and Bennett, *Theatre Audiences*.
11 Francis Merbury, *The Marriage between Wit and Wisdom*, in *English Moral Interludes*, ed. Wickham, 167–84.
12 While I am theorizing the queer scopophilia of the early English stage, I do not wish to obscure the likelihood of heteroerotic scopophilia functioning simultaneously, with many female members of the audience similarly finding visual pleasure in viewing the actors staging dramas for their pleasure, too. Lesbian scopophilia would be faced with the potential obstacle of male actors playing female roles, but certainly any such obstacle would never be insurmountable, as the ensuing discussions of "Adam" in the Chester Mystery Cycle (in this chapter) and the Digby *Mary Magdalen* (in the following chapter) illuminate.
13 John Hazel Smith, ed., *A Humanist's "Trew Imitation."* Text references are to act, scene, and line.
14 Aloni and Sharon-Zisser, "Judaism and Jouissance," 182.
15 *Thersites*, in *Three Tudor Classical Interludes*, ed. Marie Axton, 37–63.
16 *The Interlude of Youth*, in *The Broadview Anthology of Medieval Drama*, ed. Fitzgerald and Sebastian, 436–48.
17 Epp, *The Towneley Plays*.
18 Lumiansky and Mills, *The Chester Mystery Cycle*.
19 The issue of Jesus's nudity sparked some interesting debates in medieval drama, such as in *Lucidus and Dubius*. Dubius wonders, "Was Crist leyde in his tombe al naked?" (499); Lucidus replies, "ʒe, syr, that he was," and further explains, "Sir, he is almyʒty and euer was / and the eyre he turned anone / jn-to clothis thurgh his myʒt" (500, 503–5). See *Lucidus and Dubius*, in *Non-Cycle Plays and The Winchester Dialogues*, ed. Davis, 179–91.
20 Crowder, "Children, Costume, and Identity," 15.
21 *The Castle of Perseverance*, in *The Macro Plays*, ed. Eccles, 1–111.
22 *Mundus et Infans*, in *Three Late Medieval Morality Plays*, ed. Lester, 107–57.
23 *Gismond of Salerne*, in *Early English Classical Tragedies*, ed. Cunliffe, 161–216. Text references are to act, scene, and line.
24 T. Lupton, *All for Money*, in *English Morality Plays*, ed. Schell and Shuchter, 419–73.
25 Medwall, *Nature*, in *The Plays of Henry Medwall*, ed. Nelson, 91–161.
26 *Impatient Poverty*, in *The Tudor Interludes*, ed. Tennenhouse, 127–91.
27 Tydeman, "Costumes and Actors," 184.
28 Orgel, *Impersonations*, 104. On fashion and costumery for early English drama see Cunnington and Cunnington, *Handbook of English Mediaeval Costume*; Norris, *Tudor Costume and Design*; and Lublin, *Costuming the Shakespearean Stage*.

29 Spector, *The N-Town Play*.
30 *Mary Magdalen*, in *The Late Medieval Religious Plays*, ed. Donald Baker, Murphy, and Hall, 24–95.
31 Ulpian Fulwell, *Like Will to Like*, in *Four Tudor Interludes*, ed. Somerset, 128–64.
32 John Foxe, *Two Latin Comedies*, ed. John Hazel Smith. Text references are to act, scene, and line.
33 Beadle, ed., *The York Plays*. Text references are to play and line.
34 Schelling, *Tom Tyler and His Wife*, 253–89.
35 Edwards, *The Works of Richard Edwards*, 160–1.
36 Alan Bray, *Homosexuality in Renaissance England*, 52.
37 Udall, *Royster Doyster*, in *Tudor Plays*, ed. Creeth, 215–314; text references are to act, scene, and lines of this edition. *Oxford English Dictionary*, s.v. "malkin," 1(a) and 2.
38 *Oxford English Dictionary*, s.v. "capon," (2); *Middle English Dictionary*, s.v. "capoun," 2(a). The *Middle English Dictionary*'s accompanying definition 2(b) awkwardly pairs *eunuch* with "?surname."
39 *Four Elements*, in *Three Rastell Plays*, ed. Richard Axton, 30–68.
40 *Middle English Dictionary*, s.v. "dighten" 1(a) and 7.
41 Skelton, *Magnificence*, 84.
42 Walker, *Medieval Drama*, 358.
43 Shakespeare, *Henry IV, Part 1*, in *The Riverside Shakespeare*, ed. Evans, 912.
44 *Oxford English Dictionary*, s.v. "pole" 1(f). The poem "A Man's Yard," c. 1600, includes the lines "It is a stiffe shorte flesshly pole, / That fittes to stopp a Maydens hole" (Burford, *Bawdy Verse*, 49, lines 5–6).
45 Partridge, *Shakespeare's Bawdy*, 106.
46 Wever, *Lusty Juventus*, in *Four Tudor Interludes*, ed. Somerset, 97–127. See also Noseworthy, *Lusty Juventus*.
47 *Oxford English Dictionary*, s.v. "pudding" 9 (a).
48 Epp, "Into a womannys lyckenes," 65.
49 *King Darius*, in *Anonymous Plays*, ed. John Farmer, 72.
50 George Whetstone, *Promos and Cassandra*, in Chadwyck-Healey Database.
51 Dawson and Brown, *July and Julian*.
52 As evident from its prologue and epilogue, *July and Julian* was performed by boys: "we are come hither to troble yow as boyes. / and after sage thinges to shewe oᵗ trifflinge toyes" (7–8). The relative youth of the actors would not preclude sexual connotations in the play-script, particularly as it uses such epithets as *whore* (637, 809). Also, characters express explicitly their erotic desire for each other, as in Wilkin's statement about Bettrice: "canst not thow borow her for me, I wold do a thing wᵗʰ her" (778).

53 *Oxford English Dictionary*, s.v. "trim," 7.

54 Shakespeare, *Titus Andronicus*, in *The Riverside Shakespeare*, ed. Evans, 1065–100; text references are to act, scene, and line.

55 G. Wapull, *The Tide Tarrieth No Man*, in *English Morality Plays*, ed. Schell and Shuchter, 309–66.

56 More work remains to be done on this topic, but several excellent studies have focused on the intersection of language and sexuality in medieval literature. See such volumes as Carissa Harris, *Obscene Pedagogies*; Gust, *Chaucerotics*; and Sidhu, *Indecent Exposure*.

57 Neal, *The Masculine Self*, 25.

58 Bynum, *Fragmentation and Redemption*, 151; italics in the original.

59 Fitzgerald, *The Drama of Masculinity*, 164.

60 Whitney, "What's Wrong with the Pardoner?," 360; italics in the original.

61 *The History of Iacob and Esau*, in *Reformation Biblical Drama in England*, ed. Paul Whitfield White, 67–133.

62 *Candlemes Day and the Kyllyng of þe Children of Israelle*, in *The Late Medieval Religious Plays*, ed. Donald Baker, Murphy, and Hall, 96–115.

63 *The Prodigal Son*, in *Collections, Part 1*, ed. Greg, 27–30.

64 Beadle, *"Occupation and Idleness,"* 7–47.

65 All citations of Chaucer refer to *The Riverside Chaucer*, 3rd ed., ed. Benson, and are noted parenthetically; text references are to line.

66 *Common Conditions*, in *Five Anonymous Plays*, ed. Farmer. See also Brooke, *Common Conditions*.

67 Heywood, *Johan Johan*, in *The Plays of John Heywood*, ed. Axton and Happé, 75–92.

68 Preston, *Cambises*, in *Tudor Plays*, ed. Edmund Creeth, 443–503.

69 R.B., *Apius and Virginia*, in *Tudor Interludes*, ed. Happé, 271–317.

70 Braunmuller, "Bearded Ladies in Shakespeare," 209.

71 Thomas Garter, *Virtuous and Godly Susanna*, in Chadwyck-Healey Database.

72 James D. Clark, *The Bugbears*; text references are to act, scene, and line.

73 For Ovid's version of this myth, see his *Metamorphoses*, bk. 4, pp. 204–5, lines 375–9. This scene is discussed in greater detail in chapter 6. For the figure of the hermaphrodite in medieval literature see Rollo, *Kiss My Relics*.

74 Bale, *Thre Lawes of Nature, Moses, and Christ*, in *The Complete Plays of John Bale*, ed. Happé, 2:64–124.

75 Gascoigne, *The Glasse of Governement*, in *The Complete Works of George Gascoigne*, ed. Cunliffe, 2.28.

76 *The Enterlude of Godly Queene Hester*, in *Medieval Drama*, ed. Walker, 408–31.

77 Arbona is identified as a eunuch in the biblical account of Esther: "cum rex esset hilarior et post nimiam potionem incaluisset mero, pracepit Mauman

et Bazatha et Arbona et Bagatha et Abgatha et Zarath et Charchas, septem eunuchis qui in conspectu eius ministrabant" (Esther 1:10; when the king was merry, and after very much drinking was well warmed with wine, he commanded Mauman, and Bazatha, and Harbona, and Bagatha, and Abgatha, and Zethar, and Charcas, the seven eunuchs that served in his presence). The Vulgate is cited from *Biblia Sacra iuxta Vulgatam Versionem*, with translations taken from *Holy Bible: Douay-Rheims Version*.

78 On Chaucer's influence on Heywood see Boocker, "Heywood's Indulgent Pardoner," 21–30. On the ambiguous gender of Chaucer's Pardoner see Sturges, *Chaucer's Pardoner and Gender Theory*.

79 Heywood, *The Pardoner and the Frere*, in *The Plays of John Heywood*, ed. Axton and Happé, 93–109.

80 Peter Houle, "A Reconstruction," 259–77.

81 Medwall, *The Plays of Henry Medwall*, ed. Nelson, 200 n442; text references are to line.

82 *Wisdom*, in *The Macro Plays*, ed. Eccles, 113–52.

83 Klausner, *Two Moral Interludes*, 67n751; see also Pamela Allen Brown and Peter Parolin, *Women Players in England*. Whetstone's *Promos and Cassandra* features a similar stage direction – "Fiue or sixe, the one halfe men, the other women, neare vnto the Musick, singing on some stage" (pt. 2, following 1.9.30) – which indicates such a moment was not anomalous in early English theatre. See also Twycross, "'Transvestism' in the Mystery Plays," 185–236.

84 Butler, "Critically Queer," 28.

85 Sedgwick, *Touching Feeling*, 61.

86 Case, *Feminist and Queer Performance*, 150.

87 Enders, "Of Miming and Signing," 17.

88 Epp, "To 'Play the Sodomits,'" 189.

89 On the tensions arising from cross-dressing in the medieval and early modern era, see such key studies as Normington, *Gender and Medieval Drama*; Chess, *Male-to-Female Crossdressing*; and Levine, *Men in Women's Clothing*.

90 *Robin Hood and the Friar*, in *The Early Plays of Robin Hood*, ed. David Wiles, 76.

91 Gosson, *Markets of Bawdrie*, 178.

92 *Oxford English Dictionary*, s.v. "prick" 12 (b). The *Medieval English Dictionary* does not include "penis" as a definition of *prick*.

93 Heywood, *The Foure PP*, in *The Plays of John Heywood*, ed. Axton and Happé, 111–42.

94 Walker, *Medieval Drama*, 362n66.

95 John Redford, *Wit and Science*, in *Medieval Drama*, ed. Bevington, 1029–61.

96 The anonymously penned *The Marriage of Wit and Science*, inspired by Redford's play, contains a similar scene of Wit resting in Idleness's lap

(4.4.1130–57), with similar queer potential; see Lennam, ed., *Sebastian Westcott*, 119–74.

97 *The Contention between Liberalitie and Prodigalitie*, ed. Greg.
98 *Nice Wanton*, in *The Tudor Interludes*, ed. Tennenhouse, 64–125.
99 Barber, *Misogonus*.

2 Themes of Friendship and Sodomy

1 Studies of homosocial friendships illuminate their exalted position in Western culture during various historical eras, as well as the anxieties they provoked. Key texts in this subfield of queer studies include David Clark, *Between Medieval Men*; MacFaul, *Male Friendship*; Alan Bray, *The Friend*; Rocke, *Forbidden Friendships*; Bruce R. Smith, *Homosexual Desire*; and the special issue of *GLQ: A Journal of Lesbian and Gay Studies* addressing "The Work of Friendship" (*GLQ* 10, no. 3 [2004]: 319–541).

2 Cicero concludes *De amicitia* with the following exhortation: "vos autem hortor ut ita virtutem locetis (sine qua amicitia esse non potest) ut ea excepta nihil amicitia praestabilius putetis" (but I exhort you both so to esteem virtue [without which friendship cannot exist], that, excepting virtue, you will think nothing more excellent than friendship; Cicero, *De senectute*, 210–11). For a brief review of Cicero's status in the Middle Ages and the legacy of his ideas on friendship see Laurens Mills, *One Soul in Bodies Twain*, 1–15; and Ailes, "The Medieval Male Couple," 214–37, esp. 215–16.

3 *Everyman*, ed. Cawley.

4 For excerpts of these authors and their homoerotic verse see Byrne R.S. Fone, ed., *The Columbia Anthology of Gay Literature*, 103–10. See also Kenneth Boris, ed., *Same-Sex Desire in the English Renaissance*.

5 On the homoeroticism of Ganymede in art and narrative see Boswell, *Christianity, Social Tolerance, and Homosexuality*, particularly the chapter "The Triumph of Ganymede," 243–66; Saslow, *Ganymede in the Renaissance*; and on this figure's pivotal role in medieval drama, Kolve, "Ganymede / Son of Getron," 1014–67.

6 Thomas Eliot, *The Bankette of Sapience* (1534), fols. B3v–4r.

7 Stretter, "Engendering Obligation," 501–2. See also Alan Bray, "Wedded Brother," in *The Friend*, 13–41; and my "For to be sworne bretheren til they deye," in *Chaucer's (Anti-) Eroticisms*, 65–97.

8 Quoted from Alan Bray, *The Friend*, 16, as taken from London, British Library, Harleian MS 2259, fol. 27v. See also London, "Some Medieval Treatises on English Heraldry."

9   Critiques of Boswell's work include Paglia, "Plighting Their Troth"; and Woods, "Same-Sex Unions or Semantic Illusions?" 321.

10   Schultz, *Courtly Love*, 95.

11   Wever, *Lusty Juventus*, in *Four Tudor Interludes*, ed. Somerset, 97–127.

12   *Wealth and Health*, in *Recently Recovered "Lost" Tudor Plays*, ed. John Farmer, 282.

13   A. Esdaile, *Love Feigned and Unfeigned*, in *Collections, Part 1*, ed. Greg, 17–25.

14   *The Four Cardinal Virtues*, in Chadwyck-Healey Database.

15   Lancashire, *Two Tudor Interludes*, 157–238.

16   As much as bed-sharing need not carry any homoerotic undertones in medieval and early modern culture, it could be used to imply the moral depravity of men, such as in *The Trial of Treasure* when Just observes of the Vice characters, "But Lust is lusty, and full of porridge: / Cogitation and he in one bed doth lie" (*The Trial of Treasure*, in *Anonymous Plays*, 3rd series, ed. Farmer, 221).

17   Sedgwick, *Between Men*, esp. 1–25.

18   *The Marriage of Wit and Science*, in *Sebastian Westcott*, ed. Lennam, 119–74; text references are to act, scene, and line.

19   Udall, *Royster Doyster*, in *Tudor Plays*, ed. Creeth, 215–34.

20   Fulwell, *Like Will to Like*, in *Four Tudor Interludes*, ed. Somerset, 128–64.

21   On the genealogy of the Titus and Gisippus legend, see Sorieri, *Boccaccio's Story*. Sorieri traces this story of homosocial brotherhood to a range of sources, including *The Arabian Nights*, the *Disciplina clericalis*, and the *Gesta Romanorum*. It also serves as a source for Shakespeare's *Two Gentlemen of Verona*.

22   Foxe, *Two Latin Comedies*.

23   Epp, "John Foxe and the Circumcised Stage," 291.

24   *Damon and Pythias*, in Edwards, *The Works of Richard Edwards*, ed. King, 108–84.; text references are to scene and line.

25   Jennifer Richards documents a performance of *Palamon and Arcite* at Christ Church in 1566; see her "Male Friendship and Counsel," 296. Richards posits that Edwards questions the viability of male friendships in *Damon and Pythias*.

26   John Philip, *Pacient and Meeke Grissell*, in Chadwyck-Healey Database.

27   Littleton, *Clyomon and Clamydes*.

28   Gascoigne, *The Glasse of Governement*, in *The Complete Works of George Gascoigne*, ed. Cunliffe, 2.9.

29   Gascoigne, 2.72.

30   *Albion Knight* (fragment), in Chadwyck-Healey Database.

31   *Four Elements*, in *Three Rastell Plays*, ed. Richard Axton, 30–68.

32   *The Conversion of St. Paul*, in *The Late Medieval Religious Plays*, ed. Donald Baker, Murphy, and Hall, 1–23.

33 Woodes, *The Conflict of Conscience*, in *English Morality Plays*, ed. Schell and Shuchter, 475–550.

34 Wager, *"The Longer Thou Livest,"* ed. Benbow.

35 The quotation of Aelred's *De spiritali amicitia* is taken from Aelred of Rievaulx, *Aeldredi Rievallensis Opera Omnia*, ed. Hoste and Talbot, 295, with translations from Aelred of Rievaulx, *Spiritual Friendship*, trans. Laker, 59.

36 Aelred of Rievaulx, *Aeldredi Rievallensis Opera Omnia*, 313; Aelred of Rievaulx, *Spiritual Friendship*, 84.

37 Jaeger, *Ennobling Love*, 111–12.

38 Newman, *From Virile Woman to WomanChrist*, 39–40, with her quotations of Guibert of Nogent taken from *De virginitate*, in *Patrologia Latina*, 156:579–80, 608bc.

39 Olsen, *Of Sodomites*, 14.

40 Jonathan Goldberg, *Sodometries*, 17. The semantic slipperiness of *sodomy* in Reformation discourse is discussed in greater detail in chapter 5 of the present volume.

41 Northbrooke, *A Treatise against Dicing*, 183.

42 Stubbes, *The Anatomie of Abuses*, ed. Kidnie, 204.

43 Stubbes, 35.

44 John Hazel Smith, *A Humanist's "Trew Imitation,"* text references are to act, scene, and line; *King Darius*, in *Anonymous Plays*, ed Farmer, 74; Beadle, *Occupation and Idleness*, 7–47.

45 Barber, *Misogonus*; text references are to act, scene, and line.

46 Somerset, *Four Tudor Interludes*, 181nn87–88.

47 James D. Clark, *The Bugbears*.

48 Gascoigne, *Supposes*, in *The Complete Works of George Gascoigne*, ed. Cunliffe, 1:208, 1:237.

49 Heywood, *The Foure PP*, in *The Plays of John Heywood*, ed. Axton and Happé, 111–42.

50 Heywood, *The Play of the Wether*, in *The Plays of John Heywood*, ed. Axton and Happé, 183–215.

51 *Tom Tyler and His Wife*, ed. Schelling, 253–89.

52 *The Enterlude of Godly Queene Hester*, in *Medieval Drama*, ed. Walker, 408–31. Phalaris's story is also addressed in George Whetstone's *Promos and Cassandra* (part 2, 2.5.30, in Chadwyck-Healey Database).

53 Lupton, *All for Money*, in *English Morality Plays*, ed. Schell and Shuchter, 419–73.

54 Medwall, *Fulgens and Lucrece*, in *The Plays of Henry Medwall*, ed. Nelson, 31–89; text references are to part and line.

55 Walker, *Medieval Drama*, 319n35; text references are to part and line.

56 Walker, 325n55.

57 Fitzgerald and Sebastian, *The Broadview Anthology of Medieval Drama*,

415n6. See also Peter Meredith with Meg Twycross, "'Farte Pryke in Cule' and Cock-Fighting," 30–9, who note that the two most prominent features of this game are "the joust-like nature of the contest" and "its association with asses" (31). The scholarly discussion of "farte prycke in cule" continues in Alan Fletcher, "Fart Prycke in Cule," 132–9, and in Twycross with Jones and Fletcher, "'Fart Prycke in Cule': The Pictures," 100–21.

58 All citations of Chaucer refer to *The Riverside Chaucer*, ed. Benson, and are noted parenthetically. Text references are to line.

59 *Oxford English Dictionary*, s.v. "needle" IV (16); www.oed.com. John Lyly, *Gallathea*, in *The Complete Works of John Lyly*, ed. Bond, act 4, scene 2, lines 86–7.

60 McFadyen, "What Was Really Lost?," 9–13.

61 Whitworth, *Gammer Gurton's Needle*; text references are to act, scene, and line.

62 *Oxford English Dictionary*, s.v. "breech" 1 and 4 (a).

63 *Oxford English Dictionary*, s.v. "meat" 6 (b), with the citation from the poem "Buckleye" of the Arundel Harington Manuscript: "The baker he did cram the cockes / wth bread well baked for ye nonce / and she her meatie mouth well stoppes / wth pleasinge meate quite free from bones" (Hughey, *The Arundel Harington Manuscript of Tudor Poetry*, 2:285, stanza 61).

64 Toole, "The Aesthetics of Scatology," 258.

65 On the issue of female friendships in the medieval and early modern eras see Verini, "Medieval Models of Female Friendship," 365–91; and Herbert, *Female Alliances*.

66 Robert Mills, *Seeing Sodomy in the Middle Ages*, esp. 264–70, for his reading of the *Ancrene Wisse*. See also Sautman and Sheingorn, *Same Sex Love*; and Giffney, Sauer, and Watt, *The Lesbian Premodern*.

67 Lochrie, *Covert Operations*, 187; italics in the original.

68 Sautman and Sheingorn, "Charting the Field," in *Same Sex Love*, 24–5.

69 *Mary Magdalen*, in *The Late Medieval Religious Plays*, ed. Donald Baker, Murphy, and Hall, 24–95.

70 Coletti, *Mary Magdalene and the Drama of Saints*, 183.

3 York Corpus Christi Plays

1 Krummel, "Him Jesus, That Jew!," 298. On closeted and outed identities, Krummel cites Diana Fuss's "Inside/Out," 1–10.

2 Kolve, *The Play Called Corpus Christi*, 32.

3 R.B. Dobson advocates a "big bang" theory of the York Corpus Christi Plays, suggesting that they emerged in the 1370s in a relatively finished form; see his "Craft Guilds and City," in *The Stage as Mirror*, ed. Knight, 101.

Other scholars propose a more evolutionary development to the cycle, including Stevens, "The York Cycle," 37–61; Tydeman, *The Theatre in the Middle Ages*, 102; and P.J.P. Goldberg, "From Tableaux to Text," 247–76.

4 Johnston and Rogerson, *Records of Early English Drama: York*, 1:16–26. See also Davies, *Municipal Records*, 230–3.

5 Johnston and Rogerson, *Records of Early English Drama: York*, 1:355.

6 On the York Realist, see Robinson, "The Art of the York Realist," 241–51; and Davidson, "The Realism of the York Realist," 270–83.

7 Foundational studies of typology in the English mystery cycles include Woolf, "The Effect of Typology," 805–25; Meyers, *A Figure Given*; Arnold Williams, "Typology and the Cycle Plays," 677–84; and Keenan, *Typology and English Medieval Literature*. More recently, see Fitzgerald, *The York Corpus Christi Play*, 16–17.

8 Meyers, "Typology and the Audience," in *Typology and English Medieval Literature*, ed. Keenan, 262.

9 Beckwith, *Signifying God*, 3.

10 Gash, "Carnival against Lent," 75 and 96. See also Munson, "Audience and Meaning," 44–67, in which he advocates situating the York Corpus Christi Plays and other medieval drama among "the festivity of civic holiday … in which there was procession, liturgy, and feast organized under the supervision of the town authorities" (46).

11 Sturges, *The Circulation of Power*, 4.

12 Sponsler, *Drama and Resistance*, 140.

13 Biddick, *The Typological Imaginary*, 6.

14 Tinkle, "York's Jesus," 97.

15 Powell, "John Mirk," in *Oxford Dictionary of National Biography*, ed. Matthew and Harrison, 369.

16 Powell, *John Mirk's Festial*, 1:3 (from the prologue).

17 Powell, 1:90–1 (from the sermon "4 Lent").

18 Powell, 1:74 (from the sermon "Quinquagesima").

19 Woolf, "The Effect of Typology," 806. The exception to the typological pattern that Woolf notes occurs in the Towneley Plays.

20 Cohen, *Living Letters of the Law*, 2, 5. See also Lampert, *Gender and Jewish Difference*, 21–57. Further pertinent readings include Tomasch on the "virtual Jew" in "Postcolonial Chaucer and the Virtual Jew," 243–60; and Kruger on the "spectral Jew," in *The Spectral Jew*.

21 For additional Pauline passages on the necessity of typological interpretation, see Romans 5:12–14; 1 Corinthians 10:6, 10:11, 15:21; Galatians 4:21–31; Colossians 2:16–17; and Hebrews 9:11–14. The Vulgate is cited from *Biblia Sacra iuxta Vulgatam Versionem*, with translations taken from *Holy Bible: Douay-Rheims Version*.

22 Auerbach, *Mimesis*, 75.

23 Quotations of the plays are taken from *The York Plays*, ed. Beadle, and are cited parenthetically by play and line numbers; italics in the original.

24 Davidson, *The York Corpus Christi Plays*, 410n15. Richard Beadle observes that these lines appear to be a loose paraphrase of Psalms 73 (*The York Plays*, 2:83n16).

25 Arnold Williams, "Typology and the Cycle Plays," 679.

26 On the complex relationship between Jesus, Judaism, and a nascent Christianity see Daniel Boyarin, *The Jewish Gospels*, esp. the chapter "Jesus Kept Kosher," 102–28. See also Boyarin's works on cultural constructions of Jewish difference, including *Border Lines*, *Unheroic Conduct*, and, with Jonathan Boyarin, *Jews and Other Differences*.

27 Normington, *Gender and Medieval Drama*, 38–9; italics in the original. From the preponderance of evidence it is clear that women were marginalized on the medieval stage, yet P.J.P. Goldberg, in tracing the development of the York plays, proposes that women may have participated in the cycle's early productions that took place in the form of *tableaux vivants* and in their subsequent transition into plays with speaking parts, with female participation ending "once the cycle evolved from being essentially 'owned' by the city's many craft groups – and hence participation was an act of devotion on the part of craft members – to being 'owned' by the city government and hence a projection of civic pride" ("From Tableaux to Text," 262).

28 Robert L.A. Clark and Claire Sponsler, "Queer Play," 319, 320, and 338.

29 Lampert, *Gender and Jewish Difference*, 101. In an amusing typographical error, I originally cited Lampert as referring to "men or *goys* in 'drag'" – an apropos solecism that highlights the ways in which gendered and religious identities were always in flux in the production of these plays.

30 On Noah and birthing themes see also Fitzgerald, *The Drama of Masculinity*, 70–2.

31 On the gendering of Jewish men in Christian traditions see Resnick, "Medieval Roots," 241–63; Willis Johnson, "The Myth of Jewish Male Menses," 273–95; Jay Geller, "(G)nos(e)ology, 243–82; and Kruger, "The Bodies of Jews," 301–23.

32 The definitive study of medieval conceptions of a maternal and effeminized Jesus remains Caroline Walker Bynum's *Jesus as Mother*.

33 See Utley, "The One Hundred and Three Names," 426–52.

34 Rice and Pappano, *The Civic Cycles*, 181.

35 Lumiansky and Mills, *The Chester Mystery Cycle*, 1:50, lines 203–4.

36 It should be noted that within the play's typological imaginary, Mary adapts Balaam's prophecy to her particular circumstances. He predicts that "orietur stella ex Iacob et consurget virga de Israhel" (Numbers 24:17;

a star shall rise out of Jacob and a sceptre shall spring up from Israel), but describes this figure more as a conqueror of enemies than as a saviour of souls: "De Iacob erit dominetur et perdat reliquias civitatis" (Numbers 24:19; Out of Jacob shall he come that shall rule, and shall destroy the remains of the city). It is likely that *virga* (sceptre) was mistranslated or misunderstood as *virgo* (virgin).

37 Powell, *John Mirk's Festial*, 1:95 (from the sermon "Annunciation of the Virgin").

38 Joseph here cites the Septuagint version of Habakkuk 3:2: "thou shalt be known between the two living creatures"; see *The Septuagint with Apocrypha*, ed. Brenton, 1108.

39 As Clifford Davidson notes, this scene "conflates the Purification ritual with that of the Presentation, which in Jewish tradition was a different ceremony" (*The York Corpus Christi Plays*, 424); see also Shorr, "The Iconographic Development," 17–32.

40 Resnick, "Medieval Roots," 248.

41 Dutka, *Music in the English Mystery Plays*, 100.

42 Carleton Brown, *Religious Lyrics of the XVth Century*, 30–3, lines 15–16.

43 Perry, *Religious Pieces*, 79–82, lines 75–6.

44 Chaucer, "An ABC," in *The Riverside Chaucer*, ed. Benson, 637–40, lines 84, 86. Furthermore, the idiom *dere bought* is employed in a variety of more secular literary circumstances, referring simply to the high price a character has paid to achieve their objectives.

45 Augustine, "Sermon CCLXXXVIII," 38.1304.

46 Lynn Staley Johnson, "St. John the Baptist," 109.

47 Staging Paul's life would likely be challenging for pageant plays, although this difficulty should not be construed as an insurmountable obstacle, as evident in the Digby *Conversion of St. Paul*.

48 On medieval Jewish life in England and the 1290 Jewish expulsion see Mundill, *The King's Jews*; Skinner, *The Jews in Medieval Britain*; and Roth, *A History of the Jews in England*. On the slaughter at Clifford's Tower see Sarah Rees Jones and Watson, *Christians and Jews in Angevin England*.

49 Pearsall, *Arthurian Romance*, 21.

50 On Herod's unique role in medieval dramatic typology see Christopher Taylor, who explains how the "English mystery plays complicate supercessionary typology by uniquely foregrounding the degree to which Herod *knows* the severity of his actions" ("The Once and Future Herod," 145; italics in the original).

51 As Clifford Davidson notes, the Vulgate identifies Emmaus as a *castellum* (Luke 24:13), based on a mistranslation of the Septuagint (*The York Corpus Christi Plays*, 485). This piece of courtly imagery may be unintentional, yet it nonetheless influenced the staging, scenery, and themes of the

cycle. Anachronistic castles appear in other medieval plays, such as the Digby *Mary Magdalen*, in which Lazarus, upon his father's death, informs his sisters of their inheritance: "Thys castell is owerys wyth all þe fee!" (Donald Baker, Murphy, and Hall, *The Late Medieval Religious Plays*, line 299, cf. 417), with the stage directions later detailing how the Vice characters lay siege to it until Mary capitulates (following line 439).

52 Tiner, "English Law in the York Trial Plays," 140. See also such studies as Nicholson, "The Trial of Christ in the York Cycle," 125–69; and Kastleman, "Impersonating the Law," 37–56.

53 Nisse, *Defining Acts*, 41. With these words Nisse refers specifically to Pilate's words in "The Remorse of Judas," but her wider point applies well to the various court scenes of the York plays.

54 Quinn, "The Chosen and the Chastised," 149.

55 *Middle English Dictionary*, s.v. "perverten," 1 (a).

56 Woolf, "The Theme of Christ the Lover-Knight," 2.

57 Jacobus de Voragine, *Legenda aurea*, ed. Graesse, 509; Jacobus de Voragine, *The Golden Legend*, trans. Ryan, 2:82.

58 Justin, *Dialogus cum Tryphone*, in *Die ältessten Apologeten*, ed. Goodspeed, 100, 4–6, 215; qtd. and trans. in Maja Weyermann, "The Typologies of Adam-Christ," 616.

59 Neuss, *The Creacion of the World*, 28, following line 343. In the Norwich *Grocers' Play*, the Father clothes Adam and Eve in leather aprons, further testifying to the utility of such costuming. In his words, "Beholde, theis letherin aprons unto yourselves now take" (Davis, *Non-cycle Plays and Fragments*, 8–18, at B.94).

60 Coldewey, "Thrice-Told Tales," 18.

61 Wyclif, *Select English Works of John Wyclif*, ed. Arnold, 1:129.

4 Mankind

1 Nathaniel Woodes, *The Conflict of Conscience*, in *English Morality Plays and Moral Interludes*, ed. Schell and Shuchter, 475–550, line 47.

2 Bevington, *From "Mankind" to Marlowe*, 9.

3 Angus Fletcher, *Allegory*, 2, 7; italics in the original.

4 Indeed, even the apparently clear term *subtext* invites interpretative problems when dealing with medieval allegory, for one could question in many instances precisely which elements constitute the text and which the subtext. For example, Mercy is both a friar and a personal quality in *Mankind*, as well as assuming additional significations that broaden his thematic role. For the purposes of this argument I refer to the play's subtext when considering meanings potentially unintended by the author

but nonetheless adumbrated in the tension between and among allegorical registers.

5   On the queerness of these allegories see such studies as Michael Johnson, "Sodomy, Allegory, and the Subject of Pleasure," 1–12; Paxson, "Queering *Piers Plowman*," 21–9; and my "Abandoning Desires, Desiring Readers, and the Divinely Queer Triangle of *Pearl*," in *Sexuality and Its Queer Discontents*, 21–47.

6   Burger, *Chaucer's Queer Nation*, xii.

7   For example, Neville Denny, in outlining *Mankind*'s plot, concludes that the title character is "finally saved by Mercy from degeneracy" ("Aspects of the Staging of *Mankind*," 252); Hardin Craig condemns the play as "probably degenerate" (*English Religious Drama of the Middle Ages*, 351). Garrett P.J. Epp tackles the homoerotic shenanigans of *Mankind*, in his "Vicious Guise," in *Becoming Male in the Middle Ages*, ed. Cohen and Wheeler, 303–20. This study expands on his by theorizing the play's disidentified audience and the queerness of allegory in its treatment of excremental and sodomitical themes. See also Garrison, "*Mankind* and the Masculine Pleasure of Penance," 46–62.

8   Eccles, *The Macro Plays*, cited parenthetically by line number; see also Bevington, *The Macro Plays*.

9   Bouchard, "*Every Valley Shall Be Exalted*," 2.

10 The Vulgate is cited from *Biblia Sacra iuxta Vulgatam Versionem*, with translations taken from *Holy Bible: Douay-Rheims Version*.

11 Bakhtin, *Rabelais and His World*, 11.

12 Bevington, *From "Mankind" to Marlowe*, 48.

13 Eccles, *The Macro Plays*, xliii.

14 Gash, "Carnival against Lent," 82.

15 Dollimore, *Sexual Dissidence*, 219.

16 Muñoz, *Disidentifications*, 97.

17 Muñoz, 5.

18 Paulson, *Theater of the Word*, 108.

19 On medieval conceptions of the human body see Kay and Rubin, *Framing Medieval Bodies*; in his chapter therein, "The Image and the Self" (62–99), Michael Camille addresses hierarchies of human corporality.

20 In his disquisitions on adolescent lust in book 2 of his *Confessions*, Augustine includes an apt illustration of an embarrassing erection: "quin immo ubi me ille pater in balneis vidit pubescentem et inquieta indutum adulescentia" (when we were at the baths my father saw that I was becoming a man and clothed with the turbulence of adolescence). See Augustine, *Confessions, Books 1–8*, ed. Hammond, 66–7.

21 Thomas Aquinas, *Quaestiones de anima*, 7, in *Quaestiones diputatae*, ed. Spazzi et al.; qtd. in Kay, "Women's Body of Knowledge," 229.

22 Thomas Aquinas, *Truth*, ed. McGlynn, 2:391.

23 Morris, *Old English Homilies*, 152–3.

24 As Michael Camille notes, many medieval illuminated manuscripts depict the mouth as "a hole in the crucial barrier between inside and outside," with this ambiguity illustrated in depictions of dying: "As the last breath or *spiritus* left the defunct corpse, a little homunculus, representing *through* a body its very antithesis, was shown escaping into the arms of an angel or devil" ("The Image and the Self," 70; italics in the original). In such ironic images, the soul is freed from the body yet is concurrently represented by the body.

25 Lactantius, *Divinae Institutiones*, ed. Brandt, 165 (lib. II.14); qtd. and trans. in Bayless, *Sin and Filth in Medieval Culture*, 122.

26 Tanner, *Decrees of the Ecumenical Councils*, 1:360.

27 Guibert of Nogent, *Tractatus de incarnatione contra Judaeos*, in *Patrologia Latina*, ed. Migne, vol. 156, col. 499A; Rubenstein, *Guibert of Nogent*, 119.

28 Rubenstein, *Guibert of Nogent*, 119.

29 *The Lost Books of the Bible*, 43. Although tracing the motifs of apocryphal sources as they travelled from the Middle East to Western Europe presents a daunting scholarly challenge, another source with documented presence in fourteenth-century England, *Quomodo Maria et Ioseph fugerunt in Aegyptum cum Ihesu et de latrone, quem inuenerunt in deserto*, details a similar account of Jesus's miraculous bath-water. See Mark Glen Bilby, "Hospitality and Perfume of the Bandit." My thanks go to Stephen Hopkins for helping me to locate this source.

30 Gray, "The Five Wounds of Our Lord," 50.

31 Grumett, *Material Eucharist*, 176.

32 Morrison, *Excrement in the Late Middle Ages*, 80 and 191n61.

33 Rubin, *Corpus Christi*, 37.

34 Ashley, "*Mankind*: The Omnibus Text," 104. See also Charlotte Steenbrugge, "O, yowr louely wordys," 28–57.

35 Steenbrugge, *Staging Vice*, 160.

36 On the varying depictions of and anxieties surrounding Jesus's penis see Steinberg, *The Sexuality of Christ*.

37 Guynn, *Allegory and Sexual Ethics*, 4.

38 May, "A Medieval Stage Property," 88.

39 Billington, "Suffer Fools Gladly," 48.

40 Davidson, *A Tretise of Miraclis Pleyinge*, 96.

41 Epp, "Ecce Homo," 238.

42 *Middle English Dictionary*, s.v. "wantoun," 1 (d).

43 For the respective quotations, see Panton and Donaldson, *The Gest Hystoriale*, vol. 1, lines 2911–12; and Blayney, *Fifteenth-Century Translations*, 8, lines 23–7.

44 New Gyse omits the intervening passages: "cum viro innocente innocenter ages, cum electo electus eris" (and with the innocent man thou wilt be innocent. And with the elect thou wilt be elect).
45 On satiric treatments of friars see Szittya, *The Antifraternal Tradition*.
46 Epp, "The Vicious Guise," 308.
47 *Oxford English Dictionary*, s.v. "head," 19 (d).
48 Richard Axton, "Popular Modes," 37.
49 Chaucer, *The Riverside Chaucer*; cited parenthetically.
50 *Respublica*, ed. Greg; text references are to act, scene, and line.
51 *Medieval English Dictionary*, s.v. "fop," 1.
52 *Oxford English Dictionary*, s.v. "fop," 1(a) and 3.
53 Epp, "The Vicious Guise," 306.
54 Sponsler, *Drama and Resistance*, 86.
55 This is a variant reading of line 3322 of *The Miller's Tale*, as documented in Tatlock and Kennedy, *A Concordance*, 480.
56 *Mum and the Sothsegger*, ed. Day and Steele, line 375.
57 *The Castle of Perseverance*, in *The Macro Plays*, ed. Eccles, 1–111, lines 1054–7.
58 Ashley and NeCastro, *Mankind*, 59.
59 Smart, "Some Notes on *Mankind* (Concluded)," 303–5; Smart cites *The Statutes at Large*, ed. Raithby, 3:362. See also Smart, "Some Notes on *Mankind*," 45–58.
60 Kendrick, "In bourde and in pleye," 272.
61 *Like Will to Like*, in *Four Tudor Interludes*, ed. Somerset, 133, lines 145, 149, and 150.
62 Ashley, "Titivillus and the Battle of Words," 138–9.
63 Jaeger, *Ennobling Love*, 136.
64 Lester, *Three Late Medieval Morality Plays*, 53, note to lines 839–41.
65 *The Castle of Perseverance*, in *The Macro Plays*, ed. Eccles, lines 3229–32.
66 "þe first of þaim was cald merci; / þe toþer was cald sothfastness; / þe thrid of þaim, rightwisnes; / Pes þe ferde syster hiht," in *Cursor Mundi*, ed. Morris, 551, lines 9544–7.
67 Michael J. Preston, "Re-presentations," 226.

5 John Bale's Interludes

1 Shrank, *Writing the Nation*, 80.
2 See Blatt, *The Plays of John Bale*, 30–1; and McCusker, *John Bale*, 5 and 74. Paul Whitfield White documents that "Bale was under Cromwell's direct patronage" from early 1537 to early 1540 (*Theatre and Reformation*, 16).
3 For a fuller account of Bale's life see Jesse W. Harris, *John Bale*, 14–59; and Happé, *John Bale*, 1–25.
4 For his interludes see Bale, *The Complete Plays of John Bale*, ed. Happé. Quotations from these texts are cited parenthetically, with the following

abbreviated titles indicating the respective plays: *KJ, CPG, JBP, TOL,* and *ThrL*. See also Adams, ed., *John Bale's "King Johan."*

5 Happé, "John Bale's Lost Mystery Cycle," 2.

6 John N. King, *English Reformation Literature: The Tudor Origins of the Protestant Tradition,* 69. The references to Bale as a compiler appear in Bale, *The Complete Plays of John Bale,* ed. Happé, 2.34, 2.50, 2.63, and 2.124. Within the realm of medieval drama itself, the Poeta character of *The Conversion of St. Paul* extols the work of compilers: "Howbeyt vnable, as I dare speke or say, / The compyler hereof shuld translat veray / So holy a story, but wyth fauorable correccyon / Of my honorable masters, of þer benygne supplexion" (Baker, Murphy, and Hall, *The Late Medieval Religious Plays,* 13, lines 356–9).

7 Hughes and Larkin, *Tudor Royal Proclamations,* proclamation 240, 1:341–2. See also proclamation 344, 1:478–9, by which Edward VI in 1549 similarly forbad certain theatrical productions. On culture and the Tudor court see Penry Williams, *The Tudor Regime,* 293–310.

8 Gerald Bray, *Documents of the English Reformation,* 113.

9 House, "Cromwell's Message to the Regulars," 124.

10 Christianson, *Reformers and Babylon,* 16.

11 Simpson, "John Bale, *Three Laws,*" 118.

12 Tyndale, *The Obedience of a Christen Man,* 65; qtd. in Butterworth, *Magic on the Early English Stage,* 127. Tyndale's subtitle registers his anti-theatrical stance: *Howe Christen Rulers Ought to Gouerne, Where in Also (If Thou Marke Diligently) Thou Shalt Fynde Eyes to Perceive the Crafty Conveyaunce of All Iugglers.*

13 Brokaw, "Music and Religious Compromise," 326–7.

14 Butler, "Baleus Prolocutor," 106.

15 Frantzen, "Bede and Bawdy Bale," 28–9. On Bale's multivalent view of sodomy see also Garrett P.J. Epp, who states that "Bale's Sodomy signifies, among other things, bestiality, masturbation, pederasty, heterosexual promiscuity, and even clerical celibacy" ("Into a womannys lyckenes," 64).

16 The Vulgate is cited from *Biblia Sacra iuxta Vulgatam Versionem,* with translations taken from *Holy Bible: Douay-Rheims Version.*

17 Levy-Navarro, "Burning in Sodom," 72 and 88.

18 Raithby, *The Statutes at Large,* 3:145.

19 Hyde, *The Love That Dared Not Speak Its Name,* 40. The acts of recriminalization were passed in 1536, 1539, 1541, and 1548.

20 One could reasonably argue that Bale's phrase "children with mennis so carnallye consent" refers to heteroerotic passions, and, because *children* is an unspecific term regarding gender, indeed it could. Still, male-male carnal sin would be envisioned in such a scenario as well, and given Bale's predominant focus on men throughout his interludes, an interpretation

that focuses on the homoerotic aspects of these lines appears more in congruence with his thinking.

21 Bale, *Select Works of John Bale*, 259–60. On Bale's conception of femininity, the Whore of Babylon, and the Catholic Church, see McEachern, "A Whore at the First Blush," 245–69.

22 Bale, *The Examination of Lord Cobham*, in *Select Works of John Bale*, ed. Christmas, 12.

23 Bale, *The Image of Both Churches*, 454, 497.

24 Bale, 427, 444, 336, and 633.

25 Mager, "John Bale and Early Tudor Sodomy Discourse," 156.

26 Pamela King, "Morality Plays," 235.

27 Brokaw, "Music and Religious Compromise," 330.

28 On the identification of "Our Lady of Grace" with the Rood of Grace at Boxley, Kent, see Farmer, *The Dramatic Writings of John Bale*, 341. See also Groeneveld, "A Theatrical Miracle," 12–48, in which she examines this enigmatic crucifix and its theatrical properties.

29 On the depictions of Muslims in the Crusades see Manion, *Narrating the Crusades*, esp. "Refiguring Catholic and Turk," 146–211. See also Elst, *The Knight, the Cross, and the Song*. Several contemporary authors still strongly advocated for the continuation of the Crusades, such as Thomas More in such works as *A Dialogue Concerning Heresies* (1529) and *A Dialogue of Comfort against Tribulation* (1534). In another passage Englande seems to portray herself as the victim of Catholic rape, telling Johan, "Alas, yowre clargy hath done very sore amys / In mysusyng me ageynst all ryght and justyce" (*KJ*, 27–8).

30 Bale, *The Image of Both Churches*, 517 and 410.

31 Strohm, *Hochon's Arrow*, 5–6.

32 Herschel Baker, *The Race of Time*, 24.

33 Bale, preface to *The Actes of Englysh Votaryes*, v.

34 Guy-Bray, Nardizzi, and Stockton, *Queer Renaissance Historiography*, 6. For additional theorizations of sexual historiography see Dinshaw, *Getting Medieval*, and Fradenburg and Freccero, *Premodern Sexualities*.

35 Bale, *The Complete Plays of John Bale*, ed. Happé, 2:173, for note L1335–36.

36 Bale, *The Actes of Englysh Votaryes*, 74 (in the chapter "Sygnes and plages folowynge these myschefes").

37 Weir, *Eleanor of Aquitaine*, 252.

38 Ralph V. Turner, *King John*, 117.

39 Matthew Paris, *Chronicles of Matthew Paris*, 28 and 58.

40 Gerald of Wales, *The Historical Works*, 163.

41 Gerald of Wales, 174.

42 Bale, *The Examination of Lord Cobham*, in *Select Works of John Bale*, ed. Christmas, at 58.

43 Impelluso, *Nature and Its Symbols*, 267.

44 Cervone, "The King's Phantom," 195.

45 Munday, *The Downfall of Robert*, act 2, scene 1.

46 Peele, *The Troublesome Reign*, cited parenthetically. Text references are to act, scene, and line.

47 Shakespeare, *The Life and Death of King John*, in *The Riverside Shakespeare*, ed. Evans, 805–40; cited parenthetically.

48 Goldman, *The Lion in Winter*. These lines are taken from Goldman's screenplay of the film version of his play, *The Lion in Winter*, dir. Anthony Harvey (1968). It should be mentioned that Richard is the more obviously queer character in Goldman's narrative, having loved and still pining for Philip II of France. On Richard the Lionheart and narrative accounts of his queerness see Stock, "He's Not an Ardent Suitor," 61–78, in which she summarizes historical accounts of Richard's sexuality before analysing his portrayal in DeMille's film *The Crusades* (1935).

6 *Ane Satyre of the Thrie Estaitis*

1 *Ane Satyre of the Thrie Estaitis* was first performed publicly in 1552 in Cupar, Fife; an earlier private production dates to 1540.

2 Lindsay, *Ane Satyre of the Thrie Estaitis*, ed. Lyall; cited parenthetically. It should be noted that Lyndsay's name is spelled in alternate ways, including *Lindsay* and *Lyndesay*; I employ *Lyndsay* as the default spelling in this chapter, while retaining the alternate spellings used by various scholars and in various editions. In quoting Lyndsay, I have glossed the more challenging words for readers unfamiliar with Middle Scots, and all glosses are confirmed with *Dictionary of the Scots Language*.

3 Mill, "The Influence of the Continental Drama," 434–5.

4 Sontag, *Against Interpretation and Other Essays*, 280.

5 For this brief biographical account of Lyndsay's life I have benefited greatly from Janet Hadley Williams, *Sir David Lyndsay*, vii–xxvi, and Edington, *Court and Culture*, 11–66. For documentation of a David Lyndsay attending St. Andrews see Anderson, *Early Records*, 203.

6 Paul, *Accounts of the Lord High Treasurer*, 4:441.

7 Paul, 4:313.

8 Quotations from Lyndsay's works, other than *Ane Satyre of the Thrie Estaitis*, are taken from Lyndesay, *Sir David Lyndesay's Works, Parts I–IV*, ed. Small and Hall; cited parenthetically.

9 Paul, *Accounts of the Lord High Treasurer*, 5:432.

10 Janet Hadley Williams, *Sir David Lyndsay*, ix.

11 On the play's performance history see Lindsay, *Ane Satyre of the Thrie Estaitis*, ed. Lyall, ix–xiv, and Mill, "The Original Version," 65–75.

12 MacQueen, "*Ane Satyre of the Thrie Estaitis*," 136, 139, and 140.

13 In *Ane Satyre of the Thrie Estaitis* the character aligned with Dissimulance is named Dissait, and both characters employ deception to advance their objectives.

14 Reid, "Rule and Misrule," 11.

15 Carpenter, "Early Scottish Drama," 206 and 205.

16 Edington, *Court and Culture*, 159.

17 McGinley, "That Every Man May Knaw," 3.

18 Goldstein, "Normative Heterosexuality," 349.

19 Hamilton, *The Catechism of John Hamilton*, ed. Law, 89.

20 On the various meanings of sodomy in Reformation discourse see the relevant sections of the chapters "Themes of Friendship and Sodomy" and "Sodomy, Chastity, and Queer Historiography in John Bale's Interludes" herein.

21 Hamilton, *The Catechism of John Hamilton*, 92, 94.

22 Conroy, *Theatre and the Body*, 74 and 15.

23 In a play illustrating the sexual transgressions of the clergy, Wantonnes's comparison of the sexual innocence of Rex Humanitas to that of a novice is somewhat ironic, particularly because Lyndsay rarely allows the possibility of the religious order's sexual probity. It nonetheless appears that these lines characterize Rex Humanitas as sexually inexperienced, yet, as with many moments in a satire, the precise identity of the author's satirical target may be hazy.

24 Kantrowitz, *Dramatic Allegory*, 94; italics in the original.

25 Janet Hadley Williams, "Women Fictional and Historic," 48 and 57.

26 Rastall, "Female Roles in All-Male Casts," 27–8.

27 Lindsay, *Ane Satyre of the Thrie Estaitis*, ed. Lyall, 180n312. Lyall's citation of Douglas Hamer refers to his edition of *The Works of Sir David Lindsay*, 4:175.

28 Epp, "Chastity in the Stocks," 64.

29 Dynes, *Encyclopedia of Homosexuality*, 1:189.

30 Ross, "Uses of Camp," 58.

31 Walker, "Personification," 247 and 253.

32 Core, *Camp*, 77.

33 Intersex Society of North America, "What Is Intersex?"

34 Ovid, *Metamorphoses*, trans. Miller, book 4, pages 204–5, lines 375–9. For Ovid's influence on early modern conceptions of the body see Stanivukovic, *Ovid and the Renaissance Body*, as well as Long, *Hermaphrodites in Renaissance Europe*.

35 Augustine, *The City of God against the Pagans*, 7:46–7.

36 Augustine, 7:46–7.

37 Augustine, 7:46–7.

38 Lemay, *Women's Secrets*, 117.

39 I recognize the anachronism of referring to the theatre's "fourth wall" for productions prior to the proscenium-arch stage and use it to refer to moments of metatheatricality in which actors confront their audiences with the staged nature of their performance.

40 *Christ's Burial*, in *The Late Medieval Religious Plays*, ed. Baker, Murphy, and Hall, 142–68.

41 Thomas Garter, *The Most Virtuous and Godly Susanna*, in Chadwyck-Healey Database.

42 John Philip, *Pacient and Meeke Grissell*, in Chadwyck-Healey Database.

43 Goldie, "Dragging Out the Queen," 130.

44 Butler, *Bodies That Matter*, 132; cited in Goldstein, "Normative Heterosexuality," 361.

45 Murphy, "Antifeminism in the Service of Anticlericalism," 408.

46 Murphy, 409–10.

47 Epp, "Chastity in the Stocks," 67. Murphy concurs with Epp on most points but disagrees on the performance's significations: "I take issue with Epp's interpretation of the dichotomy between allegorical and 'actual' women as evidence that Lindsay 'denies any licit expression onstage' of what Epp calls 'feminine power'" ("Antifeminism in the Service of Anticlericalism," 399).

48 As the *DSL* attests, *quhat rak* is an interrogative phrase that denotes such queries as "what matter?," "what does it matter?," and "why not?"

49 *DSL*, s.v. "lume," 1(b).

50 *DSL*, s.v. "lume," 2.

51 On the gloss of *unpysalt* as "with an erection," see Lindsay, *Ane Satyre of the Thrie Estaitis*, ed. Lyall, 100.

52 A number of sexually suggestive denotations are assigned to the verb *bend* in Middle Scots, including "to draw (a bow, etc.) in order to shoot," "to cock, or make ready for firing," "to aim *against*," "to pull or draw tight; to apply with force or vigour," and "to bring into a state of exaltation or excitement."

53 Walker, *The Politics of Performance*, 151.

54 Eagleton, *Walter Benjamin*, 145–6; italics in the original.

55 A thorough cataloguing of camp on the Renaissance stage remains to be written. Susan Sontag famously identified William Shakespeare's *Titus Andronicus* as camp (*Against Interpretation*, 284). For exemplary studies of Christopher Marlowe and camp see Bowers, "Hysterics," 95–106; and Grantley, "What Meanes This Shew?," 224–38.

56 Meyer, introduction to *The Politics and Poetics of Camp*, 11.

Conclusion

1 For overviews of medievalism see Utz, *Medievalism*, and Pugh and Weisl, *Medievalisms*.

2 D'Arcens, "Medievalism," 2.

3 Sponsler, *Ritual Imports*, 183. For additional studies of the vagaries of medieval drama performed across the centuries, see David Mills, *Recycling the Cycle*; Elliott, *Playing God*; and Normington, *Modern Mysteries*.

4 On film and medievalism see Finke and Shichtman, *Cinematic Illuminations*. Theatrical medievalisms have been the focus of much less scholarly attention than have cinematic medievalisms, presumably owing to issues of accessibility: a film can be watched in its entirety in the comforts of one's home, but a play can only be read, without the benefit of an accompanying performance.

5 Matthews, *Medievalism*, 37–8.

6 For representative studies of the queerness of twentieth-century drama see O'Connor, *Straight Acting*; Sinfield, *Out on Stage*; and Marra and Schanke, *Staging Desire*.

7 McNally, *Corpus Christi*; text references are to page.

8 In addition to Butterworth's *Staging Conventions*, see Southern's works, *The Medieval Theatre in the Round* and *The Staging of Plays before Shakespeare*, although several of his points have been subsequently challenged.

9 While this costuming strategy succeeds in de-individualizing (and thus, to some extent, universalizing) the characters, it also served to whitewash the production in its initial production, presenting a virtually uniform vision of whiteness for the characters (with the exception of James the Less, as played by Ken Leung).

10 I have edited this dialogue slightly to indicate the common features of the actor and character introductions. The characters are introduced in the following order: Andrew, James, Bartholomew, Simon, Matthew, Thomas, James the Less, Thaddeus, Philip, Peter, Joshua. Joshua then repeats the blessing for John and Judas.

11 Brustein, "McNally on the Cross," 35 and 36.

12 Currier, "A Dramatic Crucifixion," 27.

13 Fish, "Demanding the Divine," 35.

14 Barnes, "Just How Lousy Is the 'Gay Jesus' Play?," 41.

15 Green, "Review: *Corpus Christi*," 196.

16 Miller and Román, "Preaching to the Converted," 173.

Bibliography

Plays

The majority of the plays under consideration in this volume are anonymously authored, and so the following list proceeds alphabetically by title, with cross-references to editions included parenthetically and with full citations in the subsequent "Works Cited and Consulted." This list includes all early English plays examined for their potentially queer content, even if they are not directly addressed in the preceding chapters. Composition dates for all titles except the mystery cycles and Latin plays are cited from Darryll Grantley's English Dramatic Interludes, 1300–1580: A Reference Guide. *Most plays are available from the Chadwyck-Healey Database (CHD), even if not specifically noted in their entries.*

Absalom. By Thomas Watson. 1535–45. (John Hazel Smith, *Humanist's "Trew Imitation."*)

Albion Knight (fragment). 1537–66. (CHD.)

All for Money. By Thomas Lupton. 1559–77. (Schell and Shuchter, *English Morality Plays*, 419–73.)

The Andria. 1516–33. (Twycross, *Terence in English.*)

Apius and Virginia. By R.B. (Richard Bower?). 1559–67. (Happé, *Tudor Interludes*, 271–317.)

The Ashmole Fragment. C. 1500. (Davis, *Non-cycle Plays and Fragments*, 120.)

The Bugbears. 1563–6. By John Jefferes? (James D. Clark, *The Bugbears.*)

Calisto and Mélebea. 1527–30. (Richard Axton, *Three Rastell Plays*, 60–96.)

Cambises. 1558–69. By Thomas Preston. (Creeth, *Tudor Plays*, 443–503.)

The Cambridge Prologue. Late thirteenth century. (Davis, *Non-cycle Plays and Fragments*, 114–15.)

Candlemes Day and the Kyllyng of þe Children of Israelle. 1480–90. (Baker, Murphy, and Hall, *The Late Medieval Religious Plays*, 96–115.)

The Castle of Perseverance. 1382–1425. (Eccles, *The Macro Plays*, 1–111.)

The Chester Mystery Cycle. Early fifteenth century. (Lumiansky and Mills, *The Chester Mystery Cycle.*)

Christ's Burial. C. 1520. (Baker, Murphy, and Hall, *The Late Medieval Religious Plays*, 141–68.)

Christ's Resurrection. C. 1520. (Baker, Murphy, and Hall, *The Late Medieval Religious Plays*, 169–93.)

Christus Triumphans. By John Foxe. 1556. (John Hazel Smith, *Two Latin Comedies*, 199–371.)

Clyomon and Clamydes. 1570–83. (Littleton, *Clyomon and Clamydes.*)

Common Conditions. Printed 1576. (Farmer, *Five Anonymous Plays*, 181–256.)

The Conflict of Conscience. By Nathaniel Woodes. 1570–81. (Schell and Shuchter, *English Morality Plays*, 475–550.)

The Contention between Liberalitie and Prodigalitie. 1567–8. (Greg, *The Contention between Liberalitie and Prodigalitie* [1913].)

The Conversion of St. Paul. C. 1500–25. (Baker, Murphy, and Hall, *The Late Medieval Religious Plays*, 1–23.)

The Creacion of the World. Performed c. 1550. MS 1611. (Neuss, *The Creacion of the World.*)

The Croxton *Play of the Sacrament.* C. 1450–1500. (Davis, *Non-cycle Plays and Fragments*, 58–89.)

Damon and Pythias. By Richard Edwards. 1564–8. (Edwards, *The Works of Richard Edwards*, 108–84.)

The Disobedient Child. By Thomas Inglelend. 1559–70. (Farmer, *The Dramatic Writings of Richard Wever and Thomas Inglelend*, 44–92.)

The Durham Prologue. Late fourteenth to early fifteenth century. (Davis, *Non-cycle Plays and Fragments*, 118–19.)

Dux Moraud. Early to mid fifteenth century. (Davis, *Non-cycle Plays and Fragments*, 106–13.)

Enough Is as Good as a Feast. By W. Wager. 1559–70. (Wager, "The Longer Thou Livest," 79–146.)

Everyman. Ca. 1519. (Cawley, *Everyman.*)

The Four Cardinal Virtues (fragment). 1537–47. (CHD.)

Four Elements. By John Rastell. 1517–18. (Richard Axton, *Three Rastell Plays*, 30–68.)

The Foure PP. By John Heywood. 1520–8. (Heywood, *The Plays of John Heywood*, 111–42.)

Fulgens and Lucrece. By Henry Medwall. C. 1497. (Medwall, *The Plays of Henry Medwall*, 31–89.)

Gammer Gurton's Needle. By Mr. S. 1552–63. (Whitworth, *Gammer Gurton's Needle.*)

Gentleness and Nobility. Attributed to John Heywood. 1527–30. (Richard Axton, *Three Rastell Plays*, 97–124.)

Gismond of Salerne. By Rodney Stafford, Henry Noel, G. Al. (?), Christopher Hatton, and Robert Wilmot. 1567–8. (Cunliffe, *Early English Classical Tragedies*, 161–216.)

The Glasse of Governement. By George Gascoigne. Printed 1575. (Gascoigne, *The Complete Works of George Gascoigne*, 2.1–90.)

(The Enterlude of) Godly Queene Hester. 1525–9. (Walker, *Medieval Drama*, 408–31.)

God's Promises. By John Bale. 1538. (Bale, *The Complete Plays of John Bale*, 2.1–34.)

Good Order, or Old Christmas (fragment). Printed 1533. (CHD.)

Gorboduc (or *Ferrex and Porrex*). By Thomas Norton and Thomas Sackville. 1562. (Tydeman, *Two Tudor Tragedies*, 47–125.)

Hick Scorner. 1513–16. (Lancashire, *Two Tudor Interludes*, 157–238.)

Horestes. By John Pickering. Printed 1567. (Marie Axton, *Three Tudor Classical Interludes*, 94–138.)

(The History of) Iacob and Esau. 1550–7. (White, *Reformation Biblical Drama in England*, 67–133.)

Impatient Poverty. 1547–58. (Tennenhouse, *The Tudor Interludes*, 127–91.)

Jack Juggler. 1553–8. (Marie Axton, *Three Tudor Classical Interludes*, 64–93.)

Jacob and Esau. See *(The History of) Iacob and Esau*.

Jocasta. By George Gascoigne and Francis Kinwelmershe. 1566. (Gascoigne, *The Complete Works of George Gascoigne*, 1.244–326.)

Johan Baptystes Preachynge. By John Bale. 1538. (Bale, *The Complete Plays of John Bale*, 2:35–50.)

Johan Johan. By John Heywood. 1520–33. (Heywood, *The Plays of John Heywood*, 75–92.)

Johan the Euangelyst. 1520–7. (CHD.)

July and Julian. 1547–53. (Dawson and Brown, *July and Julian*.)

King Darius. Published 1565. (Farmer, *Anonymous Plays*, 41–92.)

King Johan. By John Bale. 1538. (Bale, *The Complete Plays of John Bale*, vol. 1.)

Liberalitie and Prodigalitie. See *The Contention between Liberalitie and Prodigalitie*.

Like Will to Like. By Ulpian Fulwell. 1562–8. (Somerset, *Four Tudor Interludes*, 128–64.)

The Longer Thou Livest. By W. Wager. 1559–68. (Wager, *"The Longer Thou Livest,"* 1–78.)

(A Play of) Love. By John Heywood. 1520s to early 1530s. (Heywood, *The Plays of John Heywood*, 143–81.)

Love Feigned and Unfeigned (fragment). By A. Esdaile. 1540–60. (Greg, *Collections, Part 1*, 17–25.)

Lucidus and Dubius. Mid-fifteenth century. (Davis, *Non-cycle Plays and The Winchester Dialogues*, 179–91.)

(The Play of) Lucrece. Early sixteenth century. (Greg, *Collections, Part II*, 137–42.)

Lusty Juventus. By Richard Wever. 1547–53. (Somerset, *Four Tudor Interludes*, 97–127.)

Magnyfycence. By John Skelton. 1520–2. (Skelton, *Magnyfycence*, ed. Ramsey.)

Mankind. 1465–70. (Eccles, *The Macro Plays*, 153–84.)

The Marriage between Wit and Wisdom. By Francis Merbury. 1571–9. (Wickham, *English Moral Interludes*, 167–84.)

The Marriage of Wit and Science. C. 1569. (Lennam, *Sebastian Westcott*, 119–74.)

Mary Magdalen (Digby). Late fifteenth or early sixteenth century. (Baker, Murphy, and Hall, *The Late Medieval Religious Plays*, 24–95).

Misogonus. 1564–77. (Barber, *Misogonus*.)

Mundus et Infans. 1500–22. (Lester, *Three Late Medieval Morality Plays*, 107–57.)

Nature. By Henry Medwall. 1496. (Medwall, *The Plays of Henry Medwall*, 91–161.)

New Custome. 1550–73. (CHD.)

Nice Wanton. 1547–53. (Tennenhouse, *The Tudor Interludes*, 64–125.)

The N-Town Play. 1450–1500. (Spector, *The N-Town Play*.)

Occupation and Idleness. Mid-fifteenth century. (Beadle, "*Occupation and Idleness*.")

(*The Commodye of) Pacient and Meeke Grissell*. By John Philip. 1558–61. (CHD.)

The Pardoner and the Frere. By John Heywood. 1513–21. (Heywood, *The Plays of John Heywood*, 93–109.)

The Pedlers Prophecie. 1561–3. (CHD.)

The Pride of Life. C. 1350–1450. (Davis, *Non-cycle Plays and Fragments*, 90–105.)

The Prodigal Son. Early sixteenth century. (Greg, *Collections, Part I*, 27–30.)

Promos and Cassandra, Parts I and II. By George Whetstone. 1578. (CHD.)

Respublica. Attributed to Nicholas Udall. 1553. (Greg, *Respublica*.)

The Resurrection of Our Lord (fragments). 1530–60. (CHD.)

The Reynes Extracts. Later half of fifteenth century. (Davis, *Non-cycle Plays and Fragments*, 121–3.)

The Rickinghall (Bury St. Edmunds) Fragment. Early fourteenth century. (Davis, *Non-cycle Plays and Fragments*, 116–17.)

Robin Hood and the Friar. 1560. (Wiles, *The Early Plays of Robin Hood*, 72–6.)

Robin Hood and the Potter (fragment). 1560. (Wiles, *The Early Plays of Robin Hood*, 76–9.)

Robin Hood and the Sheriff or *Robin Hood and the Knight* (fragment). C. 1475. (Wiles, *The Early Plays of Robin Hood*, 71.)

(*Ralph) Royster Doyster*. By Nicholas Udall. 1552–4. (Creeth, *Tudor Plays*, 215–314.)

Ane Satyre of the Thrie Estaitis. By Sir David Lyndsay. 1540–52. (Lindsay, ed. Lyall.)

Somebody and Others, or The Spoiling of Lady Verity. 1547–50. (Houle, "A Reconstruction of the English Morality Fragment.")

The Student and the Girl (fragment). (*Interludium de clerico et puella*.) 1290–1335. (CHD.)

Supposes. By George Gascoigne. 1566. (Gascoigne, *The Complete Works of George Gascoigne*, 1.187–243.)

Temperance and Humility (fragment). 1521–35. (CHD.)

The Temptation of Our Lord. By John Bale. 1538. (Bale, *The Complete Plays of John Bale*, 2:51–63.)

Thersites. 1537. (Marie Axton, *Three Tudor Classical Interludes*, 37–73.)

Thre Lawes of Nature, Moses, and Christ. By John Bale. 1538. (Bale, *The Complete Plays of John Bale*, 2:64–124.)

The Tide Tarrieth No Man. By George Wapull. Printed 1576. (Schell and Shuchter, *English Morality Plays and Moral Interludes*, 309–66.)

Titus et Gesippus. By John Foxe. 1544. (John Hazel Smith, *Two Latin Comedies*, 51–197.)

Tom Tyler and His Wife. C. 1561. (Schelling, *Tom Tyler and His Wife*.)

The Towneley Plays. Fifteenth to mid-sixteenth century. (Epp, *The Towneley Plays*.)

The Trial of Treasure. Published 1567. (Farmer, *Anonymous Plays*, 203–46.)

(The Commody of the Moste) Virtuous and Godly Susanna. By Thomas Garter. 1563–9. (CHD.)

Wealth and Health. 1553–5. (Farmer, *Recently Recovered "Lost" Tudor Plays*, 273–309.)

(The Play of the) Wether. By John Heywood. 1527–33. (Heywood, *The Plays of John Heywood*, 183–215.)

Wisdom. 1460–70. (Eccles, *The Macro Plays*, 113–52.)

(The Play of) Wit and Science. By John Redford. 1539. (Bevington, *Medieval Drama*, 1029–61.)

Witty and Witless. By John Heywood. 1520–33. (Heywood, *The Plays of John Heywood*, 55–73.)

The World and the Child. See *Mundus et Infans.*

The York Corpus Christi Cycle. Late fourteenth century to mid-fifteenth century. (Beadle, *The York Plays*.)

(The Interlude of) Youth. 1513–14. (Fitzgerald and Sebastian, *The Broadview Anthology of Medieval Drama*, 436–48.)

Works Cited and Consulted

Adams, Barry, ed. *John Bale's "King Johan."* San Marino, CA: Huntington Library, 1969.

Aelred of Rievaulx. *Aeldredi Rievallensis opera omnia.* Edited by A. Hoste and C.H. Talbot. Turnhout, Belgium: Brepols, 1971.

– *Spiritual Friendship.* Translated by Mary Eugenia Laker. Kalamazoo, MI: Cistercian Publications, 1977.

Ailes, M. J. "The Medieval Male Couple and the Language of Homosociality." In *Masculinity in Medieval Europe*, edited by D.M. Hadley, 214–37. London: Longman, 1999.

Aloni, Gila, and Shirley Sharon-Zisser. "Judaism and Jouissance in Two
Medieval Texts." *Canadian Review of Comparative Literature / Revue
Canadienne de Littérature Comparée* 28, no. 2–3 (2001): 159–92.

Anderson, James Maitland, ed. *Early Records of the University of St. Andrews:
The Graduation Roll, 1413–1579, and the Matriculation Roll, 1473–1579.*
Edinburgh: Scottish Historic Society, 1926.

Ashley, Kathleen. "*Mankind*: The Omnibus Text." *Studies in Medieval and
Renaissance Teaching* 21, no. 2 (2014): 101–9.

– "Titivillus and the Battle of Words in *Mankind.*" *Annuale Mediaevale*, no. 16
(1975): 128–50.

Ashley, Kathleen, and Gerard NeCastro, eds. *Mankind.* Kalamazoo, MI:
Medieval Institute Publications, 2010.

Auerbach, Erich. *Mimesis: The Representation of Reality in Western Literature.*
Princeton, NJ: Princeton University Press, 1973. First published 1953.

Augustine. *The City of God against the Pagans.* Edited and translated by Eva
Matthews Sanford and William McAllen Green. 7 vols. Cambridge, MA:
Harvard University Press, 1988. First published 1965.

– *Confessions: Books 1–8.* Edited by Carolyn J.-B. Hammond. Cambridge, MA:
Harvard University Press, 2014.

– "Sermon CCLXXXVIII." In *Patrologia Latina*, edited by J.-P. Migne, 38:1304.
Paris, 1863.

Axton, Marie, ed. *Three Tudor Classical Interludes.* Cambridge: D.S. Brewer, 1982.

Axton, Richard. "Popular Modes in the Earliest Plays." In *Medieval Drama*,
edited by Neville Denny, 13–39. New York: Crane, Russack, 1973.

–, ed. *Three Rastell Plays: "Four Elements," "Calisto and Mélebea," "Gentleness
and Nobility."* Cambridge: D.S. Brewer, 1979.

Baker, Donald, John Murphy, and Louis Hall, eds. *The Late Medieval Religious
Plays of Bodleian MSS Digby 133 and E Museo 160.* Early English Text Society,
o.s. 283. Oxford: Oxford University Press, 1982.

Baker, Herschel. *The Race of Time: Three Lectures on Renaissance Historiography.*
Toronto: University of Toronto Press, 1967.

Bakhtin, Mikhael. *Rabelais and His World.* Translated by Hélène Iswolsky.
Bloomington: Indiana University Press, 1984.

Bale, John. *The Actes of Englyish Votaryes.* London: John Tysdale, 1560.

– *The Actes of Englysh Votaryes.* University of Oxford Text Archive. http://ota
.ox.ac.uk/tcp/headers/A02/A02573.html.

– *The Complete Plays of John Bale.* Edited by Peter Happé. 2 vols. Cambridge:
D.S. Brewer, 1985.

– *Select Works of John Bale, D.D., Bishop of Ossory, Containing "The Examinations
of Lord Cobham, William Thorpe, and Anne Askewe" and "The Image of Both
Churches."* Edited by Henry Christmas. Cambridge: Cambridge University
Press and the Parker Society, 1849.

Barber, Lester E., ed. *Misogonus*. New York: Garland, 1979.

Barish, Jonas. *The Antitheatrical Prejudice*. Berkeley: University of California Press, 1981.

Barnes, Clive. "Just How Lousy Is the 'Gay Jesus' Play? Alas, *Corpus Christi* Is Boring." *New York Post*, 14 October 1998, 41.

Bayless, Martha. *Sin and Filth in Medieval Culture: The Devil in the Latrine*. New York: Routledge, 2012.

Beadle, Richard, ed. "*Occupation and Idleness*." *Leeds Studies in English*, n.s., 32 (2001): 7–47.

– *The York Plays: A Critical Edition of the York Corpus Christi Play as Recorded in British Library Additional MS 35290*. 2 vols. Early English Text Society, s.s., 23. Oxford: Oxford University Press, 2009.

Beckwith, Sarah. *Signifying God: Social Relation and Symbolic Act in the York Corpus Christi Plays*. Chicago: University of Chicago Press, 2001.

Bennett, Susan. *Theatre Audiences: A Theory of Production and Reception*. London: Routledge, 1997.

Betteridge, Thomas, and Greg Walker, eds. *The Oxford Handbook of Tudor Drama*. Oxford: Oxford University Press, 2012.

Bevington, David. *From "Mankind" to Marlowe: Growth of Structure in the Popular Drama of Tudor England*. Cambridge, MA: Harvard University Press, 1962.

–, ed. *The Macro Plays: A Facsimile Edition with Facing Transcriptions*. Washington, DC: Folger Shakespeare Library, 1972.

–, ed. *Medieval Drama*. Boston: Houghton Mifflin, 1975.

Biblia Sacra iuxta Vulgatam Versionem. Stuttgart: Deutsche Bibelgesellschaft, 1969.

Biddick, Kathleen. *The Typological Imaginary: Circumcision, Technology, History*. Philadelphia: University of Pennsylvania Press, 2003.

Bilby, Mark Glen. "Hospitality and Perfume of the Bandit." *E-Clavis: Christian Apocrypha*. Accessed 16 February 2019, www.nasscal.com/e-clavis-christian-apocrypha/hospitality-and- perfume-of-the-bandit.

Billington, Sandra. "'Suffer Fools Gladly': The Fool in Medieval England and the Play *Mankind*." In *The Fool and the Trickster: Studies in Honour of Enid Weisford*, edited by Paul V.A. William, 36–54. Cambridge: D.S. Brewer, 1979.

Bjork, David. "On the Dissemination of *Quem quaeritis* and the *Visitatio sepulchri* and the Chronology of Their Early Sources." *Comparative Drama* 14, no. 1 (1980): 46–69.

Blatt, Thora Balslev. *The Plays of John Bale: A Study of Ideas, Technique, and Style*. Copenhagen: Gad Publishers, 1968.

Blayney, Margaret, ed. *Fifteenth-Century Translations of Alain Chartier's "Le Traité de l'Espérance" and "Le Quadrilogue Invectif*." Early English Text Society, o.s., 270. Oxford: Oxford University Press, 1974.

Bleeker, Maaike. *Visuality in the Theatre: The Locus of Looking*. Houndmills, UK: Palgrave Macmillan, 2008.

Boehrer, Bruce Thomas. *Monarchy and Incest in Renaissance England: Literature, Culture, Kinship, and Kingship*. Philadelphia: University of Pennsylvania Press, 1992.

Boocker, David. "Heywood's Indulgent Pardoner." *English Language Notes* 29, no. 2 (1991): 21–30.

"Book Review Forum: *The Swerve: How the World Became Modern*." *Exemplaria* 25, no. 4 (2013): 313–70.

Boris, Kenneth, ed. *Same-Sex Desire in the English Renaissance: A Sourcebook of Texts, 1470–1650*. New York: Routledge, 2004.

Boswell, John. *Christianity, Social Tolerance, and Homosexuality: Gay People in Western Europe from the Beginning of the Christian Era to the Fourteenth Century*. Chicago: University of Chicago Press, 1980.

– *Same-Sex Unions in Premodern Europe*. New York: Villard, 1994.

Bouchard, Constance Brittain. *"Every Valley Shall Be Exalted": The Discourse of Opposites in Twelfth-Century Thought*. Ithaca, NY: Cornell University Press, 2003.

Bowers, Rick. "Hysterics, High Camp, and *Dido, Queene of Carthage*." In *Marlowe's Empery: Expanding His Critical Contexts*, edited by Sarah Munson and Robert Logan, 95–106. Newark: University of Delaware Press, 2002.

Boyarin, Daniel. *Border Lines: The Partition of Judaeo-Christianity*. Philadelphia: University of Pennsylvania Press, 2004.

– *The Jewish Gospels: The Story of the Jewish Christ*. New York: New Press, 2012.

– *Unheroic Conduct: The Rise of Heterosexuality and the Invention of the Jewish Man*. Berkeley: University of California Press, 1997.

Boyarin, Jonathan, and Daniel Boyarin, eds. *Jews and Other Differences: The New Jewish Cultural Studies*. Minneapolis: University of Minnesota Press, 1997.

Braunmuller, A.R. "Bearded Ladies in Shakespeare." In *The Forms of Renaissance Thought: New Essays in Literature and Culture*, edited by Leonard Barkan, Bradin Cormack, and Sean Keilen, 201–24. Houndmills, UK: Palgrave Macmillan, 2009.

Bray, Alan. *The Friend*. Chicago: University of Chicago Press, 2003.

– *Homosexuality in Renaissance England*. New York: Columbia University Press, 1995.

Bray, Gerald, ed. *Documents of the English Reformation*. Minneapolis, MN: Fortress Press, 1994.

Brenton, Lancelot, ed. *The Septuagint with Apocrypha: Greek and English*. Peabody, MA: Hendrickson, 1986.

Brokaw, Katherine Steele. "Music and Religious Compromise in John Bale's Plays." *Comparative Drama* 44, no. 3 (2010): 325–49.

Brooke, Tucker, ed. *Common Conditions*. New Haven, CT: Yale University Press, 1915.

Brown, Carleton, ed. *Religious Lyrics of the XVth Century*. Oxford: Clarendon, 1939.

Brown, Pamela Allen, and Peter Parolin, eds. *Women Players in England, 1500–1600: Beyond the All-Male Stage*. Aldershot, UK: Ashgate, 2005.

Brustein, Robert. "McNally on the Cross." *New Republic* 219, no. 22 (30 November 1998): 34–6.

Burford, E.J., ed. *Bawdy Verse: A Pleasant Collection*. London: Penguin, 1982.

Burger, Glenn. *Chaucer's Queer Nation*. Minneapolis: University of Minnesota Press, 2003.

Butler, Judith. *Bodies That Matter: On the Discursive Limits of "Sex."* New York: Routledge, 1993.

– "Critically Queer." In *The Routledge Queer Studies Reader*, edited by Donald Hall and Annamarie Jagose, 18–31. London: Routledge, 2013.

Butler, Michelle. "Baleus Prolocutor and the Establishment of the Prologue in Sixteenth-Century Drama." In *Tudor Drama before Shakespeare, 1485–1590: New Directions for Research, Criticism, and Pedagogy*, edited by Lloyd Kermode, Jason Scott-Warren, and Martine Van Elk, 93–109. New York: Palgrave Macmillan, 2004.

Butterworth, Philip. *Magic on the Early English Stage*. Cambridge: Cambridge University Press, 2005.

– *Staging Conventions in Medieval English Theatre*. Cambridge: Cambridge University Press, 2014.

Bynum, Caroline Walker. *Fragmentation and Redemption: Essays on Gender and the Human Body in Medieval Religion*. New York: Zone, 1991.

– *Jesus as Mother: Studies in the Spirituality of the High Middle Ages*. Berkeley: University of California Press, 1982.

Camille, Michael. "The Image and the Self: Unwriting Late Medieval Bodies." In *Framing Medieval Bodies*, edited by Sarah Kay and Miri Rubin, 62–99. Manchester, UK: Manchester University Press, 1994.

Carpenter, Sarah. "Early Scottish Drama." In *Origins to 1660*, edited by R.D.S. Jack and Craig Cairns, 199–212. Vol. 1 of *The History of Scottish Literature*. Aberdeen, Scotland: Aberdeen University Press, 1998.

Case, Sue-Ellen. *Feminist and Queer Performance*. Houndmills, UK: Palgrave Macmillan, 2009.

Cawley, A.C., ed. *Everyman*. Manchester, UK: Manchester University Press, 1961.

Cervone, Thea. "The King's Phantom: Staging Majesty in Bale's *Kynge Johan*." In *Defining Medievalism(s)*, edited by Karl Fugelso, 185–202. Cambridge: D.S. Brewer, 2009.

Chaucer, Geoffrey. *The Riverside Chaucer*. 3rd ed., edited by Larry D. Benson. Boston: Houghton Mifflin, 1987.

CHD (Chadwyck-Healey Database). http://collections.chadwyck.com.

Chess, Simone. *Male-to-Female Crossdressing in Early Modern English Literature: Gender, Performance, and Queer Relations*. New York: Routledge, 2016.

Christianson, Paul. *Reformers and Babylon: English Apocalyptic Visions from the Reformation to the Eve of the Civil War*. Toronto: University of Toronto Press, 1978.

Cicero. *De senectute, De amicitia, De divinatione*. Edited and translated by William Falconer. Cambridge, MA: Harvard University Press, 1979.

– *On the Good Life*. Translated by Michael Grant. London, 1971.

Clark, David. *Between Medieval Men: Male Friendship and Desire in Early Medieval English Literature*. Oxford: Oxford University Press, 2009.

Clark, James D., ed. *The Bugbears: A Modernized Edition*. New York: Garland, 1979.

Clark, Robert L.A., and Claire Sponsler. "Queer Play: The Cultural Work of Crossdressing in Medieval Drama." *New Literary History* 28, no. 2 (1997): 319–44.

Clopper, Lawrence. *Drama, Play, and Game: English Festive Culture in the Medieval and Early Modern Period*. Chicago: University of Chicago Press, 2001.

Cohen, Jeffrey Jerome, and Bonnie Wheeler, eds. *Becoming Male in the Middle Ages*. New York: Garland, 2000.

Cohen, Jeremy. *Living Letters of the Law: Ideas of the Jew in Medieval Christianity*. Berkeley: University of California Press, 1999.

Coldewey, John C., ed. *Early English Drama: An Anthology*. New York: Garland, 1993.

– "Thrice-Told Tales: Renegotiating Early English Drama." *European Medieval Drama*, no. 1 (1997): 15–31.

Coletti, Theresa. *Mary Magdalene and the Drama of Saints: Theater, Gender, and Religion in Late Medieval England*. Philadelphia: University of Pennsylvania Press, 2004.

Conroy, Collette. *Theatre and the Body*. Houndmills, UK: Palgrave Macmillan, 2010.

Core, Philip. *Camp: The Lie That Tells the Truth*. New York: Delilah Books, 1984.

Craig, Hardin. *English Religious Drama of the Middle Ages*. Oxford: Clarendon, 1955.

Creeth, Edmund, ed. *Tudor Plays: An Anthology of Early English Drama*. Garden City, NY: Anchor Books, 1966.

Crowder, Susannah. "Children, Costume, and Identity in the Chester Midsummer Show." *Early Theatre* 10, no. 1 (2007): 13–34.

Cunliffe, John, ed. *Early English Classical Tragedies*. Oxford: Clarendon, 1912.

Cunnington, C. Willett, and Phillis Cunnington. *Handbook of English Mediaeval Costume*. 2nd ed. London: Faber & Faber, 1973.

Currier, Jameson. "A Dramatic Crucifixion: *Corpus Christi.*" *Lambda Book Report* 8, no. 4 (November 1999): 27.

D'Arcens, Louise. "Medievalism: Scope and Complexity." In *The Cambridge Companion to Medievalism,* edited by Louise D'Arcens, 1–13. Cambridge: Cambridge University Press, 2016.

Davidson, Clifford, ed. *Deliver Us from Evil: Essays on Symbolic Engagement in Early Drama.* New York: AMS Press, 2004.

–. "The Realism of the York Realist and the York Passion." *Speculum* 50, no. 2 (1975): 270–83.

–, ed. *A Tretise of Miraclis Pleyinge.* Kalamazoo, MI: Medieval Institute Publications, 1993.

–, ed. *The York Corpus Christi Plays.* Kalamazoo, MI: Medieval Institute Publications, 2011.

Davies, Robert, ed. *Municipal Records of the City of York, during the Reign of Edward IV, Edward V, and Richard III.* London: Nichols and Son, 1843.

Davis, Norman, ed. *Non-cycle Plays and Fragments.* Early English Text Society, s.s., 1. London: Oxford University Press, 1970.

–, ed. *Non-cycle Plays and The Winchester Dialogues: Facsimiles of Plays and Fragments in Various Manuscripts and the Dialogues in Winchester College MS 33.* Leeds, UK: University of Leeds School of English, 1979.

Davril, Anselme, OSB. "Johann Drumbl and the Origin of the *Quem quaeritis*: A Review." Translated by Fletcher Collins, Jr. *Comparative Drama* 2, no. 1 (1986): 65–75.

Dawson, Giles, and Arthur Brown, eds. *July and Julian.* Oxford: Malone Society Reprints, 1955.

Day, Mabel, and Robert Steele, eds. *Mum and the Sothsegger.* Early English Text Society, o.s., 199. London: Oxford University Press, 1936.

Denny, Neville. "Aspects of the Staging of *Mankind.*" *Medium Aevum* 43, no. 3 (1974): 252–63.

DiGangi, Mario. *The Homoerotics of Early Modern Drama.* Cambridge: Cambridge University Press, 1997.

Dinshaw, Carolyn. *Getting Medieval: Sexuality and Communities, Pre- and Postmodern.* Durham, NC: Duke University Press, 1999.

Dobson, R.B. "Craft Guilds and City: The Historical Origins of the York Mystery Plays Reassessed." In *The Stage as Mirror: Civic Theatre in Late Medieval Europe,* edited by Alan Knight, 91–105. Cambridge: D.S. Brewer, 1997.

Dollimore, Jonathan. *Sexual Dissidence: Augustine to Wilde, Freud to Foucault.* Oxford: Clarendon, 1991.

Donaldson, E. Talbot. *The Swan at the Well: Shakespeare Reading Chaucer.* New Haven, CT: Yale University Press, 1985.

DSL: Dictionary of the Scots Language / Dictionar o the Scots Leid. www.dsl.ac.uk.

Dutka, JoAnna. *Music in the English Mystery Plays*. Kalamazoo, MI: Medieval Institute Publications, 1980.

Dynes, Wayne R., ed. *Encyclopedia of Homosexuality*. 2 vols. New York: Garland, 1990.

Eagleton, Terry. *Walter Benjamin, or Towards a Revolutionary Criticism*. London: Verso, 1981.

Eccles, Mark, ed. *The Macro Plays: "The Castle of Perseverance," "Wisdom," "Mankind."* Early English Text Society, o.s., 262. London: Oxford University Press, 1969.

Edington, Carol. *Court and Culture in Renaissance Scotland: Sir David Lindsay of the Mount*. Amherst: University of Massachusetts Press, 1994.

Edwards, Richard. *The Works of Richard Edwards*. Edited by Ros King. Manchester, UK: Manchester University Press, 2001.

Eliot, Thomas. *The Bankette of Sapience*. 1534.

Elliott, John R. *Playing God: Medieval Mysteries on the Modern Stage*. Toronto: University of Toronto Press, 1989.

Elst, Stefan Vander. *The Knight, the Cross, and the Song: Crusade Propaganda and Chivalric Literature, 1100–1400*. Philadelphia: University of Pennsylvania Press, 2017.

Enders, Jody. "Of Miming and Signing: The Dramatic Rhetoric of Gesture." In *Gesture in Medieval Drama and Art*, edited by Clifford Davidson, 1–25. Kalamazoo, MI: Medieval Institute Publications, 2001.

Epp, Garrett P.J. "Chastity in the Stocks: Women, Sex, and Marriage in *Ane Satyre of the Thrie Estaitis*." In *Woman and the Feminine in Medieval and Early Modern Scottish Writing*, edited by Sarah Dunnigan, C. Marie Harker, and Evelyn Newlyn, 61–73. Houndmills, UK: Palgrave Macmillan, 2004.

– "Ecce Homo." In *Queering the Middle Ages*, edited by Glenn Burger and Steven Kruger, 236–51. Minneapolis: University of Minnesota Press, 2001.

– "'Into a womannys lyckenes': Bale's Personification of Idolatry." *Medieval English Theatre*, no. 18 (1996): 63–73.

– "John Foxe and the Circumcised Stage." *Exemplaria* 9, no. 2 (1997): 281–313.

– "To 'Play the Sodomits': A Query in Five Actions." In *The Ashgate Research Companion to Queer Theory*, edited by Noreen Giffney and Michael O'Rourke, 181–97. Farnham, UK: Ashgate, 2009.

–, ed. *The Towneley Plays*. Kalamazoo, MI: Medieval Institute Publications, 2017.

– "The Vicious Guise: Effeminacy, Sodomy, and *Mankind*." In *Becoming Male in the Middle Ages*, edited by Jeffrey Jerome Cohen and Bonnie Wheeler, 303–20. New York: Garland, 2000.

Farmer, John, ed. *Anonymous Plays, Comprising "Jack Juggler," "King Darius," "Gammer Gurton's Needle," "New Custom," and "Trial of Treasure."* London: Early English Drama Society, 1906.

–, ed. *The Dramatic Writings of John Bale, Bishop of Ossory*. London: Early English Drama Society, 1907. Reprint 1966.

–, ed. *The Dramatic Writings of Richard Wever and Thomas Inglelend*. London: Early English Dramatic Society, 1905.

–, ed. *Five Anonymous Plays: "Apius and Virginia," "The Marriage of Wit and Science," "Grim the Collier of Croydon," "Common Conditions," and "The Marriage of Wit and Wisdom."* 4th series. London: Early English Drama Society, 1908.

–, ed. *Recently Recovered "Lost" Tudor Plays with Some Others, Comprising "Mankind," "Nature," "Wit and Science," "Respublica," "Wealth and Health," "Impatient Poverty," "John the Evangelist."* Guildford, UK: Charles W. Traylen, 1966. First published 1907.

Finke, Laurie, and Martin Shichtman. *Cinematic Illuminations: The Middle Ages on Film*. Baltimore, MD: Johns Hopkins University Press, 2010.

Fish, Thomas. "Demanding the Divine: Terrence McNally's Gay Passion Play *Corpus Christi*." *Ecumenica: A Journal of Theatre and Performance* 2, no. 2 (2009): 29–40.

Fitzgerald, Christina. *The Drama of Masculinity and Medieval English Guild Culture*. New York: Palgrave Macmillan, 2007.

–, ed. *The York Corpus Christi Play: Selected Pageants*. Peterborough, ON: Broadview, 2018.

Fitzgerald, Christina, and John Sebastian, eds. *The Broadview Anthology of Medieval Drama*. Peterborough, ON: Broadview, 2013.

Fletcher, Alan. "'Fart Prycke in Cule': A Late Elizabethan Analogue." *Medieval English Theatre* 8, no. 2 (1986): 132–9.

Fletcher, Angus. *Allegory: The Theory of a Symbolic Mode*. Ithaca, NY: Cornell University Press, 1964.

Folse, Keith. *The Grammar Answer Key*. Ann Arbor: University of Michigan Press, 2018.

Fone, Byrne R.S., ed. *The Columbia Anthology of Gay Literature: Readings from Western Antiquity to the Present Day*. New York: Columbia University Press, 1998.

Fradenburg, Louise, and Carla Freccero, eds. *Premodern Sexualities*. New York: Routledge, 1996.

Frantzen, Allen. "Bede and Bawdy Bale: Gregory the Great, Angels, and the 'Angli.'" In *Anglo-Saxonism and the Construction of Social Identity*, edited by Allen Frantzen and John Niles, 17–39. Gainesville: University Press of Florida, 1997.

Fuss, Diana. "Inside/Out." In *Inside/Out: Lesbian Theories, Gay Theories*, edited by Diana Fuss, 1–10. New York: Routledge, 1991.

Garrison, Jennifer. "*Mankind* and the Masculine Pleasure of Penance." *Exemplaria* 31, no. 1 (2019): 46–62.

Garter, Thomas. *The Most Virtuous and Godly Susanna*. Edited by B. Evans and W.W. Greg. Oxford: Malone Society Reprints, 1936.

Gascoigne, George. *The Complete Works of George Gascoigne*. Edited by John Cunliffe. 2 vols. New York: Greenwood, 1969. First published 1907.

Gash, Anthony. "Carnival against Lent: The Ambivalence of Medieval Drama." In *Medieval Literature: Criticism, Ideology, and History*, edited by David Aers, 74–88. New York: St. Martin's, 1986.

Gassner, John, ed. *Medieval and Tudor Drama*. New York: Applause, 1987. First published 1963.

Geller, Jay. "(G)nos(e)ology: The Cultural Construction of the Other." In *People of the Body: Jews and Judaism from an Embodied Perspective*, edited by H. Eilberg-Schwartz, 243–82. Albany: State University of New York Press, 1992.

Gerald of Wales. *The Historical Works of Giraldus Cambrensis*. Edited by Thomas Wright. London: Bell & Sons, 1913.

Giffney, Noreen, Michelle Sauer, and Diane Watt, eds. *The Lesbian Premodern*. New York: Palgrave Macmillan, 2011.

Goldberg, Jonathan, ed. *Queering the Renaissance*. Durham, NC: Duke University Press, 1994.

– *Sodometries: Renaissance Texts, Modern Sexualities*. Stanford, CA: Stanford University Press, 1992.

Goldberg, P.J.P. "From Tableaux to Text: The York Corpus Christi Play, ca. 1378–1428." *Viator* 43, no. 2 (2012): 247–76.

Goldie, Terry. "Dragging Out the Queen: Male Femaling and Male Feminism." In *Revealing Male Bodies*, edited by Nancy Tuana, William Cowling, Maurice Hamington, Greg Johnson, and Terrance MacMullan, 125–45. Bloomington: Indiana University Press, 2002.

Goldman, James. *The Lion in Winter*. New York: Viking, 1966.

Goldstein, R. James. "Normative Heterosexuality in History and Theory: The Case of Sir David Lindsay of the Mount." In *Becoming Male in the Middle Ages*, edited by Jeffrey Jerome Cohen and Bonnie Wheeler, 349–65. New York: Garland, 2000.

Gosson, Stephen. *Markets of Bawdrie: The Dramatic Criticism of Stephen Gosson*. Edited by Arthur Kinney. Salzburg: Institut für Englishe Sprache und Literatur, 1974.

Grantley, Darryll. *English Dramatic Interludes, 1300–1580: A Reference Guide*. Cambridge: Cambridge University Press, 2004.

– "'What Meanes This Shew?': Theatricalism, Camp, and Subversion in *Doctor Faustus* and *The Jew of Malta*." In *Christopher Marlowe and English Renaissance Culture*, edited by Darryll Grantley and Peter Roberts, 224–38. Aldershot, UK: Ashgate, 1996.

Gray, Douglas, ed. "The Five Wounds of Our Lord." *Notes and Queries* 10, no. 4 (1963): 50–1, 82–9, 127–34.

Green, Sharon. "Review: *Corpus Christi*." *Theatre Journal* 51, no. 2 (1999): 194–6.

Greenblatt, Stephen. *The Swerve: How the World Became Modern*. New York: Norton, 2011.

Greg, W.W., ed. *Collections, Part I*. Oxford: Malone Society, 1907.

–, ed. *Collections, Part II*. Oxford: Malone Society, 1908.

–, ed. *The Contention between Liberalitie and Prodigalitie*. Oxford: Malone Society Reprints, 1913.

–, ed. *Respublica: An Interlude for Christmas 1553 Attributed to Nicholas Udall*. Early English Text Society, o.s., 226. London: Oxford University Press, 1952.

Groeneveld, Leanne. "A Theatrical Miracle: The Boxley Rood Grace as Puppet." *Early Theatre* 10, no. 2 (2007): 12–48.

Grumett, David. *Material Eucharist*. Oxford: Oxford University Press, 2016.

Guibert of Nogent. *Tractatus de incarnatione contra Judaeos*. In *Patrologia Latina*, vol. 156, edited by J.-P. Migne, cols. 489–528. Paris, 1880.

Gust, Geoffrey. *Chaucerotics: Uncloaking the Language of Sex in the "Canterbury Tales" and "Troilus and Criseyde."* Cham, Switzerland: Palgrave Macmillan, 2018.

Guy-Bray, Stephen, Vin Nardizzi, and Will Stockton, eds. *Queer Renaissance Historiography: Backward Gaze*. Farnham, UK: Ashgate, 2009.

Guynn, Noah. *Allegory and Sexual Ethics in the High Middle Ages*. New York: Palgrave Macmillan, 2007.

Hamilton, John. *The Catechism of John Hamilton, Archbishop of St. Andrews*. Edited by Thomas Graves Law. Oxford: Clarendon, 1884.

Happé, Peter. *John Bale*. New York: Twayne, 1996.

– "John Bale's Lost Mystery Cycle." *Cahiers Élisabéthains* 60 (2001): 1–12.

–, ed. *Tudor Interludes*. Harmondsworth, UK: Penguin, 1972.

Harris, Carissa. *Obscene Pedagogies: Transgressive Talk and Sexual Education in Late Medieval Britain*. Ithaca, NY: Cornell University Press, 2018.

Harris, Jesse W. *John Bale: A Study in the Minor Literature of the Reformation*. Freeport, NY: Books for Libraries, 1970. First published 1940.

Herbert, Amanda. *Female Alliances: Gender, Identity, and Friendship in Early Modern Britain*. New Haven, CT: Yale University Press, 2014.

Heywood, John. *The Plays of John Heywood*. Edited by Richard Axton and Peter Happé. Cambridge: D.S. Brewer, 1991.

Holy Bible: Douay-Rheims Version. Charlotte, NC: St. Benedict Press, 2009.

Houle, Peter, ed. "A Reconstruction of the English Morality Fragment *Somebody and Others*." *Papers of the Bibliographical Society of America* 71, no. 3 (1977): 259–77.

House, Seymour Baker. "Cromwell's Message to the Regulars: The Biblical Trilogy of John Bale, 1537." *Renaissance and Reformation / Renaissance et Réforme* 15, no. 2 (1991): 123–38.

Hughes, Paul, and James Larkin, eds. *Tudor Royal Proclamations*. 3 vols. New Haven, CT: Yale University Press, 1964.

Hughey, Ruth, ed. *The Arundel Harington Manuscript of Tudor Poetry*. 2 vols. Columbus: Ohio State University Press, 1960.

Hyde, Montgomery. *The Love That Dared Not Speak Its Name: A Candid History of Homosexuality in Britain*. Boston: Little Brown, 1970.

Impelluso, Lucia. *Nature and Its Symbols*. Translated by Stephen Sartarelli. Los Angeles: J. Paul Getty Museum, 2003.

Inglelend, Thomas. *The Disobedient Child*. In *The Dramatic Writings of Richard Wever and Thomas Inglelend*, ed. John Farmer, 44–92. London: Early English Dramatic Society, 1905.

Intersex Society of North America. "What Is Intersex?" www.isna.org/faq /what_is_intersex.

Jacobus de Voragine. *The Golden Legend: Readings on the Saints*. Translated by William Granger Ryan. 2 vols. Princeton, NJ: Princeton University Press, 1993.

– *Legenda aurea*. Edited by Th. Graesse. Leipzig: Impensis Librariae Arnoldianae, 1850.

Jaeger, C. Stephen. *Ennobling Love: In Search of a Lost Sensibility*. Philadelphia: University of Pennsylvania Press, 1999.

Johnson, Lynn Staley. "St. John the Baptist and Medieval English Ideology." *American Benedictine Review* 27 (1976): 105–25.

Johnson, Michael. "Sodomy, Allegory, and the Subject of Pleasure." In *Queer Sexualities in French and Francophone Literature and Film*, edited by James Day and William Edmiston, 1–12. Amsterdam: Rodopi, 2007.

Johnson, Willis. "The Myth of Jewish Male Menses." *Journal of Medieval History* 24, no. 3 (1998): 273–95.

Johnston, Alexandra F. "An Introduction to Medieval English Theatre." In *The Cambridge Companion to Medieval English Theatre*, 2nd ed., edited by Richard Beadle and Alan Fletcher, 1–25. Cambridge: Cambridge University Press, 2008.

Johnston, Alexandra F., and Margaret Rogerson, eds. *Records of Early English Drama: York*. 2 vols. Toronto: University of Toronto Press, 1979.

Jones, Charles, ed. *The Edinburgh History of the Scots Language*. Edinburgh: Edinburgh University Press, 1997.

Jones, Sarah Rees, and Sethina Watson, eds. *Christians and Jews in Angevin England: The York Massacre of 1190, Narratives and Contexts*. Rochester, NY: Boydell, 2013.

Justin. *Die ältessten Apologeten*. 2nd ed., edited by Edgar Goodspeed. Göttingen, Germany: Vandenhoeck & Ruprecht, 1984.

Kantrowitz, Joanne Spencer. *Dramatic Allegory: Linday's "Ane Satyre of the Thrie Estaitis."* Lincoln: University of Nebraska Press, 1975.

Kastleman, Rebecca. "Impersonating the Law: The Dramaturgy of Legal Action in the York Corpus Christi Pageant and John Bale's *Three Laws*." *Theatre Journal* 68, no. 1 (2016): 37–56.

Kay, Sarah. "Women's Body of Knowledge: Epistemology and Misogyny in the *Romance of the Rose.*" In *Framing Medieval Bodies*, edited by Sarah Kay and Miri Rubin, 211–35. Manchester, UK: Manchester University Press, 1994.

Kay, Sarah, and Miri Rubin, eds. *Framing Medieval Bodies*. Manchester, UK: Manchester University Press, 1994.

Keenan, Hugh T., ed. *Typology and English Medieval Literature*. New York: AMS Press, 1992.

Kelley, Michael. *Flamboyant Drama: A Study of "The Castle of Perseverance," "Mankind," and "Wisdom."* Carbondale: Southern Illinois University Press, 1979.

Kendrick, Laura. "'In Bourde and in Pleye': *Mankind* and the Problem of Comic Derision in Medieval English Religious Plays." *Etudes anglaises* 58, no. 3 (2005): 261–75.

King, John N. *English Reformation Literature: The Tudor Origins of the Protestant Tradition*. Princeton, NJ: Princeton University Press, 1986.

King, Pamela. "Morality Plays." In *The Cambridge Companion to Medieval English Theatre*, 2nd ed., edited by R. Beade and A.J. Fletcher, 235–62. Cambridge: Cambridge University Press, 2008.

Klausner, David, ed. *Two Moral Interludes: "The Pride of Life" and "Wisdom."* Kalamazoo, MI: Medieval Institute Publications, 2009.

Knight, Alan, ed. *The Stage as Mirror: Civic Theatre in Late Medieval Europe*. Cambridge: D.S. Brewer, 1997.

Kobialka, Michal. "The *Quem Quaeritis*: Theatre History Displacement." *Theatre History Studies*, no. 8 (1988): 35–51.

Kolve, V.A. "*Ganymede / Son of Getron*: Medieval Monasticism and the Drama of Same-Sex Desire." *Speculum* 73, no. 4 (1998): 1014–67.

– *The Play Called Corpus Christi*. Stanford, CA: Stanford University Press, 1966.

Kruger, Steven. "The Bodies of Jews in the Late Middle Ages." In *The Idea of Medieval Literature: New Essays on Chaucer and Medieval Culture in Honor of Donald R. Howard*, edited by James M. Dean and Christian Zacker, 301–23. Newark: University of Delaware Press, 1992.

– *The Spectral Jew: Conversion and Embodiment in Medieval Europe*. Minneapolis: University of Minnesota Press, 2006.

Krummel, Miriamne Ara. "'Him Jesus, That Jew!' Representing Jewishness in the York Plays." In *Jews in Medieval Christendom: "Slay Them Not,"* edited by Kristine Utterback and Merrall Llewelyn Price, 287–311. Leiden: Brill, 2013.

Lactantius. *Divinae Institutiones et epitome diviniarum institutionum*. Edited by Samuel Brandt. Vienna: CSEL, 1890.

Lampert, Lisa. *Gender and Jewish Difference from Paul to Shakespeare*. Philadelphia: University of Pennsylvania Press, 2004.

Lancashire, Ian, ed. *Two Tudor Interludes: "The Interlude of Youth" and "Hick Scorner."* Manchester, UK: Manchester University Press, 1980.

Lemay, Helen Rodnite, ed. and trans. *Women's Secrets: A Translation of Pseudo-Albertus Magnus's "De secretis mulierum" with Commentary.* Albany: State University of New York Press, 1992.

Lennam, Trevor. *Sebastian Westcott, the Children of Paul's, and "The Marriage of Wit and Science."* Toronto: University of Toronto Press, 1975.

Lester, G.A., ed. *Three Late Medieval Morality Plays: "Mankind," "Everyman," "Mundus et Infans."* London: A. & C. Black, 2006.

Levine, Laura. *Men in Women's Clothing: Anti-Theatricality and Effeminization, 1579–1642.* Cambridge: Cambridge University Press, 1994.

Levy-Navarro, Elena. "Burning in Sodom: Sodomy as the Moral State of Damnation in John Bale's *The Image of Both Churches.*" *Reformation* 9, no. 1 (2004): 67–98.

Lindsay, Sir David, of the Mount. *Ane Satyre of the Thrie Estaitis.* Edited by Roderick Lyall. Edinburgh: Cannongate, 1989.

– *The Works of Sir David Lindsay of the Mount, 1490–1555.* Edited by Douglas Hamer. 4 vols. Edinburgh: Blackwood & Sons, Scottish Text Society, 1936.

– *See also* Lyndesay, Sir David.

The Lion in Winter. Directed by Anthony Harvey. Screenplay by James Goldman. Haworth Productions, 1968. DVD.

Littleton, Betty J., ed. *Clyomon and Clamydes: A Critical Edition.* The Hague: Mouton, 1968.

Lochrie, Karma. *Covert Operations: The Medieval Uses of Secrecy.* Philadelphia: University of Pennsylvania Press, 1999.

London, H. Sanford. "Some Medieval Treatises on English Heraldry." *Antiquaries Journal* 33 (1953): 169–83.

Long, Kathleen. *Hermaphrodites in Renaissance Europe.* Aldershot, UK: Ashgate, 2006.

The Lost Books of the Bible: Being All the Gospels, Epistles, and Other Pieces Now Extant Attributed in the First Four Centuries to Jesus Christ. New York: Alpha House, 1926.

Lublin, Robert. *Costuming the Shakespearean Stage: Visual Codes of Representation in Early Modern Theatre and Culture.* Farnham, UK: Ashgate, 2011.

Luis-Martinez, Zenón. *In Words and Deeds: The Spectacle of Incest in English Renaissance Tragedy.* New York: Rodopi, 2002.

Lumiansky, R.M., and David Mills, eds. *The Chester Mystery Cycle.* 2 vols. Early English Text Society, s.s., 3. London: Oxford University Press, 1974.

Lyly, John. *The Complete Works of John Lyly.* Edited by Warwick Bond. 3 vols. Oxford: Clarendon, 1967. First published 1902.

Lyndesay, Sir David. *Sir David Lyndesay's Works, Parts I–IV.* Edited by J. Small and F. Hall. Early English Text Society, o.s., 11, 19, 35, and 37. Woodbridge, UK: Boydell & Brewer, 1999.

– *See also* Lindsay, Sir David, of the Mount.

MacFaul, Tom. *Male Friendship in Shakespeare and His Contemporaries.* Cambridge: Cambridge University Press, 2007.

MacQueen, John. *"Ane Satyre of the Thrie Estaitis."* *Studies in Scottish Literature* 3, no. 3 (1966): 129–43.

Mager, Donald. "John Bale and Early Tudor Sodomy Discourse." In *Queering the Renaissance,* ed. Jonathan Goldberg, 141–61. Durham, NC: Duke University Press, 1994.

Manion, Lee. *Narrating the Crusades: Loss and Recovery in Medieval and Early Modern English Literature.* Cambridge: Cambridge University Press, 2014.

Marra, Kim, and Robert Schanke, eds. *Staging Desire: Queer Readings of American Theater History.* Ann Arbor: University of Michigan Press, 2002.

Masten, Jeffrey. *Queer Philologies: Sex, Language, and Affect in Shakespeare's Time.* Philadelphia: University of Pennsylvania Press, 2016.

Matthew Paris. *Chronicles of Matthew Paris: Monastic Life in the Thirteenth Century.* Edited and translated by Richard Vaughan. New York: St. Martin's, 1884.

Matthews, David. *Medievalism: A Critical History.* Cambridge: D.S. Brewer, 2015.

May, Steven. "A Medieval Stage Property: The Spade." *Medieval English Theatre* 4, no. 2 (1982): 77–92.

McCusker, Honor. *John Bale: Dramatist and Antiquary.* Freeport, NY: Books for Libraries, 1971. First published 1942.

McEachern, Claire. "'A Whore at the First Blush Seemeth Only a Woman': John Bale's *Image of Both Churches* and the Terms of Religious Difference in the Early English Reformation." *Journal of Medieval and Renaissance Studies* 25, no. 2 (1995): 245–69.

McFadyen, Lindsay. "What Was Really Lost in *Gammer Gurton's Needle?*" *Renaissance Papers,* 1982, 9–13.

McGee, Timothy. "The Role of the *Quem quaeritis* Dialogue in the History of Western Drama." *Renaissance Drama* 7 (1976): 177–91.

McGinley, Kevin. "'That Every Man May Knaw': Reformation and Rhetoric in the Works of Sir David Lyndsay." *Literature Compass* 2 (2005, RE 144): 1–15.

McNally, Terence. *Corpus Christi.* New York: Grove Press, 1998.

Medwall, Henry. *The Plays of Henry Medwall.* Edited by Alan Nelson. Cambridge: D.S. Brewer, 1980.

Menon, Madhavi, ed. *Shakesqueer: A Queer Companion to the Complete Works of Shakespeare.* Durham, NC: Duke University Press, 2011.

Meredith, Peter, with Meg Twycross. "'Farte Pryke in Cule' and Cock-Fighting." *Medieval English Theatre* 6, no. 1 (1984): 30–9.

Meyer, Moe. "Introduction: Reclaiming the Discourse of Camp." In *The Politics and Poetics of Camp,* edited by Moe Meyer, 1–22. London: Routledge, 1994.

Meyers, Walter E. *A Figure Given: Typology in the Wakefield Plays*. Pittsburgh, PA: Duquesne University Press, 1969.

– "Typology and the Audience of the English Cycle Plays." In *Typology and English Medieval Literature*, edited by Hugh T. Keenan, 261–73. New York: AMS Press, 1992.

Middle English Dictionary. https://quod.lib.umich.edu/m/middle-english -dictionary.

Mill, Anna. "The Influence of the Continental Drama on Lyndsay's *Satyre of the Thrie Estaitis*." *Modern Language Review* 25, no. 4 (1930): 425–42.

– "The Original Version of Lindsay's *Satyre of the Thrie Estaitis*." *Studies in Scottish Literature* 6, no. 2 (1969): 65–75.

Miller, Tim, and David Román. "Preaching to the Converted." *Theatre Journal* 47, no. 2 (1995): 169–88.

Mills, David. *Recycling the Cycle: The City of Chester and Its Whitsun Plays*. Toronto: University of Toronto Press, 1998.

Mills, Laurens. *One Soul in Bodies Twain: Friendship in Tudor and Stuart Drama*. Bloomington, IN: Principia, 1937.

Mills, Robert. *Seeing Sodomy in the Middle Ages*. Chicago: University of Chicago Press, 2015.

Morris, Richard, ed. *Cursor Mundi: A Northumbrian Poem of the Fourteenth Century in Four Versions*. Early English Text Society, o.s., 59. London: Kegan Paul, 1875–6.

–, ed. *Old English Homilies and Homiletic Treatises of the Twelfth and Thirteenth Centuries*. Early English Text Society, o.s., 29 and 34. New York: Greenwood, 1969. First published 1868.

Morrison, Susan Signe. *Excrement in the Late Middle Ages: Sacred Filth and Chaucer's Fecopoetics*. New York: Palgrave Macmillan, 2008.

Munday, Anthony. *The Downfall of Robert, Earl of Huntingdon*. Oxford: Malone Society, 1964.

Mundill, Robin R. *The King's Jews: Money, Massacre, and Exodus in Medieval England*. New York: Continuum, 2010.

Muñoz, José Esteban. *Disidentifications: Queers of Color and the Performance of Politics*. Minneapolis: University of Minnesota Press, 1999.

Munson, William F. "Audience and Meaning in Two Medieval Dramatic Realisms." *Comparative Drama* 9, no. 1 (1975): 44–67.

Murphy, Sara. "Antifeminism in the Service of Anticlericalism in Sir David Lindsay's *Ane Satyre of the Thrie Estaitis*." *Journal of Medieval and Early Modern Studies* 41, no. 2 (2011): 393–416.

Neal, Derek. *The Masculine Self in Late Medieval England*. Chicago: University of Chicago Press, 2008.

Neuss, Paula, ed. *The Creacion of the World: A Critical Edition and Translation*. New York: Garland, 1983.

Newman, Barbara. *From Virile Woman to WomanChrist: Studies in Medieval Religion and Literature*. Philadelphia: University of Pennsylvania Press, 1995.

A New Theatrical Dictionary, Containing an Account of All the Dramatic Pieces That Have Appeared from the Commencement of Theatrical Exhibitions to the Present Time. London: S. Bladon, 1792.

Nicholson, R.H. "The Trial of Christ in the York Cycle." *Journal of Medieval and Renaissance Studies* 16 (1986): 125–69.

Nisse, Ruth. *Defining Acts: Drama and the Politics of Interpretation in Late Medieval England*. Notre Dame, IN: Notre Dame University Press, 2005.

Normington, Katie. *Gender and Medieval Drama*. Cambridge: D.S. Brewer, 2004.

– *Modern Mysteries: Contemporary Productions of Medieval English Cycle Drama*. Woodbridge, UK; D.S. Brewer, 2007.

Norris, Herbert. *Tudor Costume and Design*. Mineola, NY: Dover, 1997. First published 1938.

Northbrooke, John. *A Treatise against Dicing, Dancing, Plays, and Interludes, with Other Idle Pastimes*. London: Shakespeare Society, 1843.

Norton, Michael. *Liturgical Drama and the Reimagining of Medieval Theater*. Kalamazoo, MI: Medieval Institute Publications, 2017.

Nosworthy, J.M., ed. *Lusty Juventus*. Oxford: Malone Society Reprints, 1971. First published 1966.

O'Connor, Sean. *Straight Acting: Popular Gay Drama from Wilde to Rattigan*. London: Cassell, 1998.

Ogden, Dunbar. *The Staging of Drama in the Medieval Church*. Newark: University of Delaware Press, 2002.

Ogilvy, J.D.A. "Mimi, Scurrae, Histriones: Entertainers of the Early Middle Ages." *Speculum* 38 (1963): 604–19.

Olsen, Glenn. *Of Sodomites, Effeminates, Hermaphrodites, and Androgynes: Sodomy in the Age of Peter Damian*. Toronto: Pontifical Institute of Mediaeval Studies, 2011.

Orgel, Stephen. *Impersonations: The Performance of Gender in Shakespeare's England*. Cambridge: Cambridge University Press, 1996.

Ovid. *Metamorphoses*. Translated by Frank Justus Miller. Cambridge, MA: Harvard University Press, 1971.

Oxford English Dictionary. https://www.oed.com.

Paglia, Camille. "Plighting Their Troth: Review of John Boswell, *Same Sex Unions in Pre-modern Europe*." *Washington Post*, 17 July 1994, wkb1.

Panton, G.A., and D. Donaldson, eds. *The Gest Hystoriale of the Destruction of Troy: An Alliterative Romance Translated from Guido de Colonna's "Hystoria Troiana."* 2 vols. Early English Text Society, o.s., 39 and 56. London: Trübner, 1869.

Partridge, Eric. *Shakespeare's Bawdy*. 3rd ed. London: Routledge, 1968.

Paul, James Balfour, ed. *Accounts of the Lord High Treasurer of Scotland*. 12 vols. Edinburgh: H.M. General Register House, 1877–1916.

Paulson, Julie. *Theater of the Word: Selfhood in the English Morality Play*. Notre Dame, IN: Notre Dame University Press, 2019.

Paxson, James. "Queering *Piers Plowman*: The Copula(tion)s of Figures in Medieval Allegory." *Rhetoric Society Quarterly* 29, no. 3 (1999): 21–9.

Pearsall, Derek. *Arthurian Romance: A Short Introduction*. Malden, MA: Blackwell, 2003.

Peele, George. *The Troublesome Reign of John, King of England*. Edited by Charles Forker. Manchester, UK: Manchester University Press, 2011.

Perry, George G., ed. *Religious Pieces in Prose and Verse, Edited from Robert Thornton's MS (Cir. 1440) in the Lincoln Cathedral Library*. Early English Text Society, o.s., 26. New York: Greenwood, 1996. First published 1914.

Powell, Susan. "John Mirk." In *Oxford Dictionary of National Biography*, edited by H.C.G. Matthew and Brian Harrison, 368–9. Oxford: Oxford University Press, 2004.

–, ed. *John Mirk's Festial: Edited from British Library MS Cotton Claudius A.II*. 2 vols. Early English Text Society, o.s., 334 and 335. Oxford: Oxford University Press, 2009.

Preston, Michael J. "Re-presentations of (Im)moral Behavior in the Middle English Non-cycle Play *Mankind*." In *Folklore, Literature, and Cultural Theory: Collected Essays*, edited by Cathy Lynn Preston, 214–39. New York: Garland, 1995.

Pugh, Tison. *Chaucer's (Anti-) Eroticisms and the Queer Middle Ages*. Columbus: Ohio State University Press, 2014.

– *Sexuality and Its Queer Discontents in Middle English Literature*. Basingstoke, UK: Palgrave Macmillan, 2008.

Pugh, Tison, and Angela Jane Weisl. *Medievalisms: Making the Past in the Present*. New York: Routledge, 2013.

Quinn, William. "The Chosen and the Chastised: Naming Jews in the York Mystery Plays." In *Jews in Medieval England: Teaching Representations of the Other*, edited by Miriamne Ara Krummel and Tison Pugh, 141–56. New York: Palgrave Macmillan, 2017.

Raithby, John, ed. *The Statutes at Large of England and of Great Britain, from Magna Carta to the Union of the Kingdoms of Great Britain and Ireland*. 20 vols. London: George Eyre and Andrew Strahan, 1811.

Rastall, Richard. "Female Roles in All-Male Casts." *Medieval English Theatre* 7 (1985): 25–50.

Reid, David. "Rule and Misrule in Lindsay's *Thrie Estaitis* and Pitcairne's *Assembly*." *Scottish Literary Journal* 11, no. 2 (1984): 5–24.

Resnick, Irven M. "Medieval Roots of the Myth of Jewish Male Menses." *Harvard Theological Review* 93, no. 3 (2000): 241–63.

Rice, Nicole, and Margaret Aziza Pappano. *The Civic Cycles: Artisan Drama and Identity in Premodern England*. Notre Dame, IN: University of Notre Dame Press, 2015.

Richards, Jennifer. "Male Friendship and Counsel in Richard Edwards' *Damon and Pythias.*" In *The Oxford Handbook of Tudor Drama*, edited by Thomas Betteridge and Greg Walker, 293–308. Oxford: Oxford University Press, 2012.

Roach, Joseph. "Culture and Performance in the Circum-Atlantic World." In *Performativity and Performance*, edited by Andrew Parker and Eve Kosofsky Sedgwick, 45–63. New York: Routledge, 1995.

Robinson, J.W. "The Art of the York Realist." *Modern Philology* 60, no. 4 (1963): 241–51.

Rocke, Michael. *Forbidden Friendships: Homosexuality and Male Culture in Renaissance Florence*. New York: Oxford University Press, 1996.

Rodosthenous, George. "Staring at the Forbidden: Legitimizing Voyeurism." In *Theatre as Voyeurism: The Pleasures of Watching*, edited by George Rodosthenous, 1–25. Houndmills, UK: Palgrave Macmillan, 2015.

Rollo, David. *Kiss My Relics: Hermaphroditic Fictions of the Middle Ages*. Chicago: University of Chicago Press, 2011.

Ross, Andrew. "Uses of Camp," In *Camp Grounds: Style and Homosexuality*, edited by David Bergman, 54–77. Amherst: University of Massachusetts Press, 1993.

Roth, Cecil. *A History of the Jews in England*. 3rd ed. Oxford: Clarendon Press, 1964.

Rubenstein, Jay, trans. *Guibert of Nogent: Portrait of a Medieval Mind*. New York: Routledge, 2002.

Rubin, Miri. *Corpus Christi: The Eucharist in Late Medieval Culture*. Cambridge: Cambridge University Press, 1991.

Ryan, Patrick. "Marlowe's *Edward II* and the Medieval Passion Play." *Comparative Drama* 32, no. 4 (1998): 465–95.

Salvato, Nick. *Uncloseting Drama: American Modernism and Queer Performance*. New Haven, CT: Yale University Press, 2010.

Sanchez, Melissa. *Shakespeare and Queer Theory*. London: Arden Shakespeare, 2019.

Saslow, James. *Ganymede in the Renaissance: Homosexuality in Art and Society*. New Haven, CT: Yale University Press, 1986.

Sautman, Francesca Canadé, and Pamela Sheingorn, eds. *Same Sex Love and Desire among Women in the Middle Ages*. New York: Palgrave Macmillan, 2001.

Savran, David. *A Queer Sort of Materialism: Recontextualizing American Theater*. Ann Arbor: University of Michigan Press, 2003.

Schechner, Richard. *Between Theater and Anthropology*. Philadelphia: University of Pennsylvania Press, 1985.

Schell, Edgar, and J.D. Shuchter, eds. *English Morality Plays and Moral Interludes*. New York: Holt, Rinehart, 1969.

Schelling, Felix E., ed. *Tom Tyler and His Wife*. *PMLA* 15, no. 3 (1900): 253–89.

Schultz, James A. *Courtly Love, the Love of Courtliness, and the History of Sexuality*. Chicago: University of Chicago Press, 2006.

Sedgwick, Eve Kosofsky. *Between Men: English Literature and Male Homosocial Desire*. New York: Columbia University Press, 1985.

– *Touching Feeling: Affect, Pedagogy, Performativity*. Durham, NC: Duke University Press, 2003.

Shakespeare, William. *The Riverside Shakespeare*. 2nd ed., edited by G. Blakemore Evans. Boston: Houghton Mifflin, 1997.

Sheingorn, Pamela. "The Bodily Embrace or Embracing the Body: Gesture and Gender in Late Medieval Culture." In *The Stage as Mirror*, ed. Alan Knight, 51–89. Cambridge: D.S. Brewer, 1997.

Shorr, Dorothy C. "The Iconographic Development of the Presentation in the Temple." *Art Bulletin* 28, no. 1 (1946): 17–32.

Shrank, Cathy. *Writing the Nation in Reformation England, 1530–1580*. Oxford: Oxford University Press, 2004.

Sidhu, Nicole Nolan. *Indecent Exposure: Gender, Politics, and Obscene Comedy in Middle English Literature*. Philadelphia: University of Pennsylvania Press, 2016.

Simpson, James. "John Bale, *Three Laws*." In *The Oxford Handbook of Tudor Drama*, edited by Thomas Betteridge and Greg Walker, 109–22. Oxford: Oxford University Press, 2012.

Sinfield, Alan. *Out on Stage: Lesbian and Gay Theatre in the Twentieth Century*. New Haven, CT: Yale University Press, 1999.

Skelton, John. *Magnificence*. Edited by Paula Neuss. Manchester, UK: Manchester University Press, 1980.

– *Magnyfycence: A Moral Play*. Edited by Robert Lee Ramsay. Early English Text Society, e.s., 48. London: Kegan Paul, 1906.

Skinner, Patricia, ed. *The Jews in Medieval Britain: Historical, Literary, and Archaeological Perspectives*. Woodbridge, UK: Boydell, 2003.

Smart, W.K. "Some Notes on *Mankind*." *Modern Philology* 14, no. 1 (1916): 45–58.

– "Some Notes on *Mankind* (Concluded)." *Modern Philology* 14, no. 5 (1916): 293–313.

Smith, Bruce R. *Homosexual Desire in Shakespeare's England: A Cultural Poetics*. Chicago: University of Chicago Press, 1991.

Smith, John Hazel, ed. *A Humanist's "Trew Imitation": Thomas Watson's "Absalom."* Urbana: University of Illinois Press, 1964.

–, ed. *Two Latin Comedies by John Foxe the Martyrologist: "Titus et Gesippus" and "Christus Triumphans."* Ithaca, NY: Cornell University Press, 1974.

Somerset, J.A.B., ed. *Four Tudor Interludes*. London: Athlone Press, 1974.

Sontag, Susan. *Against Interpretation and Other Essays*. New York: Anchor, 1990.

Sorieri, Louis. *Boccaccio's Story of "Tito e Gisippo" in European Literature*. New York: Institute of French Studies, 1937.

Southern, Richard. *The Medieval Theatre in the Round: A Study of the Staging of "The Castle of Perseverance" and Related Matters*. London: Faber & Faber, 1957.

– *The Staging of Plays before Shakespeare*. New York: Theatre Arts Books, 1973.

Spector, Stephen, ed. *The N-Town Play: Cotton MS Vespasian D.8*. 2 vols. Early English Text Society, s.s., 11. Oxford: Oxford University Press, 1991.

Sponsler, Claire. *Drama and Resistance: Bodies, Goods, and Theatricality in Late Medieval England*. Minneapolis: University of Minnesota Press, 1997.

– *Ritual Imports: Performing Medieval Drama in America*. Ithaca, NY: Cornell University Press, 2004.

Stanivukovic, Goran, ed. *Ovid and the Renaissance Body*. Toronto: University of Toronto Press, 2001.

–, ed. *Queer Shakespeare: Desire and Sexuality*. London: Bloomsbury, 2017.

Steenbrugge, Charlotte. "'O, yowr louely wordys': Latin and Latinate Diction in *Mankind*." *Middle English Theatre* 31 (2009): 28–57.

– *Staging Vice: A Study of Dramatic Traditions in Medieval and Sixteenth-Century England and the Low Countries*. Amsterdam: Rodopi, 2014.

Steinberg, Leo. *The Sexuality of Christ in Renaissance Art and in Modern Oblivion*. London: Faber & Faber, 1984.

Stern, Tiffany. *Making Shakespeare: From Stage to Page*. London: Routledge, 2004.

Stevens, Martin. "The York Cycle: From Procession to Play." *Leeds Studies in English* 6 (1972): 37–61.

Stock, Lorraine Kochanske. "'He's Not an Ardent Suitor, Is He, Brother?' Richard the Lionheart's Ambiguous Sexuality in Cecil B. DeMille's *The Crusades* (1935)." In *Queer Movie Medievalisms*, edited by Kathleen Coyne Kelly and Tison Pugh, 61–78. Farnham, UK: Ashgate, 2009.

Stretter, Robert. "Engendering Obligation: Sworn Brotherhood and Love Rivalry in Medieval English Romance." In *Friendship in the Middle Ages and Early Modern Age: Explorations of a Fundamental Ethical Discourse*, edited by Albrecht Classen and Marilyn Sandidge, 501–24. Berlin: de Gruyter, 2010.

Strohm, Paul. *Hochon's Arrow: The Social Imagination of Fourteenth-Century Texts*. Princeton, NJ: Princeton University Press, 1992.

Stubbes, Philip. *The Anatomie of Abuses*. Edited by Margaret Jane Kidnie. Tempe: Arizona Center for Medieval and Renaissance Studies, 2002.

Sturges, Robert. *Chaucer's Pardoner and Gender Theory: Bodies of Discourse*. New York: St. Martin's, 2000.

– *The Circulation of Power in Medieval Biblical Drama: Theaters of Authority*. Houndmills, UK: Palgrave Macmillan, 2015.

Symonds, John Addington. *Shakespere's Predecessors in the English Drama*. London: Smith, Elder, 1908.

Szittya, Penn R. *The Antifraternal Tradition in Medieval Literature.* Princeton, NJ: Princeton University Press, 1986.

Tanner, Norman, ed. and trans. *Decrees of the Ecumenical Councils.* 2 vols. London: Sheed & Ward, 1990.

Tatlock, John, and Arthur Kennedy, eds. *A Concordance to the Complete Works of Geoffrey Chaucer and to the "Romaunt of the Rose."* Gloucester, MA: Peter Smith, 1963.

Taylor, Christopher. "The Once and Future Herod: Vernacular Typology and the Unfolding of Middle English Cycle Drama." *New Medieval Literatures* 15 (2013): 119–48.

Tennenhouse, Leonard, ed. *The Tudor Interludes: "Nice Wanton" and "Impatient Poverty."* New York: Garland, 1984.

Thomas Aquinas. *Quaestiones diputatae.* 10th ed., edited by R.M. Spazzi, et al. Turin, Italy: Marietti, 1965.

– *Truth.* Edited by James McGlynn. 2 vols. Indianapolis, IN: Hackett, 1994. First published 1954.

Tiner, Elza. "English Law in the York Trial Plays." In *The Dramatic Tradition of the Middle Ages,* edited by Clifford Davidson, 140–9. New York: AMS Press, 2005.

Tinkle, Theresa. "York's Jesus: Crowned King and Traitor Attainted." *Speculum* 94, no. 1 (2019): 96–137.

Tomasch, Sylvia. "Postcolonial Chaucer and the Virtual Jew." In *The Postcolonial Middle Ages,* edited by Jeffrey Jerome Cohen, 243–60. New York: St. Martin's Press, 2000.

Toole, William "The Aesthetics of Scatology in *Gammer Gurton's Needle.*" *English Language Notes* 10 (1973): 252–8.

Turner, Ralph V. *King John.* London: Longman, 1994.

Turner, Victor. "Liminality and the Performative Genres." In *Rite, Drama, Festival, Spectacle: Rehearsals toward a Theory of Cultural Performance,* edited by John MacAloon, 19–41. Philadelphia: Institute for the Study of Human Issues, 1994.

Twycross, Meg, ed. *Terence in English: An Early Sixteenth-Century Translation of "The Andria."* Lancaster, UK: Medieval English Theatre Modern-Spelling Texts, 1987.

– "'Transvestism' in the Mystery Plays." In *The Materials of Early Theatre: Sources, Images, and Performance,* edited by Sarah Carpenter and Pamela King, 185–236. London: Routledge, 2018.

Twycross, Meg, with Malcolm Jones and Alan Fletcher. "'Fart Prycke in Cule': The Pictures." *Medieval English Theatre* 23 (2001): 100–21.

Tydeman, William. "Costumes and Actors." In *Medieval English Drama: A Casebook,* edited by Peter Happé, 180–9. London: Macmillan, 1984.

– *The Theatre in the Middle Ages: Western European Stage Conditions, c. 800–1576.* Cambridge: Cambridge University Press, 1978.

–, ed. *Two Tudor Tragedies: "Gorboduc" and "The Spanish Tragedy."* London: Penguin, 1992.

Tyndale, William. *The Obedience of a Christen Man and Howe Christen Rulers Ought to Gouerne / Where in Also (If Thou Marke Diligently) Thou Shalt Fynde Eyes to Perceaue the Crafty Conveyaunce of All Iugglers.* Marlborow, Belgium: Hans Luft; Antwerp: Johannes Hoochstraten, 1528.

Utley, Francis Lee. "The One Hundred and Three Names of Noah's Wife." *Speculum* 16, no. 4 (1941): 426–52.

Utz, Richard. *Medievalism: A Manifesto.* Kalamazoo, MI: Arc Humanities Press, 2017.

Verini, Alexandra. "Medieval Models of Female Friendship in Christine de Pizan's *The Book of the City of Ladies* and Margery Kempe's *The Book of Margery Kempe.*" *Feminist Studies* 42, no. 2 (2016): 365–91.

Wager, W. *"The Longer Thou Livest" and "Enough Is as Good as a Feast."* Edited by R. Mark Benbow. London: Edward Arnold, 1967.

Walen, Denise. *Constructions of Female Homoeroticism in Early Modern Drama.* New York: Palgrave Macmillan, 2005.

Walker, Greg, ed. *Medieval Drama: An Anthology.* Oxford: Blackwell, 2000.

– "Personification in Sir David Lyndsay's *A Satire of the Three Estates.*" In *Personification: Embodying Meaning and Emotion,* edited by Walter Melion and Bart Ramakers, 234–55. Leiden, Netherlands: Brill, 2016.

– *The Politics of Performance in Early Renaissance Drama.* Cambridge: Cambridge University Press, 1998.

Walsh, Fintan. "Touching, Feeling, Cross-Dressing: On the Affectivity of Queer Performance." In *Deviant Acts: Essays on Queer Performance,* edited by David Cregan, 55–71. Dublin: Carysfort Press, 2009.

Warning, Rainer. *The Ambivalences of Medieval Religious Drama.* Translated by Steven Rendall. Stanford, CA: Stanford University Press, 2001.

Weir, Alison. *Eleanor of Aquitaine: A Life.* New York: Ballantine, 1999.

Weyermann, Maja. "The Typologies of Adam-Christ and Eve-Mary, and Their Relationship to One Another." *Anglican Theological Review* 84, no. 3 (2002): 602–26.

White, Paul Whitfield, ed. *Reformation Biblical Drama in England: "The Life and Repentance of Mary Magdalene" and "The History of Iacob and Esau."* New York: Garland, 1992.

– *Theatre and Reformation: Protestantism, Patronage, and Playing in Tudor England.* Cambridge: Cambridge University Press, 1993.

Whitney, Elspeth. "What's Wrong with the Pardoner? Complexion Theory, the Phlegmatic Man, and Effeminacy." *Chaucer Review* 45, no. 4 (2011): 357–89.

Whitworth, Charles, ed. *Gammer Gurton's Needle.* London: A. & C. Black, 1997.

Wickham, Glynne. *Early English Stages, 1300 to 1660.* 4 vols. London: Routledge and Kegan Paul, 1963.

–, ed. *English Moral Interludes*. London: Dent, 1976.

Wiles, David, ed. *The Early Plays of Robin Hood*. Cambridge: D.S. Brewer, 1981.

Williams, Arnold. "Typology and the Cycle Plays: Some Criteria." *Speculum* 43, no. 4 (1968): 677–84.

Williams, Janet Hadley, ed. *Sir David Lyndsay: Selected Poems*. Glasgow: Association for Scottish Literary Studies, 2000.

– "Women Fictional and Historic in Sir David Lyndsay's Poetry." In *Woman and the Feminine in Medieval and Early Modern Scottish Writing*, edited by Sarah Dunnigan, C. Marie Harker, and Evelyn Newlyn, 47–60. Houndmills, UK: Palgrave Macmillan, 2004.

Williams, Penry. *The Tudor Regime*. Oxford: Clarendon, 1979.

Woodruff, Paul. *The Necessity of Theater: The Art of Watching and Being Watched*. Oxford: Oxford University Press, 2008.

Woods, Constance. "Same-Sex Unions or Semantic Illusions?" *Communio* 22 (1995): 316–42.

Woolf, Rosemary. "The Effect of Typology on the English Mediaeval Plays of Abraham and Isaac." *Speculum* 32, no. 4 (1957): 805–25.

– "The Theme of Christ the Lover-Knight in Medieval English Literature." *Review of English Studies* 13, no. 49 (1962): 1–16.

Wyclif, John. *Select English Works of John Wyclif*. Edited by Thomas Arnold. 3 vols. Oxford: Clarendon, 1869.

Young, Karl. *The Drama of the Medieval Church*. 2 vols. Oxford: Clarendon, 1951. First published 1933.

Index